Also by Stephanie South

Accessing Your Multidimensional Self: A Key to Cosmic History

2012: Biography of a Time Traveler: The Journey of José Argüelles

Time, Synchronicity and Calendar Change:
The Visionary Life and Work of José Argüelles

Daily Galactic Inspiration: 365 Quotes for your Journey in Time [eBook]

260 Keys to Synchronotron:
A Guide to the New Mind for People of the Future [eBook]

By José Argüelles and Stephanie South

Book of the Throne: Cosmic History Chronicles [Volume I]

Book of the Avatar: Cosmic History Chronicles [Volume II]

Book of the Mystery: Cosmic History Chronicles [Volume III]

Book of the Initiation: Cosmic History Chronicles [Volume IV]

Book of the Timespace: Cosmic History Chronicles [Volume V]

Book of the Transcendence: Cosmic History Chronicles [Volume VI]

Book of the Cube: Cosmic History Chronicles [Volume VII]

The Uninscribed
Initiation into the Heart of Time

A Multidimensional Love Story

Stephanie South

Law of Time Press
Ashland, Oregon

Law of Time Press
Ashland, Oregon

White Magnetic Wizard year
Cover and book design: Kelly Harding
Interior images: José Argüelles

ISBN 9780986200564

www.lawoftime.org
Law of Time Press
PO Box 156
Ashland, OR. 97520

Printed in the United State of America

Contents

❁ Part Three: Realization

Dedicated to YOU
And the Return of Light

May we
Simultaneously
Remember the
One
Behind all Form(s)

Dare to declare who you are.
It is not far from the shores of silence to the boundaries of speech.
The path is not long, but the way is deep.
You must not only walk there, you must be prepared to leap.
—Hildegard of Bingen

When will you begin the long journey into yourself? —Rumi

Preface: Blank Map

Ah, we were the blank map
Free of borders
Unbound by name
We were the wild rivers
—the fresh mind
Of the Naked Sky
Unwritten.

There are no words for what I am about to tell you. However, I will do my best through your language to communicate something you may have always known.

I am not interested in formality, but in case you are, I will tell you a bit about myself soon enough. For now, it is enough for you to know that I have come a long way from where I began. I have been sent backward in time to your planet to retrieve lost knowledge. I am on a mission of memory retrieval. I am a maker of things to come.

Since arriving in the human realm, I never felt it to be real. I always knew it must be a dream. Yet it appeared that other people were having "real" experiences, but I was not.

My first memory, after emerging from the birth canal of transmigratory amnesia, was being a child on a world that was about to explode. Everyone seemed oblivious to this impending destruction. I tried to warn anyone who would listen, but few could hear. I was young, and they didn't take me seriously.

As the mounting pressure grew, I saw people do all sorts of things to distract themselves, including much hedonistic partying into oblivion. Then the shatter! I was blasted through space, naked and weightless except for a single silver ring with an etching. I sensed a male counterpart with me, though I saw no one. I landed on another planet and then woke up.

How can I describe to you what happened next? How can I convey the true feeling of the inner experiences as they unfolded? Do you need colors and measurements? Smells and sounds? OK, I will try. But please be patient while I find the right combination in this ever-shifting time-space. With every word, my perception keeps changing.

Early on, I often felt as if I was living in other places or worlds simultaneously. I sensed a type of fence around my mind and was frustrated when I realized that all of my thoughts were just the regurgitation of someone else's thoughts. I sensed that my mind was in a type of prison. But who was the prison-keeper? I longed for originality. I longed to be shown what is NEW.

I was always interested in finding the Path unseen by the masses, a magic fairy tale path that is not fixed but ever evolving and open to being updated with new truths.

In my pursuit, I learned that there are hidden streams of knowledge that run below the threshold of normal waking consciousness. There is an invisible power that is always remembering the true nature of reality. There is a path to return to the Cosmic Source.

This Path is called different things: Path of the Initiates, Path of knowledge, Path of Self-Realization, or the Spiritual Path, etc. For clarity purposes, we will refer to it as the former.

The word initiation comes from the word "initium" which means entrance or beginning. The Path of Initiates is different from an ordinary path. The purpose of the Initiates is to cultivate a way of life that leads to truth and essence. It is the path beyond the five senses. Contemplation, reflection, and discipline are required.

Initiates are seekers of hidden knowledge. They are in a conscious process of memory retrieval. An initiate remains open and ready to see a completely different world than the masses. They understand that reality is nothing like what we have been taught; and that there is an entirely other narrative occurring that cannot be found in mainstream news nor on the internet.

An initiate knows that while it is important to know what is happening in this world, it is even more important to understand it from within. The deeper that we go within, the more we realize that this world is nothing like what we have been told.

In the depth of my childhood visions, I had often dreamed of living in the woods with a wizard and learning the secrets of the Universe. I was searching for the one who holds the Magic Map to fill in my blanks, one whose doctrines didn't represent reactions or history but the fresh slate and futures yet undreamed; one who was true by internal acts, not just outward gestures.

I imagined sitting around a warm fire, drinking fresh herbal tea, and reading by candlelight. I wanted to learn the true history of the world, of other planets and star systems. I wanted to learn about time travel and teleportation and magic spells. I wanted to know directly who God is, without intermediaries. I wanted to live a fairy tale life where happily ever after isn't just a dream.

My "dream come true" happened in my 29th year, but not quite in the way I had imagined. Life is not always logical when you are following the path of the inner dream.

On a dark and snowy winter night, deep in the forests of majestic Mt. Hood, I became the apprentice of a Galactic Mayan Avatar named Valum Votan.

I found him. And he told me:

> *In order to (reach your true essence), you have to realize that society as you have known it is misleading—if you listen to it, it will lead you away from the straight path. On this straight path, you do not deviate to the right or the left. We are continuously being distracted ...*
>
> *This means that you have to realize that there is a hidden way or a way apart from the social mainstream. The key to life is to find and cultivate your essence; this cannot be done while being absorbed in the status quo. In this late age of materialism, the straight way appears as a most elaborate, cyberspherically rigged labyrinth; this is why you must adhere to a path and maintain a discipline that cuts right through the opinion-strewn maze of the "information" revolution.*

Many are called to this inner path of the Greater Dream, but few follow it. Please follow it and Live your Dream Now. Our Future depends on It.

Now imagine that your canvas is stretched out.

Your palette is filled with endless colors—the world is yours to create.

Unwritten lands, unspoken words, unnamable space

The Blank Map

Uninscribed

This is a Telepathic Transmission
Few characters are introduced as it's about Inner vision
Open your Heart and expand your Mind
And in this story, a treasure you'll find
If some of the contents your brain can't hack
See the synchronic notes in the back

Part One
Initiation

Chapter 1

Lost in Time

Every part of the journey is of importance to the whole.
—Saint Teresa of Avilla

As a child, I had recurring visions of underground time tunnels in the earth. The tunnels were connected to a transport system with openings that led into past, present, and future. Through these tunnels, I witnessed world wars, a time of dinosaurs and giants, as well as possible futures.

I always felt that the reality I saw was only a dream, and determined that I also must exist somewhere else. Though I couldn't put my finger on it. When I was eight this feeling climaxed, and I was seized by intense energy that made me sit down and write. Flashes of tunnels filled my mind, and I kept hearing the words *lost in time, lost in time, you are lost in time!*

I grabbed a pen and my notebook, sat down at the coffee table in the living room of my trailer home, and with great urgency began writing. I determined not to get up until it was finished, all 13 pages of it. I had a feeling that the memory was already disappearing. As I wrote I could vividly see the underground libraries and classrooms that I knew so well. It felt more real than my waking life. I stapled several pieces of paper together and reflected. After a few moments I wrote the title: *Lost in Time.*

In this narrative, I was John Mathews, a seasoned time traveler, exploring underground time tunnels, searching for the right time. The entry point to these tunnels was underground in Montana. My fellow traveler was a woman named Crystal Blake. I was searching for the time I belonged in and was eager to explore, though also afraid of ending up in a bad time, which in my eight-year-old mind, I deemed as a time of violence, war or oppression, or even worse, a time when humans were extinct (which in the text I had given the date 4029).

The Bridge of All Time

This theme of time travel and underground tunnels, cities, and other realities continued to reoccur in my dreams on and off throughout my childhood. At night I would often see a circle of beings that I deemed angels flying around my bed. They would take me to other worlds, and I would experience flying through space in a warm bed. The dreams would take me to a bridge where I would see children standing before it, singing in a most haunting melody: *This is the bridge of allllll tiiiime.*

Later I realized I was sending messages of memories forward in time that I would later retrieve through a series of poems. These words sum it up:

I caught the Life Link
Of the same stream of Think
That I sent to the Sky as a child
Melted in a Pink
Bedspread
Dreaming the Dead
Awake
At age four
Praying God would use me more
Use me more, would you God, I prayed
These were how my days were made
If I should die before I wake
I pray the Lord my soul to take
I saw angels flying in orderly ranks
Under my warm soft, pink
Cotton think tank.

I had other unusual experiences as a child, which seemed normal at the time. On many occasions I would see a hand waving behind my bed when I would take naps. Sometimes it felt playful and sometimes I was scared. I would often sleep on my dresser at nap time to get away from the bed where the hand would appear. These types of experiences were normal for me and I just assumed others also had them.

I always felt connected to God or the invisible world, but the only lens I had been given was Christian-based. I was obsessed with the Book of Revelations and used to read it in my closet with a flashlight. I had read in the Bible to pray in secret and I took it literally.

When I entered first grade, the teachers wanted to skip me two grades, but my parents refused. I was socially awkward and would do things out of order. By second grade I was writing plays about time travel and fairy tales and performing them in public.

Until around the age of nine, I lived in a world of relatively limited conditioned concepts until my aunt died and my parents divorced. This was my first awakening to the fragmentation that I sought to reconcile. My will was strong as was my creative imagination. The first question I remember asking was: If I wasn't me then who would I be? I spent much time contemplating this before determining that it was impossible that I could "be" anyone else. I would often ask my father if this LIFE was a dream or not. He would always say, "It feels like it to me."

Near-Death Experience

I was 19 the first time I died. In Buffalo, New York, I was pronounced dead from an accidental drug overdose after a night of partying. As a sophomore at the State University of New York at Buffalo, I had been having a great time at a weekend party, but in my naivety and inebriated state I got on a Harley-Davidson with a man I barely knew and he gave me drugs. Before I knew it, I was found passed out on an elderly woman's front lawn on a frosty November morning.

She and two friends called 9-1-1 because I had no pulse and they thought I was dead. Apparently, I had been lying on her frozen lawn for about four hours before she found me and called for an ambulance. I watched from out of my body as the paramedics worked to revive me. I had no pulse. I was slipping in and out of consciousness, but not within the body. I later wrote:

Back to the Place of the Maker I went
And was marched through a Field
And shown the Life I had spent
Tasting death the Mission shown
Karmic action, blow by blow
Until an Unseen Angel redeemed my show

In my "death" experience, I was shown every word, action, and deed I had done throughout my short life. Then I experienced the amplified effects of each of my words and actions on others around me. When

I viewed something positive I had said or done, I enjoyed tremendous bliss. When I viewed something negative that I had said or done, I would begin writhing in the worst pain imaginable.

During the near-death experience I felt I was floating through a swirling black hole repeating, "Although I walk through the valley of the shadow of death, I shall fear no evil." I kept remembering that there is nothing to be afraid of. I felt I was riding on a type of soul boat. I was alone yet I sensed others around me on their own journey. No one could help anyone else.

What impressed me the most was seeing how our words and thoughts are pure vibrations that return to us in the most amplified way. Floating through space I sensed a magnificent FORCE, on the other side of darkness, that was pulling me toward it. As I moved toward it, more scenes flashed before me at rapid speed. Behavioral errors, as soon as seen and acknowledged, were dissolved. This was followed by a sense of relief and a deeper state of purification and joy.

All the accumulated debris and error of earth life was removed from me step by step. I was being purified and pulled by a Magnet of Omnipotent Love back to the Center Source, where I came face-to-face with what I perceived as the Christ essence. I was dazzled by the light and magnificence emanating from this Divine Being. This essence light was so pure that I could barely look at it. All I wanted was to make myself worthy to be in its Holy Presence. I began to say: "I love you. I am sorry. Forgive me."

I had a fleeting sense of shame that I had forgotten about this glory. This feeling gave way to a great warmth of what can only be described as a Divine Light exploding from within, bathing my entire essence with rapturous joy. This feeling of wholeness gave me supreme confidence that everything was ultimately going to be OK. This message, along with the message to "always be teachable," imprinted me deeply. No matter how much we learn or think we know, knowledge is ever-evolving as is our perception of it.

I was given the choice if I wanted to come back to Earth or not. I was clear that I did not want to return. Then I was shown an image of my father from a far distance. He was in great pain and crying. I saw he was at my funeral. My heart burst open when I felt his pain and his love pulled me back to Earth.

Next, I found myself seated in the center of a group of what appeared to be wise elders who telepathically showed me my Life Mission. Upon awakening I could only recall fragments, but I remembered that they communicated that all would be revealed step by step. I recalled the key part of the vision had to do with telepathy among humans and that I was here to assist with the transformation of the Earth. The one thing I do recall is that I was assured to live "happily ever after."

Three of the elder women then took me to a field and placed me back into my earth body. I was reluctant as the body felt so dense and heavy compared to the liberated feeling of freedom that I was experiencing. But I knew that my mission was not yet complete.

This experience permanently altered my perceptions about all aspects of reality. I realized that many of my previous assumptions about reality and God were incorrect. There was no one I could talk to at the time who could fully understand. At that time, near-death experiences were not so widely talked about. I suffered a period of deep depression and anxiety, feeling the contrast between this world and the one I had just experienced.

I had one year left to go in college, and in the summer of 1994, I resumed my studies in journalism. Simultaneously, and unbeknownst to me, the discovery of the tomb of the Red Queen in Temple 13 was made in the summer of 1994, in the jungle of Palenque, Mexico. Six years later, I would visit this tomb.

I graduated with a bachelor's degree in journalism in 1996, followed by a summer internship at the Pasadena Star News in California. At the time, I was practicing *A Course in Miracles* and immersed in *The Collected Works of St. John of the Cross.* I kept detailed journals of my inner world at this time, and at age 23, I wrote:

> *... Entry into the spiritual realm is triggered by anything that shakes up old beliefs and understandings. For many, the entry point experience is spontaneous and mystical as hard to explain as it is to deny. St. John of the Cross describes it as the dark night of the soul. That's also how I would describe my entry point.*

Chapter 2

Enter the Dream

Trust in dreams, for in them is the hidden gate to eternity.

—Kahlil Gibran

I felt a significant change in consciousness on my 24th birthday, January 8, 1997, Red Magnetic Serpent. I was living alone in a basement apartment in Portland, Oregon, when I noticed a mysterious energy growing within me; something was awakening, something from beyond, yet I had no context for the experiences.

The urgency to be alone in nature was triggered by heightened states of perception of the dreamlike nature of this reality. These feelings would come at inopportune times, and often while I was at work sitting at my office cubicle. This reality felt so unreal that I determined that I also must exist elsewhere.

I felt something was calling me and that I needed to pay attention. It was as though my night dreams were bleeding into my waking reality. I would often have to make an excuse to leave my desk and find a quiet spot outside.

I needed someone to talk to. I went to New Renaissance, a spiritual bookstore in Portland, and saw a flyer regarding awakening in the dream. I then made an appointment to meet with Paul Levy.

The words in the flyer that caught my eye said:

> *You discover if you see that this is a magical, synchronistic, dreamlike universe that every moment is offering you exactly what you need to wake up, it will spontaneously shapeshift and do exactly that, as it is nothing other than your own reflection. But being like a dream, this only becomes true if you see it as such.*
>
> —Paul Levy

Paul was 42, from Yonkers, New York, with short gray hair and a balanced blend of masculine and feminine energy. He was a long-time Tibetan Buddhist practitioner and the head of the Portland Padmasambhava Center, a Jungian scholar as well as a leader of Awakening in the Dream groups. We had a strong connection, and he offered to see me every "Thursday" for free, of which I obliged. At the end of our initial session, Paul intuitively said, "I need to introduce you to the [13 Moon] Mayan community."

My mind flashed when he said the word "Maya." The first time I had heard about the Maya was as a child reading *Mystery of the Maya*, a "Choose Your Own Adventure" book by Raymond Montgomery. The book was about searching for clues as to the disappearance of the Maya. The characters see a large spacecraft hovering over the pyramids. This activated my imagination.

The book says: "These Mayan ruins are contact points for other planets. Earth is seen as a leading planet. Other civilizations want to learn from us. They asked us to come to an outer galactic congress on the rights of life in the universe."

First Crystal Meeting

Soonafter our initial meeting, Paul took me to meet the 13 Moon community who were having a "Crystal Meeting" in downtown Portland, as initiated by José and Lloydine Argüelles. Copal and sage filled the air along with the sound of didgeridoos and drums. This tribal-like scene was inspired by José's vision to create a network of artists who would become a force for creative non-political change in the world, with the key objective to return the Earth back into a work of art. This was known as the Planet Art Network or PAN.

As soon as we walked in, I was "decoded" and given my "galactic signature" according to my birthdate. I felt a jolt of energy surge through my body upon hearing my galactic signature: *Red Electric Serpent.* Red was the color of initiation. Electric was the tone of Service, and its function was to "activate." Serpent was the carrier of new life-force. The Moon was my guide, signifying purification and universal water.

I was told that there are 260 frequency signatures, and that this was my "passport" into the *fourth dimension* of a new time. I had first heard of the fourth dimension from my favorite children's book, *A Wrinkle in Time* by Madeline L'Engle. I was fascinated by her description of dimensions, cubes, and tesseracts. Tesseract is explained as the "wrinkling" of time and space, allowing two points to be connected through this fifth dimension rather than forcing you to travel on a straight line. It is how the people travel to distant planets in *A Wrinkle in Time.*

During this time, I gained more in-depth insights into my often lucid dreams and kept detailed journals to record the nightly adventures. I recorded my dreams faithfully. One significant recurring dream was with a boy whom I associated with King Tut. I was always so enchanted by this boy king, who seemed empowered with charms and magic from extraordinary worlds filled with light. His presence was indescribable. The dream sequence went like this:

> *I made my way down many long, twisting, and narrow entryways that all unlocked into greater and greater storehouses of treasure—each treasure felt like a missing puzzle piece, though I kept my focus to find the boy. Finally, I would reach a large opening—a brilliant room, meticulously adorned with glittering treasures. What was this place? And why was it so familiar? I was overcome with indescribable joy and excitement. Everything felt possible.*
>
> *Then I saw him. He appeared as a boy, wise beyond his apparent years, bright, pure, and full of many charms. He was alone, but not lonely, though it felt like he was waiting—waiting for something—and it seemed he had been there for eternity.*
>
> *He was always alone playing the same ball game. The game appeared similar to basketball, but not quite. He invited me to play, and we tossed many balls that would travel in non-ordinary patterns. Often when he threw a ball it would suspend in mid-air and the boy king smiled and repeated these words in slow motion: this isssn't whhaaat wweee thiiink it iiiiss (smile). This isn't what we think it is.*

Amazingly in 2015 I would find myself in the Egyptian Museum in Cairo staring face-to-face at the gold mask of King Tutankhamen! On his headdress are a cobra and a vulture, signifying the simultaneity of ascending (into spirit) and descending (into matter).

Another recurring dream I had was of a mysterious man, a time traveler who I later recognized as José Argüelles/Valum Votan. In the dream, I met him first in the parched, barren desert. I searched for water in the salmon-colored sand where I stumbled upon a most exquisite crystal. I picked it up and was immediately transported to a crystalline stream. There across the stream, I saw a mysterious man with a glowing energy around him. We were quite a ways apart but aware of each other's every movement.

He called out to me and showed me a type of rare stone, and I knew I had been with him like this before. I met him at the King's Chamber in Egypt and other locations. I saw him again walking along a vacant street in a large city, usually crowded but strangely empty, and he was teaching me time travel. On another occasion, I met him in a simple yellow room. He put his head to mine and we exploded ecstatically in an "electrifying dissolution." These dream encounters were part of my preparation leading into my destiny.

First Encounter

I arrived at the Whole Earth Festival in Davis, California to hear José Argüelles speak on May 9, 1998, Blue Rhythmic Monkey. José was a former art history professor at UC Davis and creator of the Whole Earth Festival, which he started in 1970. It was one of the first modern gatherings ever whose sole purpose was to honor the Earth as a whole with zero waste.

Paul had invited me to join him at the festival. He had been introduced to José's work through their mutual friend Mark Comings, an independent scientific researcher. Paul was inspired to honor José as a terton for his work decoding the Telektonon Prophecy of Pacal Votan. Though I was yet to learn precisely what this all meant, I could feel the vibration in my body. Paul and Mark explained that in the Tibetan tradition, a terton is one who discovers *terma,* hidden treasure left by a concealer in a former time.

I rode from Portland to Davis with a lively group of kin who were enthusiastically following the 13 Moon calendar. There was fresh and exciting energy, as they introduced me to the basic concepts of the Thirteen Moon/28 day calendar.

They taught me that it takes the moon 28 days to orbit the Earth, and it makes this orbit 13 times each year. It is called a Moon Calendar because it is based on the female 28-day menstruation cycle, which is also the average lunar cycle. Thirteen perfect months of 28 days = 52 perfect weeks of 7 days = 364 days.

The synchronization, or new year's date of the 13 Moon calendar is July 26. This corresponds to the rising of the great star Sirius. This makes the 13 Moon Calendar a tool for harmonizing ourselves with the galaxy. There was a lot of knowledge to take in, and I eagerly absorbed it.

Upon arriving to the festival I met up with Paul and met his friend Mark and Seamus Hiestand, a drummer from Los Angeles. Seamus was White Planetary Mirror, which I would learn the significance of later. It was an appropriate synchronicity that Seamus was with me on my initial meeting of José and Lloydine, and 21 years later he would be a main encourager for me to write this book.

Meeting Destiny

When I first met José, his presence was striking. He was 59, tall and elegant, wearing a black "Prophet's Conference" shirt with a large turquoise necklace and turquoise earring in his left ear. His silver hair was short-cropped, as he had just cut it to visit the Vatican. Soft-spoken in person, he carried a mysterious, otherworldly presence about him. Lloydine, 55, had long blond hair, and glasses framed her blues eyes. She was outgoing, pretty, and talkative, with a motherly quality

When I first heard José speak, I knew I had to listen carefully. I concentrated intensely as the energies around me were loud and chaotic at this outdoor festival:

> *By living in artificial time, humanity is deviating from nature. Unless humanity adopts the 13 Moon, 28-day calendar to change its course, it would end up destroying itself and the biosphere.*

Something shifted in me and I knew that what I was hearing was more important than anything, though I could not yet grasp the full meaning and implications of José's powerful speech. I felt the urgency of the message and knew I had to learn more. He continued:

> *All revolutions have failed. We are mired in materialism beyond control. Science offers no practical solutions. Political institutions are shown to be without substance. Population increases exponentially. Day to day changes in Earth's atmosphere is met with bewilderment and arrogance. Why? Because all revolutionary endeavors from 1776*

to the present have operated on the wrong timing frequency: 12:60; 12-month calendar, 60-minute clock.

I felt an immediate resonance with José's words, or rather the energy behind the words. Memories quickly flashed through my mind and a recognition from my night dreams. He was the one who had appeared in dreams teaching me about time travel.

YOU ARE LIVING IN ARTIFICIAL TIME.
WHO OWNS YOUR TIME, OWNS YOUR MIND.
OWN YOUR OWN TIME, AND KNOW YOUR OWN MIND.

When José spoke those words, they exploded in me like a thunderbolt, reawakening forgotten memories and flooding my body with electricity. I had always sensed there was something "off" on this planet but could not articulate it. He was speaking my inner language. Hearing his words, my mind was catapulted back to my eight-year-old self sitting at my living room coffee table writing with great urgency about my recurring visions of underground time tunnels in the earth.

José's speech had world-shattering implications and spurred me to deep reflections: *What is time? What does this all mean? How is it possible that we are living in the wrong time? How do we get to the right time?*

Then my mind returned back to the festival and I heard José say: "As you run to keep ahead of the clock and pay your bills you are getting older. What do you want to have created in your life? The first step is to become receptive and to learn again what life is all about. New knowledge creates new thoughts, and new thoughts open new doors."

I remembered: *Yes, we are lost time travelers with amnesia. We are ALL here to Remember. We are here to return to the Original Time.* I focused on this with all of the power of concentration I had. It took extreme effort of will to focus on the meaning of this, to remember, to wake up. I knew I would need much more discipline.

On the journey back to Portland, we returned the rental van only to note that the odometer was 1,320! The synchronic order had been activated in my life. Little did I know that five years later, I would be living with José and Lloydine.

Chapter 3

Taming the Mind

Do not encumber your mind with useless thoughts. What good does it do to brood on the past or anticipate the future? Remain in the simplicity of the present moment.

—Dilgo Khyentse Rinpoche

My heart was open, but my mind needed discipline. I had become accustomed to a state of anxiety and often felt overwhelmed and hurried. I did not yet have the proper inner structure to understand the world holistically. I needed to learn to calm my mind if I was ever going to understand my life purpose.

Paul introduced me to Dzogchen meditation, which helped a lot. The basic method is to allow yourself to relax your mind back to its natural state without attempting to modify or chase thoughts. In Christian terms, this is similar to the practice "Be still and know I am God." Quieting the mind is easier said than done!

I also began studying the teachings of Padmasambhava, a supreme yogi and meditation master, who is known for bringing Buddhism from India to Tibet in the late eighth or early ninth century. Padmasambhava prophesied the coming darkness of the human race plagued by disaster, war, diseases, and above all, the reduced inclination to engage in any spiritual endeavor.

In the Tibetan tradition, Padmasambhava and his chief consort Yeshe Tsogyal, concealed treasures "mind terma" in stones, pillars of ancient buildings, pyramids, in cliff faces, in lakes, even in the air. Their discovery is only possible for the predicted terton and even then only at certain moments in time, which are generally revealed through synchronicity.

Padmasambhava said, "Don't investigate the root of things, investigate the root of mind! Once the mind's root has been found, you'll know one thing, yet all is thereby freed. But if the root of mind you fail to find, you will know everything but understand nothing."

Paul and I moved together into a house in Portland on October 31, 1998, White Crystal Worldbridger. Five days later, José and Lloydine moved from Tucson, Arizona, to nearby Mount Hood, Oregon. This was a time of great learning for me as I diligently worked on slowing down my mind, paying attention to my breath, and observing my habituated behaviors more closely. Paul introduced me to his teachers, two Tibetan lamas, known as the Khenpo brothers, who gave me my first meditation instructions.

As holder of the complete Nyingma lineage, the elder brother, Khenpo Palden, was recognized at a young age as a tulku and was also considered a master of Dzogchen, the highest tradition of meditation practice in Tibetan Buddhism

I had my first private meeting with the Khenpos in their bedroom when they were visiting Portland. The elder Khenpo brother was sitting on the edge of a bed, and the younger one on a chair. As I sat in a chair facing them both, I felt a lot of love and clarity but had no idea what I was supposed to do or say. I just sat there for a moment looking at them.

"Do you dream at night?" I asked the younger Khenpo. He replied, "Do you?" Then I said yes. Next, I asked, "What do you dream at night?" and they answered, "What do YOU dream at night?" My final question was: "What is your main message for humanity?" The younger Khenpo replied: "To feel more love."

That was all I needed, and I didn't have to say anything else. They both started doing blessing chants and told me to learn and recite the seven-line prayer to Guru Rinpoche (Padmasambhava). I thanked them and left.

About a year later, I took refuge, and my bodhisattva vows with the Khenpo brothers, promising to strive to liberate all sentient beings for all time. These vows are based on cultivating the qualities known as the six paramitas [perfections]—generosity, discipline, patience, exertion, meditation, and transcendental knowledge.

Soon after, another Lama stayed at our house, Lama Rinchen, and in my naivety, I asked him how to become enlightened. He smiled and said, "Just watch very carefully." The next day I came home from work, and Lama Rinchen was sitting in the middle of the living room floor. When I walked in, he told me to sit down. Then he patiently taught me the seven-line prayer to alleviate suffering and for protection, inspiration, and empowerment. The Seven-Line Prayer is said to be the "natural resonance of indestructible ultimate reality." After I learned it, Lama Rinchen said, "Now you will always have an escort." Meaning that I wouldn't have to feel alone.

Introduction to Telektonon

The back of my head would get warm and tingly whenever José and Lloydine would visit our Portland home. They would generally drop off a new teaching or booklet, and share their latest travels with Paul and I. It was from these visits that I began to learn about the Law of Time.

On one occasion, we were all four having coffee at the dining room table and discussing meditation. Both José and Lloydine had been long-time students of Chögyam Trungpa Rinpoche, the 11th descendent in the line of Trungpa tülkus. I learned that Dzogchen originated on this planet from Garab Dorje, an Indian master from the seventh century. José shared that Garab Dorje, as well as the Prophet Muhammed, were contemporaries of the Mayan sage Pacal Votan. I found this fascinating to contemplate. He also shared that there are 570 years from Buddha's birth to Christ, and 570 years from Christ's birth to Muhammad's.

On another occasion, José and Lloydine brought the Telektonon Prophecy of Pacal Votan kit. They set up the kit in my bedroom and gave me instructions on how to use it as a daily practice. In 1993 José had deciphered the Telektonon Prophecy of Pacal Votan, which had changed both he and Lloydine's lives and entered them onto a mythic journey. (For the whole story, please read *Time, Synchronicity and Calendar Change).*

The temperature and pressure of the room increased, and my face flushed with heat as they shared about the prophecy and the Tower of Babel. José explained that the "Cube of the Law" (perfect knowledge) was split, separating the mind from spirit, which created confusion in the people. From this split, ego was born with its false authority symbolized by Babylon and the Tower of Babel.

This Babylon planet manipulates death-fear for the power of a few people through insurance (and pharmaceutical) companies, through war, and through the daily news. This fear-based program is supported by the priest class of the different false spiritualities or religions. In other words, the truth of reality is covered by a false narrative held in place by corporations, banking systems, and larger institutions, who are at their root embedded in an artificial timing frequency out of synch with the laws of Nature.

José and Lloydine gave me an original writing about the Telektonon. When I read it, all my hairs stood up, and my whole body got the chills. It felt connected to my childhood memories. He wrote:

> *Telektonon = Tele (from a distance/communication), chtonic (Spirits, deities dwelling within or under the Earth). Hence, Telektonon is the earth spirit speaking tube.*
>
> *...Telektonon also refers to a type of coded text left by one intelligence to another intelligence to be found at a later distant time and appropriate moment...*

Dream the Highest Dream

In the spring of 1999 at the Time is Art Gallery in Old Town Portland, at an art walk, José suddenly appeared in front of me. He gazed into my eyes, lightly tapped my shoulder, and whispered: "Keep dreaming the highest dream." And then he walked away. A bolt of energy flashed through my body. Those words felt like a wake-up call.

I began to increase my studies of the 13 Moon calendar. I used both Eden Sky's and Randy Bruner's calendar, both of which made the knowledge more accessible. Eden started making the calendar when she was 17 years old and continues with her family to this day.

The 13 Moon Calendar has been in use for over 5500 years. From the Incan, to the Druidic count, to the Egyptian, to the Essene, to the Mayan, to the Polynesian. My daily contemplation of the 13 Moon calendar and synchronic codes deepened. I began to keep a journal to track day-to-day synchronicities. I was amazed at how rapidly my perceptions were changing. I was able to see my life pattern more clearly. These patterns are always there but are generally overlooked and filtered out by our conditioned mindset.

Paul and I watched over José and Lloydine's house while they traveled to Picarquin, Chile, to conduct a 49-day seminar on the Law of Time (Earth Wizards Seminary) at the end of 1999. This would be a pivotal event with 144 participants from around the world to lay the foundation of the knowledge of the Law of Time. José wrote that this event was "the blueprint for the entire next stage of human, terrestrial, and solar-stellar evolution."

When they returned from Chile, José and Lloydine asked me to edit the transcript of the Earth Wizards seminary, which would be called the *28 Meditations on the Law of Time.* I took this job very seriously. At the time I was working full time as a newspaper reporter and attending Paul's dream groups twice a week. I would stay up into the wee hours working on this manuscript, and would get so activated by the information that it was hard to fall sleep. I had an uncanny feeling that that this knowledge was more of a memory than "new" information. I felt (and still feel) grateful to those original ones who heard the call and dedicated seven weeks of their life to something so new.

My mind clicked into a new groove as I focused intently on understanding these teachings: Time is our greatest gift. The entire time-is-money paradigm is held together by the Gregorian calendar and mechanical clock, which creates the artificial 12:60 timing frequency.

Artificial means formed in imitation of something natural.

Our present civilization is like a simulated artifice of the natural world as we move through artificial environments with artificial lights, wearing artificial fabrics, and eating genetically modified food. To return to natural time is to return to our true essence. Disconnection from Nature results in automatons.

When humans are disconnected from Nature then they are easily swayed, readily triggered by an outer stimulus. I understood the Law of Time as a system to break free from a mass consciousness that seeks to control. I realized why I had often felt a fence around my mind, making it hard to have new perceptions. Now I had a way to articulate it that made sense.

José and Lloydine invited me as their guest to the seven-day Earth Wizards Seminar at the Resort on the Mountain in Mount Hood in the spring of 2000 in exchange for my editing assistance. I happily accepted. Here, I met a diverse group of people who were practicing the synchronic order. The energy was electric and alive, with much information being shared. I felt I had entered into a new, rarefied reality. The seven days concluded with an energetic dance party. It was here that I (and the rest of the attendees) first received the powerful Rainbow Bridge Meditation. This is the abbreviated version:

Rainbow Bridge Meditation

Visualize yourself inside Earth's octahedron crystal core (with two red and two white sides on top, and two blue and two yellow sides below).

In the center of this core is an intensely blazing point of white light. An etheric column extends north and south from the blazing center to the tops of the octahedron.

Now visualize from the center of the crystal a great beam of multicolored, plasma-filled light flows along the axis toward both of Earth's poles, shooting out from them to become two rainbow bands 180 degrees apart. As Earth revolves on its axis, the rainbow bridge remains ready and constant, unmoving.

Now take the whole vision of the rainbow bridge around the Earth and place it in your heart. Imagine the two reams of rainbow light rushing through your central column, shooting out from above your head and beneath your feet to create a rainbow bridge around your body. Now you and the rainbow bridge are one. The rainbow bridge of world peace is real. Visualized by enough people in a telepathic wave of love, the rainbow bridge will become a reality.

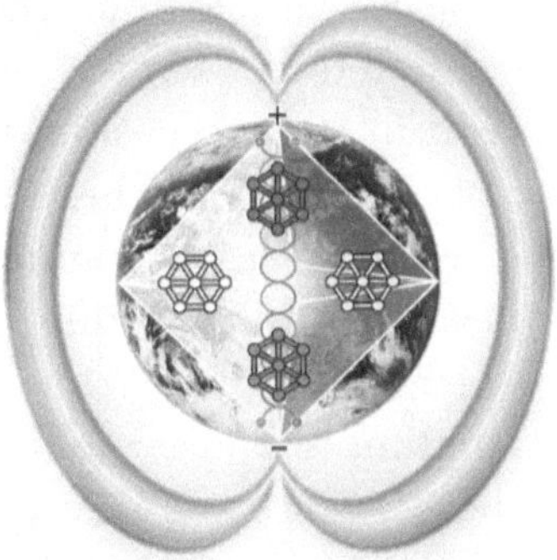

Chapter 4

Vision of the Red Queen

I ask not for any crown, but that which all may win; Nor try to conquer any world, except the one within.

—Louisa May Alcott

I arrived in Palenque, Mexico, to a massive thunder and lightning storm that began pouring down buckets of rain on June 6, 2000, Red Planetary Moon. That night our group of 10 all saw what appeared to be a fleet of unidentified orb-like objects in the sky. Everyone was awe-struck—I had never seen anything like it. Even the skeptics in our group couldn't deny it.

We looked up into heavens, and lo and behold, there was the biggest ship in the sky—we guessed that it was the Mothership, a huge glowing orb that seemed to turn in strange positions as if to communicate something. A sound that I had never heard before reverberated throughout my body, and I could not tell if it was coming from within or without. Whatever it was, it was highly activating, and the vibration was strongly felt.

Chris Coleman, a longtime supporter and friend of José, had arranged the trip. Synchronically, Chris was Yellow Galactic Sun, the same signature as Pacal Votan. José and Lloydine took me clothes shopping in downtown Portland, to prepare for my first trip to Mexico. They bought me sturdy sandals and two summer dresses, one of which I would wear the first day I visited the tomb of Pacal Votan.

Our group left Portland for Mexico a day after the sixth anniversary of the discovery of the tomb of the Red Queen, June 2, 2000, Red Rhythmic Serpent. We visited the ruins of Palenque for the first time on Chris's 42nd birthday, June 7, 2000, White Spectral Dog. That day we viewed the outside of the famous Temple of Inscriptions that contained the tomb of the Great Pacal. Also, on that fateful day, I found myself at Temple XIII, where in 1994, archeologists found a sarcophagus with the remains of a mysterious noblewoman lying on her back covered with red cinnabar powder and other objects. Temple XIII, the tomb of the Red Queen, was opened 42 years after the opening of the adjacent tomb of Pacal Votan in 1952. Mercuric oxide (cinnabar) was used by the ancient Mayans as a preservative in royal burials.

Her face, which had not been seen for 14 centuries, was covered with a shattered funeral mask, made of malachite with a diadem of jade beads adorning her skull. Her tomb bore not a single inscription. Her identity was unknown. The only clue was that her tomb was adjacent to the Great Pacal, and they both had rich burials with monolithic lidded sarcophagus, masks, and jewels.

She was called the Red Queen.

The Vision

At the time of this experience, I had not yet heard of the tomb of the Red Queen. But upon entering the ruins, I was spontaneously drawn to her tomb, where I had my first vision. I lay down on the steps of Temple XIII and closed my eyes. The UFO experience was still reverberating through me, and I had several extraordinary experiences, which were difficult to verbalize. I was taken deep within my being.

I seemed to be descending into the cellular structures of my body through my vaginal corridor. Upon fully entering myself, I came to a plateau where a mysterious light was emanating. Then I began to see flashes and images appear before me. I was shown an underground grid that connects all pyramids and sacred sites on the planet. I saw that they were all connected by electronic lines of force, some of which were now dormant, waiting to be turned "on." When these were turned on, a new "game board" would light upon planet Earth. But how to reconnect and turn on this grid?

When I came out of this experience, I felt disoriented. I felt new, yet ancient energies awakening deep within me. Still, I had not yet the skills to express or articulate it. I knew I had to get my life into further order and educate myself so that I could better understand what I was experiencing. There was a sense that something had been placed into me, or perhaps, I remembered what was always inside.

Later I was struck by the image of the shattered malachite mask of the Red Queen. The female mask was shattered, and the male mask (Pacal's jade mask) was intact. This also felt connected to my recurring childhood dream of the porcelain doll sitting high on a shelf that would fall and shatter in slow motion. I later concluded this dream was symbolic of the shattering of Maldek, the blueprint (in our solar system) of the destroyed planet. Slowly, then quickly, all of these fragmented perceptions would begin to cohere.

At the time of these experiences, I was overwhelmed with new information. Though there were many levels to this vast system of knowledge, the essence of the message was simple: *By living in artificial time, humanity is deviating from Nature. When humans deviate from natural order, strange mutations and natural catastrophes occur, and in some cases planets might even explode. Unless humanity returns to living in the cycles of nature, it will end up destroying itself and the biosphere.*

Pacal's Tomb

> *You, children of the dawn, and you, people of the book, unify yourselves the only way you can: in time, through time, as time.*
> *—Telektonon Prophecy of Pacal Votan, 4:23*

Our group made our way into the tomb of Pacal Votan on the 48th anniversary of its opening in 1952. The 13 Moon day was White Rhythmic Mirror, the signature of Pacal's death. I reflected that the mystery of this tomb and its sarcophagus lid is what had led José to decode a prophecy in the form of a terma. In the Tibetan tradition, terma was often hidden beneath rocks or in caverns and often written in a symbolic script. After visiting the tomb, I spontaneously wrote a poem that describes the feeling of the experience. The poem acknowledges each person in our group's galactic signature. Our combined signature was Kin 260: Yellow Cosmic Sun, hence the poem.

In the One
As Cosmic Sun
The Dreamers wind
Through One Mind
Thunder Beings do their dance
Down wisdom stairs — in slow entrance
Creeping through the well-kept eyes

Jaguar bellows, in timeless cries
The Sun emits its lightest rays
As Hand brings forth its knowing gaze
Three serpents breathe their life-force new
As Stars express their dreams by two.
The Eagle brings its vision's touch
As Warrior marches in fearlessness
"Free will for all," the Human cries
While Storm releases and catalyzes
Energy for the journey down
As memories spiral through holon's crown
And on the vault, a flower's thrown
Revealing truth through talking stone
And in the silence, three words, they dawn:
WELCOME TO TEL-EK-TON-ON!

I did not yet have the proper context to comprehend all the information as a whole. I was still making my way out of my inherited conditionings, though I was open and had no trouble embracing new ideas. Shortly after returning home to Portland, my life rapidly changed. I quit my job, and my relationship with Paul turned into what would become a lifelong friendship. I began to study the Law of Time in earnest, particularly the Telektonon prophecy.

According to the Telektonon Prophecy of Pacal Votan, the memory of our star origins has been virtually forgotten or distorted into various fear programs. These fear programs are based on a self-perception rooted in an artificial time-frequency (12:60), held in place by the 12-month Gregorian calendar and a 60-minute clock. These two instruments hold conditioned patterns of thought in place and reinforce concepts such as taxes, democracy, autocracy, war, money, insurance, and holidays.

This prophecy was part of a time-release that began in 1989 with the discovery of the Law of Time. This discovery made the distinction between two timing frequencies: the **12:60** artificial time and the **13:20** natural time.

The tomb of Pacal Votan was discovered in 1952, exactly **1,260** years from its dedication in 692 AD. And from its dedication in 692 AD until 2012 AD, it is precisely **1,320** years.

A few years after the initial experience at the tomb of the Red Queen, I had a dream that felt directly related. In the dream I saw the same underground grid structure that I had seen in my vision. My Tibetan teachers were showing me the circuitry of the present-day human mind. Everything appeared in a type of infrared with connecting wires. I noted that some areas looked like knots that seemed to be emitting tremendous amounts of heat. The Tibetans informed me that these were the "land mines in the human consciousness grid," the places where pockets of unconscious energy had congregated with building pressure that could explode at any moment.

They explained that explosions occur through certain vibratory triggers. The vibrations are activated by specific words that are rigged to the "land mines."

I found my dreams would become more lucid when I put the symbols of the synchronic codes under my pillow at night to sleep. I noted that José/Votan appeared more frequently in my dreams, teaching me in various locations, forests, classrooms, pyramids, caves, Tibetan monasteries as well as on spaceships and on other planets. The more I paid attention to and recorded these dreams, the more it felt as though my night dreams were merging into my waking life—until the two merged in 2002 when I came to live with José and Lloydine and became his apprentice.

WE ARE MAYA WE ARE THE MASTERS
OF ILLUSION

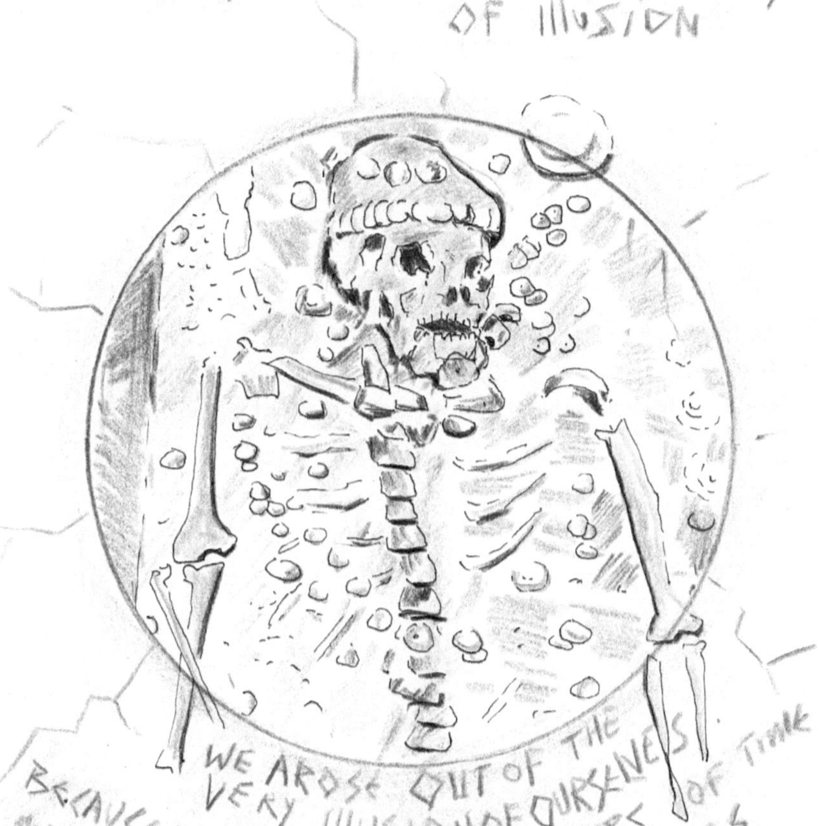

WE AROSE OUT OF THE
VERY ILLUSION OF OURSELVES.
BECAUSE WE ARE THE PRIMAL MASTERS OF TIME
AND ILLUSION, WE ARE THE FEARLESS ONES
WHO TAKE ON INCARNATION AFTER INCARNATION
TO SETTLE AND TAME ALL PLANETS — UNBECOMING
KNOWING THE SECRET OF BECOMING AND THE ILLUSION
WE OFFERED OURSELVES IN SACRIFICE TO OF
IMMORTALITY

Chapter 5

Entering GM108X

My soul is from elsewhere, I'm sure of that, and I intend to end up there.

—Rumi

The memory of the destruction of Maldek led me to my path of destiny. Twenty-four days before taking my role as an apprentice, I had an elaborate dream on New Year's Eve 2001, White Spectral Wind:

I am on Maldek. I am very young.

Many people clamor in a state of unrest like a wild, chaotic party.

Crowded and loud.

Several dreams merge into one now, but they are all with the same energy.

Like the entire red-light districts of all world systems trying to drink away the impending destruction.

An incredible pressure builds.

Voices. Movement. Panic.

Then…blast-off!

And I am hurtling through space at top speed. I sense the presence of a male counterpart with me, though I see no one.

Traveling through the stars, I unfold over myself—somersaults in space—over and over and over. I am naked. I look at my hand in attempt to wake myself up. But I am not dreaming. I see a silver ring on my finger. I look closely. It is inscribed:

Red Electric Serpent.

Later I am in a big city with tall buildings—a similar scene with lots of explosions. I am running, running, trying to warn people to get out of the buildings.

GET OUT OF THE BUILDINGS! NOW!!

Some listen. Some don't. Christmas celebrations are everywhere in large high-rise buildings. I am walking alone in a field on the outskirts of the city in an undeveloped area between buildings when I see what appears to be little bombs exploding on the horizon. They all seem connected by a time-release fuse. Then I see a fire and a huge building explode into flames.

Then I remember that I am supposed to pick someone up in one of the buildings. I am stopped by a police officer. He asks if I am responsible for what is happening. I say no. He says, "Of course you are not." He has a comforting smile—I feel safe. He keeps me close by as we navigate through chaotic bars and streets. It appears like a masquerade ball at the world's end. A final toast. People are disoriented and confused, carrying on with eating and drinking and ignoring the explosions.

I woke up feeling that this wasn't a dream but a memory. And there was much more to remember.

Brightwood

On January 24, 2002, on a dark and snowy winter evening deep in the forests of majestic Mt. Hood, I became the apprentice of Valum Votan. From here on out I will refer to José as "Votan," as this is the only name I actually knew him by.

Three weeks prior, Votan and Lloydine called me to stay and work with them for seven days, which I would later learn was a test to see if I was compatible with living with them. The rapport was high, and much work was accomplished in a short time.

In this interim, I celebrated my 29th birthday with them on January 8, 2002, White Rhythmic Dog (Saturn return). When I woke, there was a blue and purple robe with a card lovingly placed at my door, with handwritten notes by both of them. They took me to the Flying Frog for breakfast, and in the evening they cooked a special meal of rice and vegetables and got a bottle of red wine as a ceremonial toast. After dinner, we sat around the woodstove and ate pumpkin pie and mint tea as they shared with me stories of their journeys, and they showed me photo albums of their family and travels.

Four days later, the initial seven-day work experiment was complete. I returned back to Sandpoint, Idaho, where I had been living and working with Deborah and Brian Haight, who were Board members for the Foundation for the Law of Time.

A few days after returning, I received a call from Lloydine with a sense of urgency. She said that she and Votan wanted me to move in with them immediately. I was taken off guard, but also excited. I asked her to give me a few weeks to have proper closure with Deborah and Brian and their four children whom I had grown close with. Lloydine was persistent that I come sooner, and later that night, she emailed me, saying, "Don't you want to be here for Votan's birthday?"

Votan's 63rd birthday was less than a week away. I couldn't refuse her request. The next day I broke the news to the Haight family that I was moving in a few days. It was all quite abrupt. We felt sad to say goodbye so suddenly, but I knew my destiny was calling, although I had no idea what form it would take.

A few days later, I packed all of my belongings in my red Nissan pickup truck and set out on the 10-hour journey from Sandpoint, Idaho, to Brightwood, Oregon. About halfway there, I got caught in a blustering snowstorm and was sliding all over the road. I stopped for the night in Spokane, Washington. I arrived at my new home on January 20, 2002, White Overtone Wind, having no idea what to expect.

As I turned onto the long, dirt road leading to their cabin, I felt immersed in swirling portals of etheric mists that seemed to grow as I neared their place deep in the forest. The cabin was located in a small town called Brightwood, one of the communities off of Highway 26 that make up the Villages at Mount Hood. Mt. Hood, called Wy'east by the Multnomah tribe, is the tallest mountain in Oregon with a summit of 11,249 feet. It is a dormant volcano covered with glaciers and snow all year, as well as lots of waterfalls and wildflowers.

My heart was beating rapidly as I knocked at the door late in the evening. Votan and Lloydine warmly greeted me as I warmed myself at their woodstove. The table was set, and we ate baked salmon, brown rice, vegetables, and salad. They spoke animatedly of what inspired them to call me to live with them. I was excited but exhausted.

The next day I woke up, and everything felt like a dream. Votan and Lloydine told me to spend the day relaxing, decorating my room, and organizing my belongings. This day was Blue Rhythmic Night: *I organize in order to dream, balancing intuition.* This small room had a red shag carpet, two large windows, a futon bed, and a desk, and like the rest of the house it had a warm campfire kind of smell with a tinge of must.

"Welcome to your destiny," Lloydine greeted me cheerfully in my room with morning coffee as I unpacked. Later that afternoon, they both came to my room and did a formal welcoming ceremony. I had no idea what to expect but was open to the adventure. I sensed that they knew much more than me, and I trusted them both implicitly.

A New Life

The next few days, I listened as Votan and Lloydine explained to me that they had known for years that an apprentice was needed to pass this knowledge to. Lloydine made clear that this was not her role and that someone from the next generation was needed. They both shared much of their journey with me. I mostly listened and did not talk much for the first year. I asked a lot of questions.

They shared that for over a decade, beginning late in 1991, they had been galactic peace ambassadors, bringing the message of peace through time to people all over the world, without any visible means of support. This required a great sacrifice on both their parts. Their mission was to wake humanity up to the Greater Cosmic Cycles of Nature. They had started the 13 Moon Calendar Change Peace Movement, a planetary organization committed to the replacement of the irregular standard of the Gregorian calendar with the regular standard of the 13 Moon/28 day calendar. But on a personal level, there were few they trusted or confided in.

They also explained that a lineage for the Galactic Mayan transmission had to be established, and they determined it had to be returned to the matrilineal. This was the purpose of the three of us being called together at this time. Votan shared that the knowledge to be transmitted was called GM108X: Galactic Mayan mind transmissions.

He explained that the Galactic Mayans were originally a people from beyond our solar system and physical plane dimension. He explained that they first seeded our planet some 2,500 years ago. Their purpose was to create a model civilization based on galactic time in a remote part of the world far away from the Babylonian influence of the

Old World. This civilization was the means for leaving behind clues and information regarding an accurate conception of time, as well as prophecies.

Lloydine shared that while all of history is essentially the perpetuation of male lineages, hierarchies, and patriarchies, the GM108X was symbolically intended to return the pattern to its feminine origins. Many Native American tribes were matrilineal. Women were involved in the decision-making process for the greater good of the tribe. I spent many hours contemplating the meaning of this.

Time Codes

For five years prior to the apprenticeship, I had immersed myself in the studies of the Law of Time and the Dreamspell codes. The 13 Moon calendar is based on the Dreamspell codes, the integrative mathematical structure of higher-dimensional time. The entire premise of Dreamspell is that humans are lost time travelers who got amnesia and forgot their true identity. These tools lay out a mathematical guidance system that symbolizes each human's personal power and autonomy. The more I applied myself, the more I felt my awareness widen and deepen.

Votan explained to me that the sabotage of time is a part of the galactic saga known as the *time wars.* The time war on Earth is due to a low-frequency (12:60) beam that was directed at our planet to inseminate our electromagnetic mind field with artificial time. This low-frequency time beam hit Earth's ionosphere, releasing a shower of time-release projections meant to consign us to the belief that the third dimension is the only dimension of reality. This beam is what is attributed to our collective spiritual amnesia as to our true identity.

The time wars are all the conspiracies to keep people from owning their own time and, therefore, from knowing their own mind. Votan saw that the time war conspiracy reaches into all levels of society everywhere on the planet, but its primary everyday tool of control is the Gregorian calendar. This "time virus" has infiltrated religion, government, science, and virtually every institution. He reasoned that if time is the fundamental key to any new beginning, the calendar is a practical way to begin a new time.

Everything I was learning about the Law of Time only confirmed my barrage of memories and early obsession with time travel and underground tunnels, cities, and other realities. Votan's words activated images on my mental screen: The children. The Bridge. The haunting melody that would echo in my dreams: This is the bridge of all time.... The angels around my bed; Giants, dinosaurs, and my "imaginary" friend, John King. The mysterious hand that would appear during my nap time.

My inner and outer worlds were beginning to cohere. I felt I had walked onto a page of a mythic storybook.

Forever in a forest of time unknown, Votan, the Red Queen, and the Queen of the Throne.

In this mythic storybook, Lloydine, a.k.a. Bolon Ik, was the White Solar Wind. She played the role of the patroness, founder, or Mother of the Dynasty. Bolon Ik means 9 Wind in Mayan. In Palenque, there are numerous 9 Wind inscriptions that seem to be associated with the Mother of the Dynasty.

José Argüelles, a.k.a. Valum Votan, was the Blue Spectral Monkey. He was the carrier of the prophetic lineage of the Galactic Maya. He represents the heart of the people. Stephanie South, a.k.a. Red Queen, was the Red Electric Serpent. She was the receiver and renewer of knowledge. She represents the people's hearts fulfilled.

The three of us added up to the galactic signature White Planetary Mirror, the signature of Pacal's tomb opening on June 15, 1952.

There was a lot to absorb, both at the personal level and at more cosmic levels. I shared with them that when they met in 1981, I was eight years old, remembering myself as John Mathews, a seasoned time traveler, exploring underground time tunnels, searching for the right time. I brought them my 13-page Lost in Time "book."

Votan pointed out the codings in the book. For example, I gave the year 4029 as the time of human extinction. Synchronically, my apprenticeship started when I was age 29 and would conclude at age 40. There were many more synchronicities within the small book.

Votan took the booklet and made markings in it. He handed it back to me the next morning with the following words written in red on the front:

... Lost in time no more
But back to restore
The time tunnels lore

Where we last met
Between two tombs
A mystery never to forget:
The tunnel of time
Its measure of death...
Red Queen's victory, the whole planet is blessed.

People of OMA

On the morning of Votan's 63rd birthday, he woke up to a powerful dream about the "Return of the People of OMA," whom he viewed crossing the Bridge of Time among tall grasses bent by a soothing wind shimmering in the sunlight. They were accompanied by dogs and horses moving thoughtfully and yet without care into this world, purified of all its prior history. Votan wrote:

> *OMA is beginning, end and beyond, therefore do not think that this template of Vision and action called Return of the People of OMA will be anything concise nor even familiar but more like a saga and a method of action emanating from a far off star, but yet not so far from where you are, and were it not for a distant presence known as Bolon Ik we would not know of OMA and the Red Queen at all ...*
>
> *... Who would join me would join the crystal codes of primal Memnosis, put together by the two appointed queens in the time before manifestation. For from these codes, a matching pair different only in that one initiates, and the other completes lies all that can be known, sung, enacted, and done. ...*

Sex is the Beginning of Knowledge

The day of the dream of OMA was a day that stamped my destiny. I had no idea that this particular day would become the defining factor of my life mission, nor that it would later be the cause of so much misunderstanding.

The morning proceeded normally with Deb and Brian in town for a board meeting of the Foundation for the Law of Time. I brought Votan three gifts: frankincense and myrrh incense, a long-sleeved blue shirt, and Loreena McKennitt's *Mask and the Mirror* CD.

That evening Votan and Lloydine were sitting on the couch, and I was sitting on the floor in front of the cozy woodstove. After sharing about her early relationships, Lloydine began talking about the Tibetan tradition where the terton (treasure revealer) always functions with a consort who provides the inspiration and embodies the actual templates of the codes. In Tibetan Buddhism, tertons are considered to be incarnations of the 25 main disciples of Padmasambhava. The basic premise is that knowledge is locked within the body and can be released through conscious sexuality. At least that is how I interpreted it at the time.

This was the context in which a sexual relation between Votan and I began as initiated by Lloydine on the night of his 63rd birthday: White Solar Worldbridger, guided by White Solar Wind (Lloydine). I had viewed them more as a galactic Mother-Father at that point, so this was unexpected until the moment it happened, but I trusted them both implicitly. The entire evening felt like an echo choreographed in another time, another world, as if a template of forgotten knowledge was being reawakened. At this point, everything accelerated quickly, and I had no frame of reference to comprehend it all.

The next morning at breakfast, they both assured me all was well, and everything was shared openly and consciously. The apprenticeship was to last until my 40th birthday, and then I would be freed into a new path, and they would continue on theirs. They went out of their way to make me feel welcomed. I felt safe at that time, but my main interest was the teachings and knowledge. At that point, I was just in the present moment, not thinking long-term about anything or what might unfold.

Shortly after this initial encounter, Votan and Lloydine went to Mexico for six weeks, leaving me alone to reflect, work, and study. I was undergoing a whole systems reorientation of my inner and outer worlds, and had no idea what was to unfold next. They faxed me messages every day to update me on their journey and to assure me that I was in the right place. In one of the faxes they wrote:

> *The initiation of the Red Queen is the inscribing of the uninscribed and the awakening to powers wound in karmic layers around the essence soul body of the transmigratory initiate. The initiatic process is in accord with a synchronic pattern of destiny that emerges in greater moments of consciousness and self reflective clarity.*

Votan had asked me to edit his first draft of *Time and the Technosphere: The Law of Time in Human Affairs.* I immersed myself in that book and felt a buoyant sensation as I absorbed the tremendous energy vibrating beneath the words. The book offers evidence that the Earth has come to be dominated by the "technosphere," an envelope of inhuman mechanization that practically has a mind of its own and has us careening toward a cataclysmic future. It also gives an antidote: a species-wide return to natural time.

Until you make the unconscious conscious,

it will direct your life and you will call it fate.

—C.G. Jung

WE ARE MAYA
WE ARE THE NAVIGATORS OF TIME
WE ARE THE ONES WHO, IN OUR MEDITATION, PRECEDED ALL THE OTHERS FROM THE MATRIX TO THE OUTPOSTS OF THE GALAXY'S FOUR QUADRANTS -
WE ARE THE ARCHITECT MOTHERS OF ALL SYSTEMS OF KNOWING AND TRANSCENDING TIME, THOSE WHO DO NOT KNOW US OR WHO, KNOWING ABOUT US DENY OUR POWER, CONSIGN THEMSELVES TO DARKNESS.
Ω
A

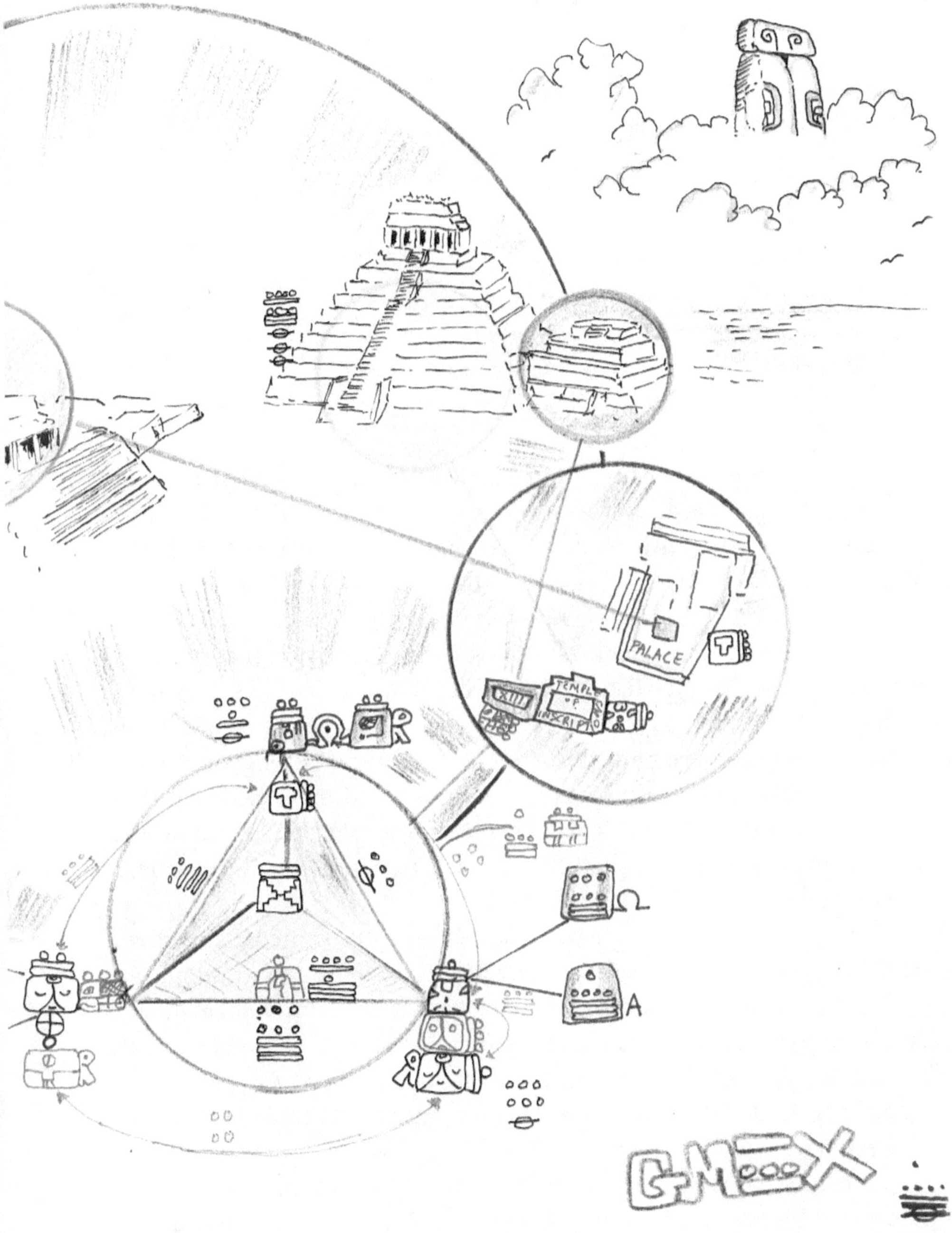
PALACE
TEMPL
OF
INXRIPTIO
XIII
A

Chapter 6

Cosmic History

You must not let your life run in the ordinary way; do something that nobody else has done, something that will dazzle the world. Show that God's creative principle works in you.

—Paramahansa Yogananda

A few days after returning from Mexico, Votan shared that the great Mayan sage, Pacal, was a seer of the distant star histories and the wisdom of the coming dawn. He also said that Pacal was the "keeper of Cosmic History." This sparked my interest, and I asked him what he meant by "Cosmic History." He said he would tell me later.

A few days later, at breakfast, Votan mentioned again that Pacal was the "knower of Cosmic History." I asked him again what that meant. He replied that "through a method of telepathy and teleportation, Pacal was able to extend his mind to different people and events throughout time."

He called Pacal, "time's special witness," and explained that he is not a personality, but rather a galactic intelligence that came to show that all teachers, teachings, and knowledge of the past, present, and future are one unified thought matrix.

This sparked my imagination, and I began to contemplate what it would be like to time travel to the greatest teachers in the world and see reality through their eyes and to have conversations with them about our cosmic origins and where the earth is at now. But still, Votan had not answered my question about Cosmic History, and the next day I asked him about it again, for the third time. This was the trigger that opened a vast process of transmission of knowledge. Ask, and ye shall receive.

On this day, I was sitting by the wood stove in our Mount Hood home, and Votan was sitting on the couch while Lloydine was out running errands. While we were sitting in silence, Votan began experiencing vertigo and lay down on the couch. He told me he was having an "optical," where his field of vision would be replaced by colorful geometric shapes.

He was accustomed to this type of experience and told me it was the way information was transmitted to him.

I felt a tingling surge of energy in the back of my head, and warmth filled my body as he began to narrate what he saw to me. He said he was viewing a parallel life through a thick interplanetary mirror. He recounted his experience of how life was lived, simultaneously, on this planet and another planet. Then, he saw the scenes change, and all of a sudden the civilization of Maldek (now the Asteroid Belt) appeared before him, before its destruction.

He narrated that he was seeing a form of humanoids moving through constructs similar to modern-day city blocks. They were engaged in activities that appeared identical to those of the present Earth world. Yet, something else was going on. The beings seemed simultaneously frantic, ecstatic, and oblivious to a catastrophe about to occur. As he narrated, my skin tingled as this memory matched precisely my own dreams.

When the intensity had subsided, Votan spoke of the similar enactment presently occurring on Planet Earth. He explained that our job is to help wake humanity up to divert it from repeating the disastrous catastrophes of Maldek and Mars. It was because of this potential replay that we were called together to receive the knowledge of what we would later call "Cosmic History."

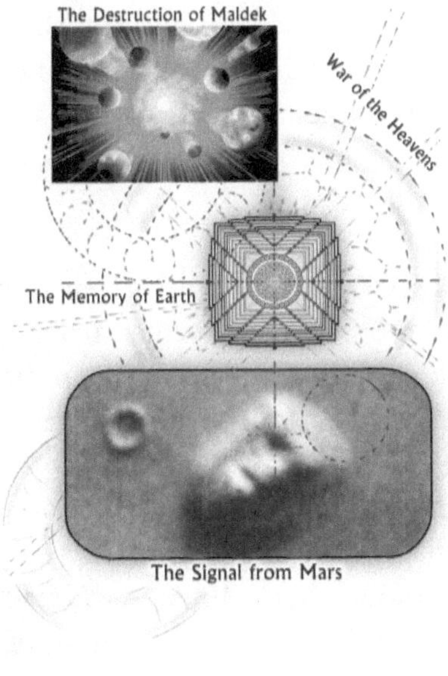

Theft in Time

Cosmic History is a continuation of the Law of Time that traces our present civilization back to the "theft in time," an interplanetary event that not only affected our solar system but which traces back to even larger cycles and other worlds.

This "theft in time" is also known as the "Fall" (from sacred to profane). This created a split of the two hemispheres of the brain (yin and yang, night and day, male and female). When this "theft" occurred, the balance of equality was lost, and the energies became dominated by the left brain (male). The planetary guardians designated Earth as a quarantine zone to isolate the problem and allow humans to correct the error matrices.

This "theft of time" accounts for the active suppression of knowledge throughout human history. Much knowledge has been lost or forgotten and replaced with various forms of entertainment designed to keep the masses asleep.

After this powerful vision, Votan realized the "Cosmic History transmission" was the vehicle to connect points of lost consciousness between Maldek and present-day Earth. There was a sense of urgency to this process, which cannot be fully articulated. The first Cosmic History transmission began the following day on March 13, 2002, White Overtone Wizard. This day was precisely 52 days after I moved in with Votan and Lloydine.

Fifty-two is a significant number in Mayan cosmology and is also the number of weeks in a solar year (plus one Day Out of Time). This particular cycle of transmissions would last for 260 days, and then the experiment would take a new form.

These sessions or tutorials were known as "between the world's transmissions." We also called them the GM108X, Galactic Mayan mind transmissions.

Mind Lineage

GM108X is the name given to a transmission circuit that is broadcast from other star systems through the center of the galaxy, the Hunab Ku. This can be understood as an information stream or knowledge template of a particular mind lineage that we called the Galactic Maya.

The GM108X is a mind lineage rather than blood and bloodlines. The basic premise of this lineage is that the origin of the universe is in time, and not in space as the present-day Earth science conceives it. Without a living lineage, the teachings cannot be authenticated. This is as true of the GM108X lineage as of any other.

Several years prior, José Argüelles had realized Valum Votan as the emanation of the code body created by Pacal Votan. He understood that mind transmission does not mean reincarnation and is not dependent on a sequence of rebirth, but rather is received through resonance to a particular system of coded knowledge. He understood Pacal Votan as a medium of transmission in what is known as a Galactic Mayan (GM) mind transmission, or GM108X. He explained that the origin of the GM108X mind transmission lies far outside the earth and predates the present historical cycle by hundreds of thousands of years. It is the information stream that contains the keys of knowledge pertaining to the science that defines how we arrived on this particular star system.

The Galactic Maya are planetary navigators and mappers of the larger psychic field of the Earth, the solar system, and the galaxy beyond. They are a telepathic culture. This means that their perceptions, modes of knowing, and communication come from telepathic attunement to the cosmos.

The experiment of the Galactic Mayan colonizers was to calibrate the time that remained on Earth before all the cosmic residue of Mars (death fear) and Maldek (sex taboo) come to a climactic point of ripening. Death-fear (Mars) manipulates the mind to feed materialism (Saturn); e.g., pharmaceutical companies. And we see false hierarchies of priests or elite (Jupiter) who manipulate sex (Maldek) and inflict fear (Mars) to maintain power over the people.

Votan wrote of our GM108X transmissions:

> *The process of tutorials and transmissions have several functions, one is to impart knowledge in a traditional sense and another is to create a particular kind of environment where it is possible for truths that have not been accessed to become accessible simply by the process of engaging in a living transmission.*

Cosmic History reveals that the dominant, historical knowledge base is a time loop that is constantly being fed back to us.

Cosmic History Chronicles, Volume I states:

> *When we think about the dominant worldview, which negates time and consciousness, we have to understand that there is a whole huge single mental order that is constantly talking to itself. In other words, when you read the newspaper, it is really only the mind talking to itself. When you watch a news program or read the news on the Internet, it is still just the mind talking to itself, because who is reading or watching it but the mind that created it?*

Preparation

My initial experience at the tomb of the Red Queen two years earlier was starting to make sense with the transmission of Cosmic History. I felt three key experiences had prepared me for this path. The first was from an early age. I never had any direction or parental expectation placed on me about who I was or what I should do. I had a powerful awakening experience at age 10 when my aunt died and my parents divorced. I realized they couldn't help me, and I made an inner vow at that time to find my own path.

The second preparation was my near-death experience in 1992. The third point of preparation was a series of ahuayasca journeys in 1999 that helped me become acquainted with non-ordinary states of reality. The beginning of my first ahuayasca journey was terrifying, with a feeling that I was being strangled by a double-headed snake. But rather than physically dying, I saw that the snake was my ally squeezing the entire matrix of conditioned reality out of my cellular structure. I saw all the fictions that had been implanted in my brain, primarily the fiction called American culture of the 1970s-80s.

During that pivotal journey, I saw our Earth civilization as a type of holographic video game. We have to make it through the maze without getting eaten by the bad guys. Then Pac-Man appeared and began to eat all of my conditionings one by one, from MTV to Lucky Charms to the White House. It was as though he was clearing my "waveform" by eating my illusory thought-forms and then digesting and transmuting my limiting perceptions and beliefs. Pac-Man then ate himself and disappeared (similar to the ororoborus archetype when the serpent bites its tail).

Everything was revealed as equally trivial from this vantage point. I was shown that this particular earth hologram is designed as a labyrinth full of meaningless distractions to see if we can find our way back to the center. I was shown how time-space holograms are constructed by a set of vibrations that translate to symbols. These conditionings also included historical figures: Marilyn Monroe, James Dean, Martin Luther King, Albert Einstein—they are all part of the same holographic software program.

After I was sufficiently "cleared," gentle guides appeared who, with soothing whispers, showed me the power of Love and that once you embrace your fears with Love, then they have no choice but to transform themselves. They reminded me that "love never fails" and advised me to always "be teachable."

Then I saw new worlds emerge; pristine, crystalline worlds, strange yet familiar. I was taken to far-off reaches of the galaxy as a type of "star tour" always with the guiding theme of Love as the answer to all. After this experience I sought a natural way to access and sustain these experiences. Then entered the Law of Time, which I found to be a psychoactive experience.

Here are my first notes from the first Cosmic History transmission:

Cosmic History Notes

Cosmic History is a teaching of liberation. These were the first seven words of the first transmission.

Cosmic History mission:

To transmit and establish in its entirety the new foundation of human knowledge completely in accord with the Law of Time; and to train and prepare the lineage holder of this transmission, otherwise known as GM108X.

Cosmic History is the sum of the codes of human knowledge in conformity with the Galactic Mayan Mind Transmission on comprehending as a whole, the moral, imaginal, and phenomenal universes.

1) Universe going from one harmonic state to another.

2) A self-reflective reflex of cosmic memory.

3) Cosmic History investigates: What is a memory? What are we trying to remember? How do we remember?

4) The root is a psychophysical premise. Everything reduces down to sensory data and what our mind does with it.

5) The normative function of mind and senses is to make things more harmonic.

Chapter 7

Daily Life

Sit down before fact like a little child, and be prepared to give up every preconceived notion, follow humbly wherever and to whatever abyss Nature leads, or you shall learn nothing.

—T.H. Huxley

I was struck by a series of disillusionments about my perceived reality during the first year of my apprenticeship. I was in the process of unlearning everything I had been taught. Non-ordinary states of consciousness became ordinary life, and paranormal phenomena became common.

In the mythic realm, Votan and I lived in the Court of Bolon Ik (Lloydine), where we strove to make domestic life a perfect mirror of the court of the star-born elders. This meant that every detail was considered: Will it put more dust on the mirror, or will it bring about a better reflection of the higher being? Though it may sound strange to some, this type of creative life fits perfectly with my childhood dreams.

The three of us were committed to up-leveling our emotional/thought structures as part of a mission that involved the complete transcendence of all conventional thoughts, ideas, and beliefs about reality. This was envisioned as a 10-year process where I agreed to live and work with them until my 40th birthday. Votan and Lloydine created an agreement that the three of us each signed and took a vow of silence as we knew other people's opinions could distract the experiment. The following is summed up in Votan's words:

... They (the three of us) have reunited on this planet to break the human species out of its hypnotic spell of self-imposed limitations and outworn belief systems. But first, they must shake off all of the fragmented karmic residuals from Maldek and Mars and redeem all memories of the war of the worlds and paradise lost through their total recollection.

Votan and Lloydine were operating as one unit, and their unified field was my anchor and guide. Lloydine's role was that of wife and partner, and mine was that of the apprentice. Their harmony as a couple was my foundation, and I felt honored to be in my role. I was so busy learning and reorienting my awareness that I didn't think much about the relationships and how they would go. Though I had never been part of an experiment such as this, it was not a question of "right" or "wrong"; it was merely what was happening.

Unlocking Knowledge

Each day, Votan and I showed up faithfully to tune into the "Cosmic History channel." Just the act of "showing up" and sitting together unlocked floods of memory simultaneously for both of us. It was a powerful force that we could not fully explain, except to say that this knowledge transmission traces back to two side-by-side tombs in Palenque, Mexico: the tomb of Pacal Votan and the tomb of the Red Queen. But it is even beyond that.

When this Cosmic History vault was unsealed between Votan and me, it was literally like being transported into another reality. We were the stargates that opened to different dimensions. Through the alignment of our energy, we could go anywhere. During the daily transmission, physical reality dissolved, and for lack of better description, it was like the movie *The Matrix*, where the coded collective paradigms that create our perception of "reality" were phased out as we vibrated into another dimension of awareness. This reality had always existed; it is just that we had never been attuned to it.

We experienced a mutual remembrance of a pact we had made in another lifetime. There was a feeling that we were performers enacting a piece of living architecture that had spanned many eons but changed appearance and name with each incarnation. It is something that cannot be fully articulated and is admittedly out of the frame of reference of most people. Still, for me, it was a natural process of the memory retrieval mission that I was prepared for.

Discipline

My circuits jammed with too much information during the beginning stages of the apprenticeship. My physical health suffered. This was compounded by the two cats, Frankie and Lucy, whom I was allergic to. For this first year, I struggled much physically and began to lighten my diet to allow space to process knowledge.

For this reason, Votan emphasized daily discipline, in both body and mind. The body had to be cultivated and cared for as a temple for transformation; otherwise, it would burn out. It was not easy in the beginning to awaken at 4 a.m. and meditate. I would drink a cup of coffee (yes, I did still drink that) and then do Dzogchen meditation: relaxing the mind back to the source, dissolving my thoughts with the out-breath.

Meditation was essential in this process as it allowed the nonconceptual mind time to breathe and experience itself apart from the ceaseless discourse of the conditioned mind. I was in the process of deprogramming old conditioning and learning new information at hyper speed. There was a sense that I was being rewired from the inside out.

Morning meditation was followed by contemplating the daily codes of the synchronic order, followed by yoga. These codes provided a lens in which to view the day and become aware of synchronicity. The three of us would have breakfast together, which was generally coffee, fruit, yogurt, and granola. A nature walk followed. There was a rushing river and wooded back trails right near the house with bears, rattlesnakes, squirrels, chipmunks, and birds. Votan was partial to ravens and considered them one of his animal spirit guides. Interesting that a group of ravens is called a "conspiracy."

On one occasion, while walking alone deep into the forest, I was absorbed in my thoughts when I heard a loud crunching sound, and a huge brown bear had made its way down the forest wall right in front of me. It stood on its hind legs, and I could feel its powerful spirit mixed with my own fear. I slowly took a step backward and then turned around and walked slowly, praying for mercy. After that, I never ventured that far into the forest again.

The best part of the day was the afternoon "Cosmic History" transmission, which transported us to other times and places. This was like tuning in to a particular radio station, which in this case was the channel GM108X. This was a multidimensional and universal channel that transcends all dogma, biases, race, and religion. This is the channel of our cosmic origins and the forgotten history of harmony.

The emphasis was first on cultivating a discerning mind. There were several types of criteria simultaneously (like logical, spiritual, etc.). Importance was stressed on understanding what was being said, how it was said, and in what context it was being said; these were important mental values critical in the development of mind, perceptions, and attitudes about the world. Votan encouraged me to examine and question everything that was presented to me to learn how to evaluate in the context of different points of view.

Learning how to operate with multiple perspectives simultaneously was all-important. One of the first things he taught me was how to experience "nothing" in the middle of daily activity. This is known as "mixing mind with space," the basis of clear perception, as taught to him by his teacher Chogyam Trungpa Rinpoche. Before practicing meditation, my mind used to run rampant, resulting in severe anxiety attacks and all sorts of other frustrations.

Daily Process

In these beginning transmissions, I made handwritten notes of key teachings, but most of the time, I just listened and absorbed. After the tutorial, I would then spend a few hours in reflection and write down notes of my understanding, and questions for what I didn't understand. The knowledge had a familiar resonance, even though I could not grasp it with my mind. There was nowhere else on Earth that I would have rather been. Great warmth and a sense of wholeness would flood my being when working with the knowledge. This feeling was accompanied by great excitement, creative wonder, and an eagerness to know or remember everything.

After my daily Cosmic History session, I would rest a bit and then meet Lloydine in her room. I was honored that she wanted me to have equal one-on-one time with her as with Votan in Cosmic History transmission. She spoke much of her early years, and we worked to trace back patterns from her childhood. She had grown up in Marin County and was close with her mother, Maya, but not as close with her father, Lloyd, who was an alcoholic and away much of her childhood. She talked about how she was bullied in school by a group of girls who formed a club against her. She studied dancing and became a Buddhist practitioner, marrying and having two children. She was 37 years old when she met José Argüelles on a 10-day silent retreat at the Rocky Mountain Dharma Center in Colorado in 1981 and married two years later. They found compatibility with their mutual divorces, and they each had two children: a boy and a girl.

In 1987 everything changed with the Harmonic Convergence, followed by the death of Votan's son, Josh. Ten years after their marriage, Lloydine was traveling the world with Votan as a messenger of the new time. While he had become realized in his mission, she admittedly felt that she had lost her own identity.

When I moved in, we all three agreed that the main focus should be on Lloydine's healing as she had been chronically sick with bronchitis on and off for years. We encouraged her to rest more, but it was challenging for her to be still, perhaps because of years of constant motion. The three of us did a 12-day juice cleanse with green vegetable juices, water, and herbal tea. This was a good bonding experience. Votan said he had been concerned for some time that the years of travel had taken their toll on her physical and mental health. Lloydine said she was at a stage in her life where she was ready to stop and enjoy family and being a grandma, which was understandable after the years of travel. Votan put me in charge of canceling all of their travels and taking over their communications. He even announced publicly that they were retiring, but did not mention the reason.

Activated Transmission

My conventional reference points were melting in light of my new life, which revolved around the daily transmission session. During these sessions, the room took on a golden glow, as otherworldly energy bathed the room. We were Votan and Red Queen, archetypal forces in a grand cosmic motion picture. "Red" is the color of initiation, and "Queen" refers to the female matrix long repressed by history. Equalization of masculine and feminine was the key that turned the ignition. Votan wrote in his moonly Rinri report:

> *The Red Queen's tomb was as uninscribed as the Great Pacal's was inscribed, though both also contained a mask and Telektonon tube. The meaning of the inscribed and the uninscribed was that as the apprentice, the Red Queen was to receive the knowledge of the Votan in its entirety and in a form consistent with the Galactic Mayan knowledge as embodied in the Great Pacal and his prophetic legacy.*

The Cosmic History sessions brought a feeling of being connected to something so vast and magnificent that everything else paled in comparison. On some occasions, I would look at Votan only to see a vibrating grid or matrix of energy, electrifying, and pulsing through him. As our resonance increased we would sit across from one another and dissolve "ourselves," allowing each other to see a parade of characters—past, future, and present—come through. This felt like a natural occurrence when we were in a field of highest trust without filters or distortion.

Votan applied all of his knowledge as a university professor to me. He had an eclectic background and had learned from many great teachers from a wide variety of styles and traditions. He told me that for my unique learning style we would start with the most advanced teachings and work backward. It was an intense education on every subject imaginable. In the initial plan, he wrote:

> *With these training programs, the Red Queen is learning intense yogic synchronization and telepathic bonding while receiving a complete instruction in all aspects of the Cosmic History, inclusive of, though by no means limited to the codes of the synchronic order, whole system design principles, third-dimensional biopsychic and astrophysical models, principles of dharma, cosmic, and sacred art; History, philosophy, and principles of organization; comparative religion, symbolic structures; psychological models of behavior; and research methods.*
>
> *Since the goal is the reformulation of the human knowledge base as one reflective of a purely sacred 13:20 order, the training is exhaustive and easily necessitates an 11-year cycle. When the training is complete, the foundations of UR shall have been established, and the noospheric basis of knowledge and behavior will be ready to be released for the benefit of all beings.*

At this time, we did not know what we would do with all the knowledge coming through. Each daily transmission was like a beautiful flower, that taken as a whole formed a brilliant bouquet in a new arrangement. It was only halfway into the 260 consecutive sessions when we determined to put this knowledge into a seven-volume series that would be known as the *Cosmic History Chronicles*. As part of the discipline, we would complete one volume per year: 2004-2011.

Chapter 8

Alchemical Cauldron

To light a candle is to cast a shadow.

—Ursula Le Guinn

After saying yes to a path of knowledge, I found many previously unseen gates that had to be opened and passed through. Many of these experiences defied all logic of the consensual mainstream framework. The concentrated absorption in this knowledge stream and its process of transmission began to inform and reshape the whole of my perceptions and daily reality. Being a cosmic whole order of knowledge, Cosmic History had to inevitably affect every detail of the life process.

I found my perceptions changing so rapidly that as soon as I would start to speak or write something down another shift would occur. I chose to remain mostly silent about my current life experience until I fully understood it.

In the case of the experiment between the three of us, it lasted from January 20, 2002 (Kin 122) to November 28, 2002 (Kin 174). About halfway through this 312-day long process, severe tests and initiations began to occur within our triad. Everything was happening so quickly. The knowledge I sought to learn felt vast and overwhelming, and I was struggling to balance all human components. I was learning at hyper speed and was relying on Votan and Lloydine's union as my emotional anchor, support, and comfort. Living in a telepathic force-field gave instantaneous feedback.

At this time I began to understand that when any time new knowledge is received, whether it be on a personal level or a planetary one, it stirs the contents of the unconscious mind, which is precisely what is happening today on a planetary scale. We are involved in the process of planetary alchemy, where all unconscious aspects of the human being have to be drawn to the surface and made conscious for us to become whole and integrated.

Fast-Track Learning

> *Alchemy is the art that separates what is useful from what is not by transforming it into its ultimate matter and essence.*
>
> —Paracelsus

Learning so much new information while uprooting subconscious programming with no let-up or "breathers" created a particular pressurized atmosphere. It was like being in an airtight alchemical vessel, and it became increasingly hard to breathe.

When inside an alchemical vessel, the intense pressure can be experienced as the contents of the unconscious mind are brought into the light. In this process, every emotion, doubt, and fear can and will be experienced for this purification to occur; this is to temper the true essence so that the pure diamond consciousness can emerge. Until the invisible forces that govern our lives are recognized, worked with, and eventually mastered, then real understanding cannot be realized.

Mystic and philosopher, G.I. Gurdjieff said that to get beyond the point of just being an automaton, sometimes different aspects of awakening occur that can be experienced as "shocks": shocking only to the conditioned persona. What I sadly came to realize is that some people will never wake up as their role is to disbelieve in any possibility other than the error they are addicted to. This is generally the result of a deep trauma that is too painful for them to look at.

Supernatural Forces

There was no denying that a Larger Force was moving the three of us. In the first 260 days of my apprenticeship with Votan, psychic phenomena increased rapidly, and telepathy was instantaneous. The three of us experienced unexplained tapping sounds, papers flying in the air, fireballs, etc. A heightened third-dimensional tension coupled this paranormal phenomenon.

One night, during a wild spring storm in 2002, I came to consciousness in my bed at our Mt. Hood home but was in a state of sleep paralysis. My room was lit in a soft glow, though no lights were turned on. Was I dreaming? It didn't feel like it. Papers were floating, suspended in mid-air, flying around my room. Music filled the air. Strangely it was the chorus of the song "Southern Cross" by Crosby, Stills, and Nash repeating over and over. In hindsight this felt to be a precognitive experience, as four years later I would be living in New Zealand and Australia beneath the Southern Cross. The main chorus of the song repeated in slow motion: "*...what heaven brought you and me cannot be forgotten...and the Southern Cross.*"

On another occasion, Votan, Lloydine, and I drove to Ashland, Oregon, for a field trip followed by a visit to Crater Lake. While in Ashland, at Lloydine's suggestion, we purchased a copy of Madame Blavatsky's biography to supplement our studies. Her mother Maya, who had been a theosophist, was also a great supporter of Votan.

Helena Petrovna Blavatsky, "Madame Blavatsky," had an uncanny ability to synthesize and connect vast amounts of knowledge, and I admired her fearlessness in speaking the truth she had discovered, however controversial it might be. We found it amazing that Blavatsky wrote of Votan as the "master magician" in her book *Isis Unveiled* and how by 1871 she had already come across the first translations of the *Popol Vuh,* which hardly anyone knew about back then. She knew of virtually every mythological advanced spiritual tradition that existed on the planet. She also had a great facility to summarize and connect these great traditions, tracing them to a previous root race. And now we were evolving into a new root race. This was similar to our work in Cosmic History, with an emphasis on memory retrieval from previous worlds and envisioning possibilities of worlds yet to come.

Mother Board

One bright autumn day, Votan and I sat on the grass in Lithia Park in Ashland, where he gave me a tutorial on the "Psychology of an Esoteric Personality," based on Madame Blavatsky (with Lloydine nearby on a walk).

Being in the park in the fresh air, we examined Blavatsky's view on fallen angels, fallen (hu)man, the serpent, and war of the heavens. Our focus then shifted to Blavatsky's cosmology of the "seven root races," which states that the human being is the recapitulation of all the previous stages of the evolution of life. Memory of the last root races is locked inside of our bodies.

In concluding the tutorial, Votan had a visionary experience in the park. He was shown the "Mother Board of the Mother Ship." This vision carried over into the following day, when we visited Crater Lake, the deepest lake in the U.S., on August 16, 2002, White Overtone Dog. This was the 15th anniversary of the Harmonic Convergence global peace meditation. To commemorate this milestone, Lloydine drove us counterclockwise around the vast body of water, stopping at seven different points to honor the seven directions: north, south, east, west, above, below, and within.

During the drive around Crater Lake, Votan once again had a visionary experience of a large circuit board with numerous wirings, that he referred to as the "Mother Board of the Mother Ship." These intricate wirings connected different spiritual aspects, inclusive of the multitude of teachers, ascended masters, guardians of the earth, and the planetary logos.

Standing by the vast body of water, Votan tuned deeply into this "Mother Board," and experienced telepathic confirmation from Master Morya of the parallelism of our work. In this parallelism, the work of Madame Blavatsky and Master Morya culminated in the founding of the Theosophical Society in the 1880s, and the major literary works *Isis Unveiled* and *The Secret Doctrine.* This paralleled the 10-year program of Cosmic History.

That night, the three of us stayed in the nearby small town of Prospect, Oregon, at the cozy, wooded home of my grandparents, Darol and Irene. It was a surreal contrast after the day at Crater Lake to stay with my grandparents. My grandmother, a joyful Christian woman, made us pumpkin pie while Votan told my grandfather about the tomb of Pacal Votan. My grandfather was on the edge of his seat with the story of the tomb's discovery. He then shared his own UFO experience as a child.

Votan played the Lakota flute for my grandmother, which sparked memories for her; she had grown up in Lakota territory in South Dakota. She was born on Pine Ridge Indian Reservation in South Dakota, home of Crazy Horse and the tragedy of Wounded Knee. Synchronically she was also Yellow Resonant Human, the signature of Blavatsky's initial meeting with Morya and my initial meeting with Votan in 1998.

Upon returning from our magical trip, we arrived to the publication of *Time and the Technosphere: The Law of Time in Human Affairs*, at our doorstep. This was a celebratory occasion. This was a pivotal book that voiced a new perception and whole systems vantage point to recent human events and worldwide developments. It defines the Tower of Babel as the root error in time that is responsible for the world system that we see today.

Transmuting Energy

> *Love is the only reality and it is not a mere sentiment. It is the ultimate truth that lies at the heart of creation.*
>
> —Rabindranath Tagore

Upon our return, Votan and Lloydine did what would be their final public event together in Eugene, Oregon. At the time Lloydine was sick with bronchitis, which worsened after the event. We all three worked sensitively with the energy as many repressed emotions began to surface. We abided by the motto *the healing of one is the healing of all.* The key reason for traveling the world as messengers of the New Time was to make conscious what was previously unconscious. What we were to learn is that these false perceptions about reality run deep and color our self-perceptions and our relationships. Votan pointed out that a result of the 12:60 beam was to separate our essence from Source and fracture our consciousness, which can create emotional body imbalances that keep us from realizing higher aspects of our being. This traces to other times and other worlds. First, we have to resolve ourselves and our relations if we are to be of genuine service to humanity.

At this point, I was taking in both Votan and Lloydine's life processes as well as the daily Cosmic History transmission and code studies. My schedule soon became exhausting and I didn't have time to process my feelings. When I realized that I could not keep up the pace, I cordially discontinued my daily sessions with Lloydine.

Most of my spare time was spent alone. I often chose to eat alone in my room as I was challenged to assimilate food and have social conversations at the same time. Votan did not talk a lot, at least in my presence, unless it was about the work. In my observation, he listened patiently to Lloydine's process, and I never heard them have any quarrel or argument the entire time. This time was an opportunity for in-depth and intensive self-study. I observed that in my process of learning I had to be silent and in a state of deep receptivity just listening and observing for long periods while all the parts became coherent.

I contemplated my life from various angles. I wrote down all the characters who ever appeared on the screen in my life. I decoded all of my family members' galactic signatures and found fascinating correspondences. I began to understand my childhood patterns.

I was born at 5:03 p.m. Electric Serpent is written 5.3. I grew up in area code 503 in Marion County in Salem, Oregon. Marion is my middle name. I was born at 1105 Sweet Road. 11 is Monkey (Votan) and 5 is Serpent. 11 + 5 = 16. There are 16 days between our birthdays, January 8 and January 24.

I thought deeply about what seemed the most mundane things through the lens of the synchronic order. For example, as a child I had an Atari 2600 and the first games I played were Asteroids and Space Invaders. In Asteroids you control a single spaceship in the Asteroid Belt where flying saucers sometimes appear. I noted that Atari means to "hit" or "strike" and that 2600 is a fractal of the 26,000-year Great Cycle. Why was I shooting at asteroids? My first computer was a Commodore 64. Was this the 64 DNA codons?

The synchronic order gave me a meaningful and interconnected lens through which to view the world. I was comforted to know and feel many other kin around the world who were also doing these same practices. I hated math prior to learning about the Law of Time. And now I loved numbers and could not get enough of them.

At this time, I was also working on stilling my mind. I examined my self-sabotage or unworthiness programmings; the places that are so painful that we will do anything to escape. I reasoned that this is why people turn to addictions of all types; to drown out the process of truly facing the depths of pain. I wondered if humanity could one day learn through love and joy, rather than so much pain and suffering. I wanted to get to the bottom of all of this.

Chapter 9

Supernatural Shock

Tradition becomes our security, and when the mind is secure it is in decay.

—Krishnamurti

Time operates in a spiral, bringing similar circumstances to our present time until they are resolved. In summer 2002, our top priority was Lloydine's healing, and secondly was the Cosmic History transmission. It was all part of one seamless tapestry, as we traced both the Work and our relations to the destruction of Maldek, which was a template for that which has been destroyed or forgotten. The three of us felt that we had returned to heal an ancient trauma set forth in another time and on another planet.

This ancient trauma traces its origins back into the War of the Heavens, the central theme of the *Telektonon Prophecy of Pacal Votan.* The War of the Heavens is an interdimensional time war that is responsible for the false time imposed at the beginning of history as the Tower of Babel and all that it implies. Babel is related to the word balal ("to confuse").

According to the Book of Genesis, the Tower of Babel was built in Babylon sometime after the Deluge. Nimrod (known in Egypt as Osiris) was the founder of the first world empire at Babel (later known as Babylon). His followers built the tower with "its tops in the heavens." There have been many speculations in regard to the actual purpose of this Tower.

It is interesting to note the Tower of Babel is first mentioned in the Book of Genesis 1:19 (911 backward). Genesis tells that God was unhappy about the creation of this Tower and so divided people's tongues into different languages. Confusion ensued and the city was never completed.

This is interesting to note that the city was never completed.

The three of us were trying to trace back the fracturing of the Original Dream. What had occurred? What were we to heal? Through our daily life experiences, the three of us were attempting to get to the root of and heal this ancient trauma on behalf of all humanity. The more we consciously worked with this, the more the energies amplified and the initiations intensified.

Those warm end-of-summer mountain days of 2002 were characterized by high pressure yet an otherworldly magic that seemed to permeate every moment. Daily life became increasingly unpredictable.

During this time, Lloydine spontaneously performed a marriage ceremony for Votan and me in which she placed a ring with 11 stars on my finger. It came with no warning and I stayed silent as she conducted the process. A few weeks later, Lloydine came to my room before sunrise and said it was time for a "Ceremony of Equalization" between she and me in regard to our relationship to Votan. This meant she wanted me to have equal intimate time with Votan as she did. After breakfast that morning, she conducted the ceremony and gave me her silver chalice and a crystal ball with a phantom pyramid, representing the European esoteric tradition. Up until now when Votan and I were not involved in the Cosmic History transmissions, he spent the remainder of his personal time with her. I was deeply steeped in studies and transmissions and did not wish to be so involved in this type of relational process.

A few weeks later Votan and Lloydine left for a retreat together to discuss the next steps of their relationship. When they returned, they informed me that they were setting forth a process of "individuation." They said it had become clear that they had developed unhealthy codependencies and were too entangled and mirroring each other in a way that wasn't helpful for each other's growth. The idea was to take some time apart. I had spoken highly of my time with the Haight family in Idaho, and Lloydine felt that might be a good space for her retreat. She wrote them:

> *Bolon Ik (Lloydine) humbly asks the Haight family to accommodate her 3 month retreat. I feel I can be most nurtured and at the same time have the chance to find myself autonomously. I calculated that 38 of my 59 years had been spent codependently in marriage, so I need to find my real face.*

At this point, everything felt unpredictable and quickly unraveling. The initial cycle completed on Thanksgiving Day, 2002, which coincided with the 260th consecutive Cosmic History transmission. A few days later, I had gone for a long drive alone, only to come back to find

Votan sitting alone by the fire and telling me Lloydine wasn't just going on retreat but that she would be moving to Idaho in a few days with the Haight family. It was all a "shock" at one level, but it was meant to lift us all into our next level.

All Things Must Pass

Lloydine asked me to arrange a U-Haul truck and to pack all of her personal belongings while she and Votan went to dinner at their favorite local restaurant, the Rendezvous Grill. I'll never forget the strangeness of that moment, being alone in their bedroom for hours packing up all of her most personal belongings. It felt like everything was happening quickly, and in some ways, in these moments I felt like an observer in their life rather than a participant.

On our last night together Lloydine was inspired to dance for Votan and me to George Harrison's song "All Things Must Pass." The dance brought forth remembrances from another time, another world. The entire evening was like a haunting déjà vu. We talked about the experiment that we started together, and we all expressed that we had no idea what the next stages of this path were. There was still hope that they would get back together.

At this point, though things felt different, it still felt like we were operating in a unified field. I didn't think that Lloydine leaving was going to be permanent; I thought she would be back. None of us knew what was to unfold next; at least I didn't. Suddenly I was left alone in the house with Valum Votan. When Lloydine arrived in Idaho a day later, I was shocked to learn that she was telling people at the Haight property that Votan had left her for another woman. The story that was told felt like it was from some other parallel universe, not the reality that I had lived.

Weeks later, Lloydine visited Votan and me unannounced. She came to declare me to be an adulteress, and generated a written document that she had a few "key" kin witnesses to sign. The document had quotes from the Quran with various punishments that were prescribed for such people, including switching. I was flabbergasted, but remained silent as she expressed herself. There was no way to get a word in edgewise. Votan, too, just listened. I didn't really feel upset, but rather just a strange and surreal feeling. It was like a whole other being had entered her. Other than this moment, Lloydine and I never had a bad word toward each other. Everything was happening at heightened speed, and it was challenging to process it all. Later I would understand it as part of the initiatory training. As we wrote in *Cosmic History Chronicles, Volume I:*

> *But for the incorporation of Cosmic History into their form bodies to occur, Votan and Red Queen underwent countless inner and outer initiations that stripped them down from outmoded habitual tendencies and finely and delicately attuned them so that the only function or purpose that remained was Cosmic History.*
>
> *All of their emotional and astral configurations have been designed to be maximally sensitive, which is heightened by a lifestyle that tends to close out forms of mass media manipulation and media in general. This only further increases the raw, sensitive space in which each resides so that the different nuances of all of these energetic embodiments can be experienced.*
>
> *Through the ongoing process of historical purification, the two vehicles of Cosmic History had to navigate through all the different programs of previous incarnations, both from this world and other worlds. This manifested as various apparent mind bombardments or a perpetual kind of psychic attack or repetitious thought-forms received by each to be transmuted and transcended through the sensitivity of their purified instruments. The necessity of witnessing all programs of the cosmic unconscious was necessary to ensure that their astral and emotional bodies were stripped down naked.*

Several weeks after Lloydine moved out, Votan left for a silent retreat at a nearby Monastery in Mount Angel to get clear on his next steps. When he returned, he felt it was time to pursue a divorce. He loved her deeply, and she loved him, but he felt their relation had run its course and that the only way she could find herself, was separate from him. He loved her enough to let her go. They still talked nearly every day for about a year.

My solace was that I knew she would be in the loving home of our dear friends, who would provide her sanctuary and the highest possibility for finding herself.

At this time, Votan wrote:

What is loyalty? Whom are we to be loyal to? We are loyal to the soul, to the true being. There is a higher love than ego love. In the conventions of the human drama, we are at a point where everything is being turned upside down. So everything that is happening here is a pure reflection of how everything is being turned upside down. So the question is what is our authentic being and how do we maintain our authentic being?

We each spent hours alone in contemplation as the rain pounded on the deck of the magical wizard cottage during that stormy winter. The only warmth came through the living flame of Cosmic History. It was as though everything else was being stripped away so that only the flame remained. For six moons, winter into spring, Votan was unwinding and making sense of his life and relation. Lloydine was in Idaho, and going through her process. I too was going through the depths of my soul and trying to make sense of what had just happened. Votan wrote in his journal:

The stream out back rages on. Within myself, I find no self. The wind blows the pine branches outside the window. At the periphery of the mind flickers of the past, flickers of the future. Flickers of nowhere else to go but here. The heart tastes its solitude, inseparable from the rain and wind. That winter, my apprentice and I experienced the deepest place of the soul where we surrender to the Absolute. Tears streaming down my face, tears of inconsolable heartbreak of all beings caught in the web of their illusions. Tears from a depth I have not known before. Tears from the deepest well of the soul's own solitude.

—Valum Votan

Part Two
Transformation

Chapter 10

Path Less Travelled

Two roads diverged in a wood, and I—I took the one less traveled by, and that has made all the difference.

—Robert Frost

People only see what they are prepared to see.

—Ralph Waldo Emerson

Sumerian goddess Inanna descends into the Underworld where she must pass through seven gates. At each gate (corresponding to the seven chakras) she is stripped of one of her powers. Finally she enters the inner sanctum, naked, and stands before the Queen of the Underworld. She is annihilated but then from the love of the people she is resurrected, regains her royal status, and arises as the Queen of Heaven.

I related to Inanna being stripped of her powers and entering the Underworld. Life, as I had previously experienced it, was over. My whole immediate reality now felt tainted by misperceptions. This was excruciating at the time, but in the end, was my greatest blessing. It forced me deep into the inner realm. This was my initiation.

New insights and knowledge were flooding my being in tandem with much third-dimensional drama. It was a complete paradox that I sought to reconcile. I slowly began to realize that our personal life experiences and relations are portals through which we can understand the greater whole of humanity.

Like so many others around the world, I was grateful for both Votan and Lloydine's work in helping lay the template to spread the 13 Moon Calendar Change and vision of a New Time. Lloydine had assisted him in the creation of Planet Art Network, which was conceived as a bridge to help awaken people to the dawning of a new time. They had awakened a worldwide movement, and while she steadfastly assisted with communication and the laying out of the worldly navigation, it was he who all the knowledge and codes came through. This would later be cause for confusion that he would have to clarify as he put her name on all of his works to honor their partnership.

Because Votan and Lloydine/Bolon Ik were well-known leaders of the 13 Moon Calendar Change Peace Movement, many had an idealistic image of them as a perfect or "heavenly" couple. This was the image that they had both projected to the public. So when they split up many felt disillusioned and perhaps a sense of betrayal. I reflected that most of us come from broken or dysfunctional families and we want to feel like somebody has it together and is embodying higher principles of divine partnership. I wanted that too. It is devastating when this doesn't work out, and like a child, we want to blame the "other" for the breakup, rather than face the pain within ourselves.

Rumors spread like wildfire. I soon found myself the recipient of many projections. At the time I had just turned 30 and it was a most fiery initiation. The three of us each had to go through our particular testings. For myself it was as though the whole field of my reality had become infected with one particular narrative, which was in sharp contrast to my direct experience. At first, it was hard to make sense of it all. If I tried to talk about my experience, even to those close to me, I would receive projections because of the role I was being cast in, which never felt like my script, but that I was living someone else's script. Even my relation with the Haight family, whom I had been so close with, became strained as particular narratives circulated. Deb Haight, who had been one of my closest friends, was now Lloydine's confidante, and it would be several years before our relation came full circle.

I was also saddened when one of our main supporters and closest confidantes, White Planetary Mirror, confronted Votan and me at a private sit-down meeting at a festival after having heard a version of the story that I had never lived. Only a handful of people ever asked me (or Votan) what our perspective was. This aspect of human psychology to only listen to one side and pass judgement, though difficult at the time, was a key to my educational process. Fortunately these connections were reestablished several years later when everything was understood. As a result of these experiences, at the time I became increasingly introspective and withdrew more and more to the inner realm. In his journal at this time, Votan wrote the following:

I pray that Lloydine, like me, is returned to her true self, for that is all each of us has to work with ultimately. That is who shows up at heaven's gate. Though I am intimate with my apprentice she is neither girlfriend nor wife, but something altogether different, an apprentice, a prophetic counterpart, my successor, a co-creator, and most fortunately, she understands the necessity of maintaining our uniqueness and autonomy, and so I am finally returning to my true self at last. If Stephanie/Red Queen had not come into our lives, as the destiny appointed apprentice, no less, I would have never seen the mosaic of habitual patterns that were keeping me from realizing my authentic self. I could no longer be a husband in the conditioned sense. I was being transformed into the final form of my terrestrial existence.

Zero Point

Through this process of initiation, I learned more about what it means to "personalize" the cosmos. That is, to see the cosmic patterns playing out in our own life. All of our personal experiences are a microcosm of what is playing out collectively on the planet, which is what is playing out in the solar system and the galaxy and ad infinitum. Before new knowledge can be received, old illusions must be cleared. This process requires courage to face the full contents of your own psyche, which includes all sorts of feelings of unworthiness, fear, anger, obstinance, etc. It can be scary at times. It can feel strange, confusing, and even foreign, like the whole of reality as you know it is being ripped from under your feet. At least that was my experience.

Around this time about five different women felt that they should be the "Red Queen" without having a clue of what journey I was living. I was so busy with the work that I didn't have time to consider myself anything or anyone in particular. I suggested to Votan that to self-proclaim any identity, however much it might be justified, such as a prophet or messenger, can become an impediment to inner growth. Not only does a particular self-identification limit you, but the projections you receive on account of this identification can actually imprison you. I did not want this. I wanted to be free of those types of identities.

I understood his guidance of self-proclamation when we first set out on the mission, as otherwise no one would know. He did not disagree with my perception, but added that the secret of many great masters is in their self-identity, not in any identity with outer form—which they are, of course, obliged to take on in order to accomplish finite tasks associated with their cosmic mission. But when the finite task has been accomplished there may be a change of form or even a temporary disappearance altogether, but the mission and journey of infinite being never ceases.

The tabloid version of this story continued to spread. The situations required me to learn lessons of sublimation and silence; to work alchemically with the energy. My test was to disarm emotional triggers and not be reactive. Who was I, and what ancient karma was I playing out? Ancient story. Ancient forces. Ancient powers at play.

I was meditating more deeply than I ever had and questing internally with all of my power. I had never felt that focused and concentrated. When your immediate reality feels against you, that is actually a great blessing as you have no choice but to plunge deep within for the answers.

I was in the process of relearning everything. I began "decoding" and mapping out all the key events and people of my own life to find the patterns. I learned the more we examine all of the experiences of our own lives and our responses to them, the more we can become aware of and break patterns that no longer serve. I revisited each year of my life to extract the lessons. I wrote letters to family members to let them know the path I had embarked on. Though they did not fully understand at the time, I felt it important that every aspect of my life was aligned.

Atisha's Seven Keys

Votan encouraged me to focus on Atisha's seven points of mind training, which spoke to many of the initiations that we were undergoing. He transmitted to me his perceptions on each of the meaning's. These writings made their way into a small booklet called, *Galactic Meditation.* The following is an excerpt from that book:

1. *Consider all phenomena as dreams.*
2. *Be grateful to everyone.*
3. *Don't be swayed by outer circumstances.*
4. *Don't brood over the faults of others.*
5. *Explore the nature of unborn awareness.*
6. *At all times rely on a joyful mind.*
7. *Don't expect a standing ovation.*

1. Consider all Phenomena as Dreams

Everyone thinks that what they are doing is the most important thing in the world. And to them it is, and to some extent, you have to have that attitude. But if everybody is thinking and acting that way all the time, then it could be problematic. If everybody's thing is equally important, then everything is reduced to the same level, and in reality, everything is equally unimportant. It is all a dream that we made up. Every dream, memory, or perception is just that—no more substantial than a passing dream. You have to consider all phenomena like this, to be as dreams, so that you don't fixate and get hung up over this or that. The point is, you do not want to solidify your thought-forms, as you become what you think. Let it all go, and you experience freedom.

2. Be Grateful to Everyone

This is important since everybody seems to have some enemy or nemesis. You have to be free of karma, so you have to be free of resentment and hatred and creeping jealousy and all of that. Instead, be grateful to everyone. Be grateful that they are giving you an obstacle to practice your patience, your tolerance, even your creativity.

Everyone we encounter in our path is there for a reason, and that is to help develop our character in the direction of the light. Be grateful to your enemy for giving you a good reason to spiritually wake up and turn the other cheek. In lak'ech! [I am another you] You could even consider that where your 'enemy' is coming from is an unenlightened place, and therefore he or she is deserving of compassion. To rise to the level of universal compassion is the purpose of being grateful to everyone.

3. Don't be Swayed by Outer Circumstances

In the cultivation of spiritual discipline, one of the greatest challenges is the unexpected effect of outer circumstances, especially those that are really upsetting. The whole point of spiritual discipline is forbearance, which means to bear with all kinds of people and circumstances and not lose it. When we are able to maintain our inner cool no matter what happens on the outside, then we are perfecting our discipline; and by not reacting to outer circumstances we are lessening the creation of negative karma for ourselves and others.

4. Don't Brood over the Faults of Others

In typical codependence there is nothing easier than spending time thinking or talking about another person's faults and relishing it. When we do this we are really making ourselves superior—to what or whom and why? To brood over the faults of others is the greatest lure for projecting blame outside of oneself and of actually avoiding personal responsibility for one's own world. The fact is that time spent in any kind of negative thinking means that we are spending our time negatively.

5. Explore the Nature of Unborn Awareness

To identify with that which is beyond the created being's perceptions and to stay identified with that is the most important step to take in the elevation of oneself beyond the buffeting winds of egoic concerns and karmic identifications—the longings, the dissatisfactions, the collisions of misperceptions—all of the suffering and pain of humanity. Only from the perspective of being identified with what is beyond human perceptions—unborn, timeless awareness—can one begin to see how one is the author of one's own suffering, and so start to take a more profound responsibility for one's world. At the same time one can develop authentic compassion for all beings.

6. At All Times Rely on a Joyful Mind

In the development of spiritual discipline, the cultivation of a genuinely positive attitude is essential. To rely at all times on a joyful mind is one of the hallmarks of true spiritual discipline. Yes, it is easy to get discouraged, to think the world is against one, that no one understands and that, therefore, it is easy or even justifiable to give in to anger, or depression, or self-defeating thoughts. And, of course, an emotional outburst is sometimes unavoidable—or is it? To rely on a joyful mind at all times means that you understand phenomena as dreams and that you have attained a certain meditative stabilization. So that what appears to be a personal disaster or negative projections directed against one may be incentive for greater spiritual practice, insight, and discipline. And to always delight in the good that befalls others—that is truly joyful!

7. Don't Expect a Standing Ovation

When one has set out on a course of being a peacemaker, a galactic crusader with a cause that will benefit the world, one becomes some type of activist. When one typically acts, one expects a response. One expects acclaim and praise of one's actions. If you are doing something because you want acclaim, then you are tainting the purity of what you are doing. So the point is—don't expect a standing ovation. Selfless giving is true love.

Chapter 11

Phoenix from the Flames

If you want to awaken all of humanity, then awaken all of yourself. If you want to eliminate the suffering in the world, then eliminate all that is dark and negative in yourself. Truly, the greatest gift you have to give is that of your own self-transformation.

—Lao Tzu

We moved into a warm and rustic rental house in Ashland, Oregon, on July 16, 2003, Yellow Magnetic Seed. Cobblestone steps led up to the front porch, which had a beautiful vista looking across Ashland and the hills to the east. Off in the distance, glimpses through the trunks and branches of redwood trees revealed the I-5 freeway, a little cascade of cars, so remote, going back and forth between California and Oregon. The house itself, virtually unchanged since 1912, exuded a kind of musty warm ambiance, perfect for hermetic work.

I took the front bedroom, just off the living room, that was designed for a study with a built-in bookcase covering one wall, perfect for the time library. A fresh feeling permeated our beings at this time, and Votan had his room at the far end of the house where he set up his art studio and slept in the loft above. The third small room was his office space, and I set up my office in the living room.

With this fresh start, we were able to gain new perspective on the previous experiences. Votan wrote of the original experiment:

The point of GM108X taking human birth is not to participate in the unconscious subculture but to transmute certain teachings of the awakening and elevation of consciousness and leave the deposits knowledge assigned to it. The 'personality' is used as a type of surfboard to negotiate certain currents of being. I am preparing through my meditation to transfer the key to my apprentice.

Like some galactic insect groomed and trained in a specialized form of transmission, I have been presented the right insect counterpart to whom I must transmit or transfer this key. Then I shall have completed a principal part of my purpose and it will then be for her to evolve this galactic evolutionary mutational key to its next level, less and less do I care to be around others, for I know that no one knows or understands who or how or why I am and what I have had to undergo to be who I am . The codes of Arcturus are what I seek to discover, to decode and decipher and to live by. Today I kept seeing myself in advancing or rising ever higher and more alone leaving all to my apprentice for her to transform.

Trial by Fire

This new tranquility didn't last long. Nine days after we moved in, Votan and I were conducting a ceremony to release the past on the Day Out of Time: Red Planetary Skywalker, July 25, 2003. At one point, we put some old scraps of paper in an outside fire pit and burned them, letting go of the old energy. After the small flames quickly passed, we hosed it all down and then went to the front porch to meditate. I noted my mind was feeling particularly agitated and I went into the house to get some water. I smelled smoke and quickly realized that part of our house was on fire! I screamed "Votan!!"

He came running, and we immediately sprung into action and worked to put out the rapidly growing flames. I called 911, while Votan grabbed the hose and did his best to fight the flames. He ended up getting third-degree burns in the process. At one point, we heard his cat Lucy loudly crying as she was trapped in his loft. I had no choice but to crawl through the window, ignoring all of the billowing smoke accumulating in the house. I climbed up the ladder to the attic and grabbed the screaming cat and pulled her down and out of the house.

The fire turned out to be caused by a few embers that had jumped from our ceremony and lit old wood in the fire pit, which somehow spread to the wall of the house. The message: When clearing from the past, even one tiny ember can burn your whole house down. Fortunately, that was not the case.

We were working on completing the first volume of *Cosmic History Chronicles* while our house was filled with the smell of smoke and loud workers worked for many moons to repair the roof.

During this period, Votan and I sought solace in nature and would go for long walks filled with silence or cosmic dialogue. We also tried to escape the noise and sometimes ended up working on Cosmic History at local coffee shops or restaurants. Everything was viewed as a Cosmic History field trip. At this time I had also begun work on what would be Votan's biography, formulating thousands of questions about his life that I posed to him over our nine-year period together.

Maiden Voyage

Shortly after that my first travels began, which included Los Angeles, Peru, Russia, and Italy. We attended the Call of the Condor vision council high up in the Peruvian mountains, which could only be accessed by a rope bridge that overlooked the Urubamba River. More than 800 people camped out in the high altitude beneath craggy mountainsides.

Gathered there were representatives of the Bioregional Movement, the Ecovillage Sustainable Community Network, the Rainbow Nation, the indigenous peoples, and the 13 Moon Calendar Change Peace Movement. Votan viewed the 13 Moon calendar as being a point of unification, bringing a sense of order to cohere these movements.

The event was organized by Alberto Ruz Buenfil, son of the archaeologist who had discovered the tomb of Pacal Votan. Alberto was a leader of the rainbow nation and wrote the seminal book *Rainbow Nation Without Borders*, which influenced many people around the world.

I was uncomfortable and felt hypersensitive on this trip. I refused to sit by Votan's side when he was giving teachings out of respect for Lloydine, even though he requested it. Instead, I chose to sit directly in front of him in the audience, which seemed more appropriate.

I camped out in a little tent with Votan in the mountains of Peru with communal showers with no hot water and no electricity. At night the rain pelted our small tent and I was always impressed by how Votan never got upset or complained about his circumstances, ever. And he never had any shame about telling the truth. He was as transparent as you could get. Here was a 64-year-old man, a visionary, a notable author, established artist, and leader of a peace movement sleeping in a tent with his young apprentice, with major thunderstorms crashing down, and it didn't faze him because he knew that all was a hologram, an illusion.

I was not quite yet that self-realized, so it was not an easy time for me. But I did have a full understanding that the outer path was appearing because certain realizations had occurred through consistent efforts in the inner realm. On this journey, I stayed mostly alone exploring the mountains while Votan attended the council meetings.

After the Vision Council, we made our way to Machu Picchu, which was extremely magical. Many theories abound regarding the purpose of Machu Picchu: a type of celestial university, a fortress for the cosmically minded last Inca emperors, an observatory, and a mystic hideaway. Because of the multiple cosmic purposes of the place, Votan told me this was my formal initiation into the power of *planetary geomancy.*

It was clear that the Inca were similar to the Maya in basing their civilization on a higher mathematical order and harmonic knowledge. The Inca had—and still do—utilize the 13 Moon/28-day Pachacuti calendar that was based on the correlation date of June 21, and it has operated for more than a thousand years. They also had an elaborate philosophy of time.

The Andeans had a great prophet and leader, Kontiki Viracocha. A contemporary of Pacal Votan, Kontiki Viracocha had much to do with the activation of the major center Tiahuanaco.

Sitting on the majestic stone formations in Machu Picchu, Votan and I conducted our first time travel projection experiments atop the ruins there on White Planetary Mirror, the signature of the opening of the tomb of Pacal Votan. We projected ourselves to Palenque 260 days later for the 52nd anniversary of the opening of the tomb of Pacal Votan. From there we experimented with traveling forward and backward in time (more on this later). While meditating at this sacred site, we simultaneously became aware of the large planetary experiment of which we were a projection. The projector was in another world, another dimension in another plane of reality.

We arrived back in the Inca capitol Cuzco, which is sometimes referred to as the "navel of the world." When Cuzco was the capital of Peru, it contained a temple of the sun, famed for its magnificence. Votan pointed out the Christian monastery built atop the ancient site of the Inca, Coricancha, which some believe covers a leyline that contains a portal to the inner earth.

I was intrigued by this land and felt much memory awaken here, particularly in the powerful Sacsayhuamán, the monumental stone fortress outside of Cuzco. I was fascinated by stories of a network of prehistoric tunnels carved by space aliens or a lost race of giants. This claim most famously appeared in Erich von Däniken's *The Gold of the Gods.*

Other researchers had also alluded to this, including Helena Blavatsky, who alleged in her book *Isis Unveiled* (1877) that a wizened Peruvian bequeathed her a map of these tunnels, and that they date back to the time of Atlantis.

Russia

We arrived at the Kremlin at midnight via Lima, Peru. I felt a deep and mysterious energy staying with Votan in our small, but cheerfully decorated Stalin-era apartment. In the rainy and dismal Moscow, I felt immediately at home. Our hosts had heard of my connection with Madame Blavatsky, and I was amazed when one of the elders brought me a relic that had belonged to her.

The highlight of the Russia trip occurred at the Third Annual International Roerich Conference at St. Petersburg University where Votan was a presenter. Situated on the same longitudinal meridian as the Great Pyramid of Egypt and at almost 60 degrees latitude north, St. Petersburg is unparalleled as a "Northern Metropolis." We stayed in a newly remodeled apartment that was converted into a type of hotel suite.

Votan first became interested in Nicholas Roerich during his tenure at Princeton in 1968, when he would visit the Roerich Museum in New York. He found Roerich's paintings highly inspiring with their universalism of cultural and spiritual values. Later, with the inception of the World Thirteen Moon Calendar Change Peace Plan in 1993, he and Lloydine began promoting the Roerich Banner of Peace as the official logo. The Banner of Peace was the basis of the Roerich Peace Pact, signifying harmony, nature, and divine spirit. It was intended to be flown over cultural monuments in times of war.

Votan gave a powerful speech at the famous Pushkin Library on October 9, 2003, Red Galactic Moon. This day was the birthday of Nicholas Roerich (as well as John Lennon). The hall was packed and the atmosphere vibrant, with women making up the majority of the audience. Votan delivered a passionate and emotionally charged speech regarding male dominance of history and the significance of a female lineage. He spoke publicly for the first time in detail about the purpose of our apprenticeship and the importance of the knowledge being transmitted from male to female.

In an unexpected turn of events, the Archbishop of the Coptic Orthodox Church of St. Petersburg was in the audience and took the stage to honor him and the emergence of the feminine. He told the audience that this man was a prophet and every word Votan had said was true. The Archbishop added that the fact that he had spoken this prophecy on this day, both Nicholas Roerich's birthday and the holy day of St. John the Prophet, was "a miracle." He repeated: "This is a miracle!" When the Archbishop was done speaking, the audience was on their feet; the atmosphere was like a revival meeting. I wish I had the transcript of that mystical evening.

From Moscow, we flew to Rome, where I experienced my first trip to the Vatican. Despite the art and ancient history, I found I had little resonance in Rome, and in fact, I couldn't wait to get out of there. Two other trips would follow to the Vatican, and every time I had the same experience. I found it claustrophobic and stuffy. We were there on the day of the canonization of Mother Teresa, which drew huge crowds. It somehow lent to the surreal nature of the entire situation and the feeling of deep inauthenticity that seemed to pervade. People felt programmed, like they were going through rote motions, wholly disassociated from their true feelings or essence.

> *The Vatican is in charge of your daily appointment schedule. If you think you have trouble getting out of this chaotic civilization and you can't stop the war, that's because these instruments are owned by corporations, organizations or fictional ghost entities from the Vatican and the Pentagon.*
>
> —José Argüelles/Valum Votan

Chapter 12

Healing Ancient Trauma

The wound is the place where the Light enters you.

—Rumi

After the move to Ashland, the fire, and then my first world travels, I was in a deep state of self-reflection and moral inventory. It was a cold, dark winter of 2004, and we were nearing the final stages of editing the first volume of Cosmic History: *Book of the Throne.*

Cosmic History was more than writing a book. It was an initiation into an entirely new model of reality, a new galaxy, and a new method for knowing. This process required tremendous concentration. The first 260 Cosmic History transmissions/tutorials formed the structure for the first two volumes of the 7 volume series. The rest of the volumes evolved in different ways. After the initial transmissions were received and later recorded, I transcribed them all. Though the first 130 transmissions were much sparser as they were taken on hand-written notes that I would have to reflect on and then transcribe into the computer. This was a very time-consuming process. The daily transmission, reflection, and transcription would take up nearly my whole day.

At this time, Votan was also very much involved in running the Foundation for the Law of Time and the 13 Moon Calendar Change Peace Movement. Though he had many "followers," he did not want that. He never sought anyone to follow him (only to follow the 13 Moon calendar). Though he put forth vision, he never told anyone what to do. He felt cautious not to gather followers, while at the same time leading a peace movement. Many people claimed that they knew him and yet misinterpreted or took literally what he said. But he never authorized anyone to follow him. The only person he had asked to do anything like that was me.

Cosmic History was the way Votan was able to focalize his knowledge, everything he had learned and all that had been revealed to him.

My job was to fully comprehend, synthesize, and embody all the information and breathe new life into it. The biggest challenge was keeping the physical body in balance and grounded while working with higher dimensional information.

As much as I tried, often the knowledge would get to a saturation point where I could not take in even another word until I had a period of silence to reflect and contemplate. At the beginning stages of the apprenticeship, I felt much anxiety. I observed how my inner dialogue would often be something like: *You need to memorize the codes. You need to be editing and studying the Cosmic History. You need to meditate more. You need to be helping people more. You need to clean the house. Hurry up you don't have much time. You better exert now. Hurry. Hurry. Hurry! You're not doing enough!*

This overwhelming urgency seemed to stem from the deeply conditioned 12:60 programming that keeps us out of synch with our own biological rhythm. I had this tendency even before the apprenticeship, as do many people. I wanted to clear this feeling once and for all.

I expressed all of my anxieties to Votan, who was extremely sensitive and gentle with me, always encouraging and uplifting. His all-encompassing sensitivity to my feelings always amazed me. He often wrote me encouraging hand-written letters such as this:

> *RQ,*
>
> *If you did not question everything, you would end up knowing nothing. Question even him who bestows everything on you. Eliminate him if he stands in the way of your truth. See your truth. Be your truth. Express your truth. Live your truth. Ask: who am I? Where am I? Why am I where I am? Is there another me to be? Is there another place to be? How can I best serve God? How can I best serve humanity?*
>
> *I am only here to serve you by prophecy's decree. If I have erred in loving you, then Gods curse be on me!*
>
> *The flow of truth through me to you cannot be stopped, except by Gods command. Since I can only be and do by this command, then you must understand that even loving you is beyond my control, something that God alone could have planned.*

A messenger, a mortal man, I have no choice but to respect you, and to raise you higher than I am. For I am but the residue of history, Adam's failed cause; but you are woman of the mystery and so to you, I transmit all of Natures Highest Laws.

—*My Love is True Love,* Votan

Science of Transmission

During the Cosmic History transmissions, it was as though Votan and I were two filaments of light. When the light bulb is plugged in, the two filaments light up and give light. When we would come into complete alignment and resonance with our highest selves with no filters, then the light turned on and began radiating.

This light was a specific state of mind, being and consciousness which we referred to as Cosmic History. A warm feeling of electricity filled our body. We felt such a vast amount of information locked into the cellular structure of our bodies, that sometimes the activation became so heightened that the transmission could only occur through intimacy. This established trust and receptivity, the keys to access increasing levels of information templates.

Only with the ventilation of the new move to Ashland was I able to redirect attention toward the cosmic aspects of the third-dimensional unfoldments that had occurred in the GM108X experiment. What had happened between the three of us and what were we here to redeem? What was the interdimensional history of the tomb of the Red Queen and the tomb of Pacal Votan which are located right next to each other in Palenque, Chiapas, Mexico? What was the role of Bolon Ik as the primal Mother? What were we playing out and why? What did Maldek have to do with it?

Maldek, once the fifth planet in our solar system, now known as the Asteroid Belt, is the blueprint of planets that have been shattered in many past world systems. It traces back to the symbolic apple that Eve tasted and into present-day (as I write this on an Apple computer with its logo of an apple).

I experienced Votan, Lloydine, and I as being sent back in time to heal a particular rupture that had occurred in the past. This wounding or trauma seemed to trace back to the planet Maldek, which is what brought us together in the first place. We all carry elements of that primal shattering and wounding.

As a prototype, Maldek can be understood as a key to the false feminine and masculine energy that manipulates reality according to its own distortion of life-force. This distortion includes tangled sexual energies that contain and perpetuate the deepest recesses of fear held in the cellular structure of the human body.

Maldek is related to life-force or sexual energy. Within the sexual energy lies all the codes and programs of the unconscious mind. The repression and misuse of sexual energy as sacred life-force leads to aggression and war, as well as the need to dominate and control. This distorted life-force contains feelings such as possessiveness, suspicion, rage and humiliation. These are destructive forces that are poisoning our planet. They stem from an ancient trauma that is carried into our earth incarnation.

This trauma seeks division and makes us not love ourselves, and so we seek validation from others. And when we don't get that, it triggers many feelings. We have been trained from birth to give our power away to external forces. A key lesson is to take full responsibility for our feelings and do not blame anyone or anything outside ourself.

I spent long hours contemplating this, as I needed to make sense of the whole situation. In my observation, the human dilemma is that certain aspects of us become frozen at some points in our lives. At these points, we stop trusting ourselves and our intuition. We begin to lose confidence in our originality and its expression, for fear of other's opinions. As this belief is reinforced and accepted by the conscious mind, then the capacity for original thought diminishes. We become like sheep, following the herd.

Our original creative spark is replaced in favor of attempting to please others and valuing opinions from the external world above our inner voice. We veer further from our connection with the Source, and this makes us agitated, anxious, angry, and resentful. When these feelings come, the tendency is to blame those outside of ourselves rather than take responsibility for our feelings and actions.

If this cycle is repeated over the years, there is a danger that we can become desensitized to our own emotions. If it continues, then at one point, we become so dissociated from our true feelings that we "forget" who we are. When this occurs, a shadow is cast around us, and we become susceptible to the forces of darkness. This is what Wilhelm Reich refers to as the "emotional plague" that is permeating our planet:

The emotional plague is the freezing cold and the draught that keeps the seed of truth from yielding the fruit. The plague reigns where it is not possible for the truth to live.

I learned that pain at any level, whether emotional or physical, is a signal to turn inward. We all have to find a way to transmute personal pain in order to assist others. We can utilize pain to develop more compassion and tolerance for others plights or we can choose to project our pain outward and blame others as the cause of our pain, thus delaying our own evolution and compounding suffering for all. But everything serves to further and our greatest adversaries can become our greatest teachers.

Sexual Amnesia

In contemplating the ancient trauma, I concluded that humans seem to suffer from sexual amnesia. Sexuality is our life-force; our creative spirit. The sacred merging of two souls with the Cosmos to create more love for humanity has been displaced by instant gratification and profanities due to the misappropriation of life-force. Sex is first in the Mind but is meant to be expressed through the Heart.

Mechanical time creates mechanical sex. Now we have the proliferation of sex robots, rote and devoid of spirit. Several years later, I had the two following dreams that helped further elucidate my reflections on this:

I was in an underground female-jail cell with concrete walls, no windows, and artificial lights. It was overcrowded, and the psychic thought-forms were suffocating, but I was relaxed as I was aware I was dreaming.

I was taken into a concrete slab dungeon with fluorescent lighting where the women were eating bad food and taking a lot of medication. I saw a sign that said: "Sexual Deviancy and Schizophrenic Ward of the Collective Unconscious." I was told that my job was to pinpoint where these women had split off from their true course and how to help guide them back, if possible.

I was given a room with a disturbed young woman. As I began talking with her, I saw that there was nothing wrong with her, except that her internal phonograph recording was skipping on the same track.

She was playing and replaying a deep wound that originated in another lifetime and that she could not seem to transcend. Her behavior was simply a reaction to this wounding of which she was mostly unconscious. I attempted to divert her from this program and help her attention to switch tracks.

How many lifetimes had the grooves of this story been etched in her consciousness? In the dream, I was shown that within the unconscious region of the planetary psi bank, there is a vast storehouse of repressed and abused life-force/kundalini energy. This accumulated storehouse contains all the programs of the unconscious mind both of this world and of destroyed worlds.

Its programs feed upon themselves and filter into and use the collective unconscious to perpetuate the misuse of life-force energy, turning it into recurring cycles of abuse, war, aggression, violence, as well as feelings of shame, guilt, etc. This is an ancient script.

In the Telektonon Prophecy of Pacal Votan, sex corresponds to Maldek. This is closely associated with death, which corresponds to Mars. Everything born of sex ends in death. Today we see that sexuality has veered far from Source, and these potent energies are being harnessed for destruction rather than spiritual evolution. Our collective life-force is being imprisoned within the concrete walls of our unconscious. This imprisoned life-force needs to be released, purified, and made conscious.

How do we bring these energies into consciousness as a collective? This brings me to my second dream.

In this dream I found myself in a futuristic parallel universe where there appeared three androgynous Amazonian lesbians. I asked them about their sexuality and they told me they were "offsetting or balancing the distorted male/female energies on Velatropa 24.3 (earth)." These women were completely empowered and supremely creative.

They had me sit down, and one of them put her hand on my third eye, another put her hand on my heart, and the third put her hand on my sacral chakra.

Then I saw a vision.

I saw the programming process and biological wiring first of the male gender as it has evolved on planet Earth. I saw in detail the circuitry of how the biological Earth male was wired, like an animal, to respond visually to different parts of the human anatomy, but mostly unconsciously (and that our society and culture exploits and is based around this). I saw that this old, animalistic program had outworn its use and that a new plan was soon to be phased in.

The female wiring was very different and far more complex and with more subtle circuitry. Though this circuitry was largely dormant during the male-dominated cycle. During this cycle the female equally abused her power by using knowledge of the male program to her advantage in an attempt to usurp the male power, though this was false power.

However, the Male programming was biologically stronger and more animalistic, thus giving way to dominance, first of the female body, then of the whole world. What is this about?

It is the exhaust of every permutation of the unconscious that originated on the primal red-light district of Maldek, with neon signs flashing: "You can never get enough of what you don't want."

Continuing with the dream, the three androgynes showed me a future potentiality to which they had evolved. In this parallel universe, each being was self-realized in the male/female energies within, and sexuality had evolved beyond physicality into an astral union in its purest form, merging with All That Is.

Chapter 13

Baghdad Portal

You will never do anything in this world without courage. It is the greatest quality of the mind next to honor.

—Aristotle

Over the years I shared with Votan, our journeys took us all over the planet, but of all the places traveled the key one that stands out to me is Baghdad, Iraq.

Votan had been invited by James Twyman and his Beloved Community to take part in a peace ceremony at the Baghdad National Theater for the first anniversary of the Iraq war. The primary mission was to conduct a Peace Vigil on March 20, 2004, Blue Magnetic Monkey, with a small, spiritually diverse group of people from the Lakota Nation, Kenya, Jerusalem, and joined by representatives of the Iraq Muslim and Christian communities among others.

We arrived first at Amman, Jordan, and upon arriving in the spacious lobby of the Crowne Plaza hotel, a piano man was playing John Lennon's song "Imagine." When the bellman took Votan and me to our room and turned on the TV to CNN, it announced that a bomb had just exploded at a hotel nearby where we had been planning to stay. The next morning our eclectic group met for breakfast to decide if we would go forth on the journey. The answer was a unanimous YES.

Before the journey, Votan and I had done much educational preparation with several Cosmic History tutorials regarding Islamic culture and the Quran. Both before and during the trip, I took notes of his narration of the history of Baghdad.

Votan emphasized to me that it is essential to understand how the course of world history and scientific knowledge transferred from Islamic civilization to European civilization. The basis of Islamic science was the Quran, the holy book that was transcribed by Muhammad as dictated over 23 years from the angel Gabriel.

Syrian Desert

Our group was picked up in a caravan of two full four-wheelers driven by Iraqi men and members of the Coptic Christian church. I felt a sense of excitement and adventure as I gazed out the window at this ancient yet strangely familiar land. We passed through several American military checkpoints with many young United States soldiers pointing their weapons at us. These checkpoints were wild with many people clamoring around in disorganized lines to show their passports and be approved to continue.

Situated between the Euphrates and Tigris Rivers, Baghdad was not only the focus of the present global conflict but the heart of the Islamic world. Before Islam, this land was known as Mesopotamia, an area between the rivers, the site of the beginnings of the modern civilized world more than 5,000 years ago. The first historical city, Uruk (Iraq), was in Iraq, and so was fabled Babylon. Babylon can also be understood as a state of mind: it is the mind of confusion, fragmentation, and compartmentalization. It is the opposite of the holo-mind, or perceiving in whole systems.

I had never felt such a palpable and otherworldly presence as on that journey to Baghdad. A profound magic was at play. I began to have experiences of seeing through the veil of the hologram and experienced the whole thing as a type of mirage, an overlay imposed into this dimension. It was one of the strangest and most pivotal experiences of my life.

I felt a type of dimensional doorway open. Internally I was taken to a place I had never been before, trackless and without a name. The words "ancient future" come to mind. I remember lying in bed at our hotel in Baghdad, hearing bombs and guns go off yet feeling like I was in a protected womb, a dark and mysterious place that felt deeply inward, yet beyond the farthest stars. It was like a memory that I had as a child when I was outside at night looking at the stars and experiencing the mystery of remembrance.

In the evenings our group would gather together to eat at a restaurant called Candle, complete with a hookah lounge. The food was quite good with a wide array of vegetarian options. In the mornings Votan and I were always the first ones up and sat in the dining room of our hotel, drinking coffee while awaiting the others. On these few mornings, Votan recounted the story of Abraham through Muhammad's journey. He said Abraham receives much attention because he initiates the historical cycle in the Old World beginning in Iraq around 2000 B.C.

When Abraham left Ur it was already corrupt and represented the primal place that fell into idolatry. Abraham had been born more than 2,000 years before Jesus in Ur, a city 200 miles southeast of present-day Baghdad. Ur is a German word that means primal, first, beginning. This is how Votan told the story to me:

> *Ur represents the primal cosmic Tollan, which is the primal state we are returning to. Following the degradation of matter, there is a return of the eternal. The return of the eternal is the UR, Universal Religion/Universal Recollection, encapsulated in the prophecy of Pacal Votan.*
>
> *Abraham with his attendant Hagar and son Ismael traveled from Ur to Palestine and then to Mecca, near the Red Sea, where an angel directed him to a black cubic stone. As the story goes, this was a celestial stone brought by an angel to Abraham from a nearby hill, where it had been preserved ever since it had reached the earth. It descended from a Paradise whiter than milk, but the sins of the sons of Adam made it black.*
>
> *The Quran tells that God showed Abraham the exact site near the "Well of Zamzam," upon which he and Ishmael must build a sanctuary. They were told its name must be Kabah (cube) because its shape is cubic with four corners that are toward the four points of the compass.*

Coffee on Maldek

Sitting with our coffee in Baghdad, I was listening to Votan tell me how the stone was a memorial (memory) fragment, which he explained came from the catastrophe of Maldek. Hearing this while in Baghdad penetrated through my whole being activating waves of remembrance. Now here we were with bombs dropping all around us, hearing the gunfire, seeing the snipers; this was planet earth, and everyone was replaying this catastrophe.

When Maldek exploded, this stone landed on Earth and was meant to be a reminder to people of Earth of what had occurred in previous worlds. The story continues with Abraham creating the Kabah shrine out of the mysterious stone, which people later began to idolize. Abraham left, but Ishmael stayed there. From Ishmael, the tribes of Koresh arose. The Koresh were the keepers of the shrine at Mecca. Also appeared the Ishmaelites, an esoteric sect of Islam.

By the time Muhammad was born a few thousand years later, the shrine had fallen into idol worship. Muhammad was the grandson of one of the Koresh tribe, and his job was to clean up the shrine that Abraham had left as it had fallen into idolatry. His mission was to make it sacred and reestablish monotheism.

Now, every day a billion people pray five times per day in the direction of this stone. This stone has a huge magnetic attraction. Mecca is synonymous with any place of great pilgrimage. Though Votan had taught me much about the cultural, spiritual, and religious history of Islam, it was during my time in Bagdad that my understanding was lifted to an entirely new level.

On the final day, we were eating at Candle restaurant, where Votan was giving a demonstration of the 13 Moon Dreamspell, when three clowns from England showed up, and they all already knew their galactic signatures! They had come to cheer up the orphaned children. The next morning we got back in the van for the 10-hour journey back to Amman, Jordan.

But the journey didn't stop there. This was just the first stop of 33 days around the world from Jordan, Baghdad, London, Japan, Australia and New Zealand. We had a three day stopover in London, and my first time to visit the city. We walked everywhere. Votan was a fantastic walker; he had long legs. Fortunately, I walk just as fast, so I naturally kept up with him. On a mysterious overcast afternoon, we walked by the last residence of Madame Blavatsky at 19 Avenue Road, followed by a visit to the Theosophical Society bookstore.

Our next stop was a great tour of Japan, from the famous Ise shrine, and then to the city of Osaka. We spent over 10 days in Tokyo, where we were put up in the penthouse at the Tokyo Dome that overlooked the whole city. I remember eating dinner with Votan at the restaurant in the hotel overlooking with the view of the city and him asking: "How did a girl from a trailer park dream up this life?" Those words were cause for reflection.

Chapter 14

Palenque and Pacal Votan

We have to stop and be humble enough to understand that there is something called mystery.

—Paul Coehlo

According to *The Mayan Factor*, the galactic Maya foresaw this time of darkness on the planet. "The time when the memory of the galactic masters would be viewed as a childish dream, the numbers of destiny would remain—the thirteen numbers and the twenty signs."

Pacal Votan lived in the seventh generation of historical Palenque and was the 11th dynastic ruler. He was born in 603 AD, and became ruler at age 12, receiving his education on cosmic, synchronic time from ages 12-28.

At 28 he came into his power (same age Buddha was when he reached enlightenment). Pacal Votan ruled from ages 28 until his death at 80 (Buddha also died at age 80). He consolidated the codes of Galactic Time on Earth during this 52-year cycle, from ages 28 to 80. He also saw to it that Palenque flourished with the highest wisdom and power during the 10th Baktun (830 - 1224 AD). Valum Votan explained that the whole of 13th baktun—AD 1618-2012—is characterized by the overlay of mechanical 12:60 time on the whole Earth, and with it, the suppression of indigenous peoples and the triumph of industrialization.

Votan and I returned to Palenque for the 52nd anniversary of the opening of the tomb of Pacal Votan on June 15, 2004, White Planetary Mirror. This was exactly 260 days from our time travel experiment at Machu Picchu. He performed a powerful ceremony and shared a riveting speech to a large group of people who gathered in a field not far from the Palace of the Winds. It was a humid summer day, and Votan's flute seemed to open a portal or the sipapu, the tunnel between the worlds.

A mysterious, ancient energy infused the entire plaza as he spoke with the backdrop of the howler monkeys that echoed throughout the jungle. I felt a deep interpenetrating awareness and a feeling of being a star traveler. There was a sense within this awareness that we never go anywhere, we are always in one place, but scenery and characters are ever-shifting around us. We call these time, spaces, planets, stars, or planes or domains. This was the knowledge of the Galactic Maya who incarnated here at a specified time to seed the earth and to leave clues to the transformation of our planetary being.

In our alone moments in Palenque, Votan narrated to me the history of Pacal Votan. He told me that once the Galactic Mayans closed Palenque (even before the prerecorded departure date of 830 AD), everything was buried, and no apparent clues were remaining other than stories gathered 1,000 years later in 1692. At this point emerged the Antonio Martinez prophecies in the Chilam Balam texts and the mysterious text *The Trials of Votan*, written by the Jesuit priests after they had burned all texts relating to or mentioning Votan. Aside from this, there was no clue until the opening of the tomb in 1952. Then, 42 years later in 1994 came the opening of the Red Queen's tomb. These were coded to be opened precisely when they were opened.

It was powerful to experience Votan pulling in the energies from ancient time to understand this galactic being. Many of these notes found their way into the *Cosmic History Chronicles.*

> *Pacal Votan is from a type 3 "Mayan" civilization, which is scattered in its different colonies through this galaxy and other galaxies and was a direct receiver of the transmission from the type 4 civilization, which is conducting the experiment here. His incarnation came after much surveillance to stabilize a cultural node in the Chiapas area of the southern Yucatan and Mexican highlands.*
>
> *In that process of cultural stabilization, he was able to create the foundations of a galactic research base where different information was taken from the resonant readings from the planetary*

field to the higher telepathic mind of himself and several other agents working closely with him.

In his disincarnation following all the laws of biological life on this planet, he left different instructions in several different ways, oral and telepathic, as to his own spiritual successor and also instructions in the noosphere as well as a prophetic lineage transmission.

All of this was to demonstrate the precise timing of Pacal Votan to plant and bury the GM108X mindstream in the earth. It was as though this knowledge had been prerecorded in another time and stored under the earth in a type of radio receiver transmission system.

Mother Tynetta Muhammad and Palenque

We are now entering into a New Time and a renewal in our history in which Telepathy is being applied in accessing higher and higher states of spiritual consciousness in which not only a few will become masters of this art, but the New Civilization will be ruled by the Minds of the Righteous in a totally New Universal World of Peace.

—Mother Tynetta Muhammad

Mother Tynetta Muhammad, widow of Hon. Elijah Muhammad, the founder of the Nation of Islam, was a close friend of Votan. Before he departed from this plane in 1975, Elijah told his wife that she should study the world's calendars and prophecies, not only those of the black people, but of the brown and red races as well, especially the prophecies of Mexico. Within twenty years, Elijah said, a time would come for a new teaching, and she should look for these signs.

Mother Tynetta was in Egypt in August 1987 where she received a leaflet about the Harmonic Convergence and soon after she discovered *The Mayan Factor* and was intrigued by the 0-19 code. She traveled to Hawaii in the early 90's to meet Votan and Lloydine. She had joined them on several travels and was now here in Palenque for the 52nd anniversary of the discovery of the tomb of Pacal Votan.

When we arrived in Palenque, Mother Tynetta requested a private meeting with both of us and shared that Lloydine had recently visited her. To my astonishment, Mother Tynetta promptly asked me to sit on one of the stones and did a video interview with me regarding what had occurred between me, Votan, and Lloydine. Though it was highly uncomfortable, I had nothing to hide and was quite relieved to be able to share my experience. In the sweltering jungle humidity, I told her precisely what is written in this book.

Even though I was able to successfully explain my perspective of what had happened between Votan, Lloydine, and me, it was strange that the truth that I had lived felt in such contrast to the stories being told. I began to realize that for people to understand the situation, they would need a broader context. Over the years to come, situations such as this would sporadically reemerge until the time of Votan's passing in 2011. I reflected on how easily people seemed influenced by what they hear or see, from other people or in the news, without bothering to investigate and reflect on the whole. This seemed to be an analogy for the world mind. It was this process of polarity and lessons learned that called forth *The Uninscribed.*

Chapter 15

Rainbow Noosphere

Live your beliefs and you can turn the world around.
—Henry David Thoreau

In late summer 2004, of the Cosmic Seed year, Votan and I moved just a few miles away from our small rustic house in the hills above Ashland, Oregon, to a large, ranch-style house on five acres of land on a small hilltop on the outskirts of town. "Rainbow Circle Ranch," as we called it, was an open plan house with many windows that allowed in a lot of light, and a deck for looking at the Milky Way Galaxy by night and a panoramic view of the southern Cascade Mountains by day. My room had a secret room within it that I turned into an art studio, and we converted our dining room into a shared office space to resume our work on the *Cosmic History Chronicles.*

Creating each of the seven *Cosmic History Chronicles* was a unique adventure. We had just completed the first volume and were well underway on the second volume with the themes of science and religion. Each theme that we entered was like a doorway that led to the multidimensional lens of Cosmic History. This way of viewing colored every aspect of our daily reality. Cosmic History was the axis that we revolved around. The space couldn't have been more perfect. It was secluded but still within range of Ashland and an abundance of wilderness, amenities and pristine forests. Our house was about a twenty-minute drive from the Padmasambhava shrine of Tashi Choling, which we occasionally visited.

We anticipated making this our permanent home for many years to come. Votan told me to enjoy the experience of setting up a home together as I may never have the opportunity to do this again with a partner. He took me to buy a new couch, tables and chairs, a bed, and all the furnishings. In the spacious kitchen of our new home, I enjoyed the process of learning to prepare delicious raw food recipes. After suffering many ailments as a child due to poor diet, I became fascinated with nutrition, herbs, and proper food combining. With all of the new information that I was inputting, my body became increasingly sensitive and could no longer process heavy or processed foods.

Votan greatly encouraged me as we both wanted to be in as high a frequency with ourselves and each other as possible. He enjoyed the changes to his diet too, enthusiastically diving into this healthy practice of eating mostly raw food for the first time in his life. We both did a variety of different cleanses, juice fasts, liver flushes, etc. We were both feeling better than we ever had, physically.

We planted a garden, which Votan loved to work in, and mature fruit trees were scattered about the property. We opened the Time is Art gallery in Ashland, a public space, that showcased Votan's incredible collection of paintings, which included a five-piece series of life-size door mandalas entitled "The Doors of Perception." This space was used as a communal hub to gather and learn about the Law of Time, meditate, and have meetings.

It was an exciting time of new beginnings for not only Votan and me but also for the group of people who had recently gathered in Ashland to support the mission of expanding awareness of the Law of Time. With our team of helpers, we started the Law of Time Press to publish the seven-volume series, the *Cosmic History Chronicles*. On Easter 2005, Votan held a three-day workshop in Ashland to help fund our new publishing company. It was a powerful gathering of eclectic people, but there were also challenges. Votan had received a death threat right before the event, and we nearly canceled but instead enlisted security for the event. Right before this event, there had been a shooting at a church in the United States, which had us even more on guard. Even though all of this intensity was going on, Votan was unflappable and fearless about the whole thing.

Psi Bank and Noosphere

Votan would often tell me, "The codes themselves become the keys, and you become the walking knowledge." He said that from the galactic perspective, it is the Earth that is conscious or that is a carrier of consciousness. The consciousness of the individual humans is actually the participation in the greater Earth consciousness. And the Earth consciousness is but an attribute of solar consciousness. He explained, for example, that the enlightenment of

"Buddha" is actually the enlightenment of the Earth. In other words it is the Earth that lends its consciousness to the individual that wakes up to the nature of mind and reality.

One morning while having coffee on our front deck, I asked Votan what he felt was the most significant disconnect of human thinking. He replied, "a lack of knowledge of the psi bank and noosphere."

The psi bank refers to the telepathic switchboard of the planet. It is a timing matrix that regulates the noosphere or planetary mind. The noosphere is the mental sheathe of the Earth. It represents the stage of Earth consciousness finally becoming self-reflective and whole. It felt logical that there is a cosmic memory field or a matrix that underlies and informs our planet. I loved the concept of this, and at first, it was just that, a concept. It must be deeply meditated on to comprehend.

Votan had been influenced by Buckminster Fuller, who he had had regular correspondence with in his later years. Fuller talked about a cosmic switchboard that could be telepathically accessed connecting us to any being throughout history. He claimed to converse with pre-Socratic philosophers while walking on the beach. This is because he had attuned his mind to this particular frequency of the pre-Socratic through forms held in place by the psi bank, the Akashic record within the earth's noosphere.

Votan explained that this psi bank, or cosmic memory field has two principal attributes:

1. It is structured by a radial telepathic template that informs all orders of reality in waves of simultaneity.
2. It is holographic in nature, or it holds the holographic structure of all forms, memories, and experiences in place.

Every human is like a radio, a transmitting and receiving station. For example, sometimes you talk (transmit), and sometimes you listen (receive). Prayer is transmission. Meditation is reception. Transmission is masculine. Reception is feminine.

Noosphere II

Shortly after we moved to Rainbow Circle Ranch, we also began the Noosphere II experiment. In the Noosphere II experiment, the whole of life would be viewed as an immersion in the experiment of Cosmic History and realization of the noosphere. Rather than give our time to media and other secondhand sources, we sought to go directly to the Source and hook up with the inner-net. This would require us to remove ourselves as much as possible from conventional thinking and media to explore different states or levels of being.

The premise was that the third-dimensional self is the evolutionary vehicle of transformation. It was created weak and fragile, without a direct connection to its higher dimensional nature. Because of this weakness fed by fear, it creates artificial systems for itself in order to maintain its body and keep it from succumbing to its weak nature. When the third-dimensional self resides exclusively in the unconscious, it merely identifies with the body and sensory experience. This is the self that we are seeking to transcend (the self that repeats the same stories and programs over and over).

Noospheric consciousness requires the ability to shift conscious attention from the physical plane (third dimension) into the planetary plane (fourth dimension) through various meditation practices. A prerequisite to experience the noosphere is to uproot conditioned subliminal mind patterns. To accelerate this process, I kept a journal and recorded my fluctuating feelings and/or behavioral patterns throughout the day. I noted trigger points of frustration or anxiety, joy or excitement. I was seeking to root out conditioned patterns of mind in the forms of particular beliefs or biases, expectations or irritations. At the end of the day, I would review what I had observed. The more I practiced this, the more clear I felt, and old conditionings seemed to be replaced by new cosmic perceptions.

When I began to place my attention on the noosphere, I began to have a distinct sense that anything I felt or thought about within my lifestream had already been considered or felt by someone else, or perhaps me in another life. At first, I felt discouraged at this realization as I wanted to feel like I was "original," but was I? Was anyone? What is originality?

I began my daily noosphere meditation by visualizing the psi bank grid around the planet. I would connect my heart with the core of the earth and imagine streams of light connected to each point of the planetary psi bank grid. Simultaneously I would see light beams emanating from space into the grid, so there was a feedback loop. When holding this visualization, I begin to increasingly experience a perception that "here" is not "here," but an illusory possibility of a set number of "here" possibilities. Each possibility exists in its own alternative universe. I also remembered at this time how, when I was a child, I used to imagine that this world was an elaborate stage where everything was set up to observe my actions and reactions to life. I wondered if all memories and histories are created and uploaded into our brain at the moment of our birth.

Teleportation

While in my bedroom one sunny afternoon, I was meditating deeply on the noosphere and single-pointedly focusing on the six mental spheres. (More about this can be found throughout the *Cosmic History Chronicles.*) After about an hour or so, I began to feel very heavy and decided to lay on my floor. I entered into a space between waking and sleeping where I experienced my first conscious "dimensional shift."

I first began to hear a static sound, like many radio stations clamoring all at once. I then felt an increasing pressure and tension in my solar plexus and began to see yellow flashes of light. The flickers became more and more rapid, and it felt like I was tuning into something vast and powerful as if a magnet was pulling me somewhere. I opened my inner eyes and looked around this hidden world. I appeared to be on board of a large ship floating through space.

Yellow lights were flashing and then changed to flickers of blue and red, like a checkerboard, that softly pulsed in a space that was warm and cold at the same time. I realized that I had penetrated some type of projection booth, and paused to take note of the space I was in and how it felt. A velvety wind began to ruffle, and I saw a stack of papers in the corner of this unusual room.

A man entered, and he appeared to be some kind of a professor with an ethereal glow. He looked at me and said something about the practice of "waking conscious mediumship" and then said he had been projecting to me to see if I would respond. He pushed a few buttons on what appeared as a type of control panel, and the room instantly changed in shape, form, and dimensions. I began to feel that I was on some type of mother ship, or rather it felt like I was in a receiving room of a smaller craft that was connected to a larger ship. The smaller craft seemed to be the symbolic storage unit of projective beams focused in a time-release fashion to open earthly minds—like mine! I was so excited, maybe overly excited as I felt my over-enthusiasm caused me to "crash land" back into my body.

I opened my eyes and was back in my bedroom with the bright sun beaming through my sliding glass door. I felt a sense of expansion and affirmed in the work we were doing. I shared this experience with Votan, which opened a dialogue about time travel and teleportation. He had these experiences frequently and they were no big deal to him.

He explained that time travel is akin to telepathic teleportation, or the ability to extend yourself through the mind into other dimensions. Some are dimensions of form, and some are not. Time is faster than the speed of light. Time is instantaneous throughout the universe. This is similar to what yogis or Buddhists describe as traveling to different places in the astral body while the physical body remains fixed in one spot.

Votan said that most people do not have these experiences, because they can only see what they have been programmed to see, or programmed to find useful, according to their intention of life. This experience led to a tutorial about the difference between conditioned knowledge and fresh sets of impressions.

> *Within the cerebral information processing and storage system, there are what is referred to as biogenetic filters. Once a conditioned, perceptual pattern is established in mind, many impressions will then be rejected or filtered out. Those impressions that are accepted will be run through the biogenetic filters of the conceptual mind that conforms to a particular preconceived perception of reality. Until these filters are de-programmed, purified and transcended, it is very difficult to say what is real.*
>
> —Valum Votan

Direct inner revelatory experiences like this one began to occur with increasing frequency in my life as a result of ongoing discipline and focus. At first, I talked a lot about it, but then I felt the experiences were enough. Votan was continuously aware of all the facets of my development. He watched over me with great care and did his best to fulfill all of my needs by providing me with diverse types of experiences. With him, I felt not just a teacher relationship but deep friendship and camaraderie.

Creative Nights

In the evenings Votan and I often had "theme" nights; we would choose a subject to absorb ourselves in. On one occasion as we were preparing for a trip to Teotihuacan, we had an "Evening of the 7 Caves."

We lit candles in the dark of the night and Votan shared with me about the heavenly city, Tollan, one of his favorite subjects. After he shared of this mystical place, we practiced entering each of the seven caves, where we found many mind treasures. At this time, we were also studying the *Popol Vuh* and *Chilam Balam,* the latter of which is written in the language of the Zuvuya, which means it is deliberately obscure, highly symbolic, and coded. The *Popol Vuh* describes four prophets that went in four directions to spread the teachings of the Maya all over the planet before returning to Lake Atitlan in Mexico.

By candlelight on a warm summer night, Votan shared that deep within the darkness of Tollan Zuvuya of the seven caves, the prophets and seers attained great power and wisdom. These ones were known as the Night Seers, or Jaguar Priests, the ones whose memory of the higher world is always being circulated through the lower realms. Tollan is the Zuvuya circuit of wisdom that connects the structure of the heavenly order with the chaos of the earthly order.

All the Mayan cities came from Tollan, so the people carried the pattern of time and created structures of the memory of heavenly Tollan. The structure and order of the heavenly Tollan is the order of the Absolute.

The seven caves refer to the power of seven as the generating power of the knowledge of the origin and return. Seven was the key also to the *Cosmic History Chronicles.* Seven caves are also the stored place of the wisdom lore of Quetzalcoatl. The return of Quetzalcoatl signifies the return of our multidimensional wholeness and our reconnection to the stars. In the seven caves is the origin of everything, including the origin of the synchronic order. These magical caves are part of the inner earth that is contacted through the mind.

Chapter 16

Southern Cross

The real voyage of discovery consists not in seeking new landscapes, but in having new eyes.

—Marcel Proust

Votan and I gazed upward at the starry moonless sky, the Milky Way bisecting the heavens and Arcturus straight above. A special magic filled the air this spring morning in 2006, and we made a decision to move to New Zealand. Several factors led up to our moving out of the United States, including the intense political situation with the Iraq War. Fear and paranoia pervaded the United States at this time. But the defining factor was when our landlord decided he did not want to sell the house, which we had talked about buying, but rather his family was moving back in. We got a three-moon notification.

Votan was at a new stage in his life and said he felt called to be in a place "uninscribed," to continue undistracted on the deeper aspects of the work we had set out for ourselves, the Noosphere II project. We first considered moving to Chile but then decided on New Zealand, as there were fewer people. Votan felt it was important to anchor our energy in the Southern Hemisphere to balance the largely technologically and militarily dominant Northern Hemisphere. I was open for the adventure.

We left the United States on July 2, 2006, Red Electric Serpent, to New Zealand. The plane ride was exhilarating, and both of us felt a deep sense of liberation and excitement. We tied up loose ends and left the day-to-day affairs of the FLT to our loyal and most trusted helpers, Jacob Wyatt and Kelly Harding.

For such a small country, New Zealand had it all, from snowy peaks and primeval forests in the South Island to desert volcanoes and white sand beaches in the North Island. It was wintertime when we arrived at a secluded vacation rental house in Taranaki between Auckland and Wellington on the North Island of New Zealand. Here, we were getting oriented with the country as well as completing the final edits on *Cosmic History Chronicles, Volume II: Book of the Avatar.*

During this time, Votan and I did not have the financial means to make such a move, but his way of operating was to first create the vision, and then let the "how" fill itself in. Most people could never dream of living like that, but it was how he had operated much of his life since he left his professional career as a professor in 1988 after the death of his son in 1987. He experimented with living by synchronicity and the philosophy that the Universe always takes care of its own if you are working on its behalf.

I admired his bravery to follow an inner calling, and he believed that there is another path and destiny that lies just beneath the realm of 9-5 consensual reality. He said that most people are too afraid to embark on this path as it requires a complete shift of perception, and the surrender of the ego into a higher cause. This is because there is no vision for a possible. human existence other than the "time is money" way of life.

He explained that the 12:60 mental field has created an artificial, yet totally illusory, mental shield around the planet. The impact of this artificial frequency creates frenzied human activities that destroy its natural environment. The root of this artificial frequency is the consensual belief that time is what is measured by the clock and Gregorian calendar. Votan felt these are the main instruments of control that keep the masses in fear and survival mode, so most choose to "play it safe" in their life.

Middle Earth

We drove four hours from Taranaki to Wellington, where we became deeply immersed in conversations about Agartha, Shambhala, and the inner earth. While driving on beautiful State Highway 3, Votan told me about Admiral Richard Byrd. He was allegedly the first person to reach both the North and South Pole by air. In his diary he tells that at the North Pole he flew into the inner earth and spoke with a leader of the city of Agartha, who gave him a message of warning to give to the "surface people" in regard to their invention of the atomic bomb.

We celebrated these musings by viewing *The Lord of the Rings: Return of the King* at the Embassy Theater in Wellington, where the world premiere had been held three years prior. Later we would note that the Wellington airport has a massive sculpture of Gollum, with his arm stretched out to catch a fish, suspended from the ceiling in the main terminal. It is startling when you first see it.

On this same day we bought *The Lord of the Rings* trilogy and immersed ourselves in the imaginal realm of J. R. R. Tolkien. The day we bought it was Blue Galactic Eagle, which synchronically is J.R.R. Tolkien's galactic signature, with the code: "I harmonize in order to create..."

Many synchronicities would continue around *The Lord of the Rings*, including a run-in with Frodo (Elijah Wood) at a Whole Foods in Venice Beach, California. This day was Red Overtone Serpent. We went to decode him that evening, and he was born on a Red Overtone Serpent. This is just to demonstrate the profundity of the synchronic order as it attunes us to patterns of the fourth dimension that govern our physical reality.

We were immersed in the Galactic Mayan mind stream and kept the third dimension as simple and close to nature as possible. Our "free" time was spent hiking and soaking in the many hot springs. We were always looking for the freshest organic produce wherever we carried our own cups and wooden bowls and made a lot of salads, even when staying in different locations.

The stunning three-hour ferry ride from the North Island to the South Island of New Zealand was a trip that we would become accustomed to. Votan commented that he felt coming to New Zealand was like having a second childhood, and called me his "favorite childhood friend." He reminisced how as a child his father had painted a mural of the South Pacific sunset on his bedroom wall, and that he would stare at it every night until he fell asleep. In 1987 he had spontaneously purchased a map of New Zealand in Nova Scotia, the day he spread the final ashes of his son Josh, who had suddenly passed away earlier that year. Since that time, Votan had carried a map of New Zealand with him on all of his travels. Now he knew why.

We made our way to Christchurch and rented a car. The first thing we did was visit the International Antarctic Center in Christchurch, as we were both fascinated by the secrets of this mysterious continent. Antarctica is home to about 70 percent of the planet's fresh water, and 90 percent of the planet's freshwater ice. But what is under the ice? Votan felt it held the key memory to the original Planetary Engineering project. We would later drive to Slope Point, the southernmost point of New Zealand with its mysterious twisted trees and howling winds.

I did all the driving as he had long ago relinquished his license. He experienced too many spontaneous visionary experiences, so it wasn't safe for him to drive. Color and geometry would overtake his field of vision and enter him into other realities. I was always amazed when he shared that he had worn glasses for much of his adult life, then in his early 50s he threw them away and his eyes improved. When I knew him he had amazing long-distance sight and only in the last three years of his life did he sometimes use a magnifying glass for fine print.

I quickly adjusted to driving on the left side of the road in New Zealand, but not without a few terrifying moments. Votan was always the navigator and loved using the big paper fold-out maps, directing me, since we didn't have cell phones at this time. (In fact I only got my first smartphone in 2016.) Maps, flutes, and clothes were the only things he really purchased for himself.

We spent the Day Out of Time, July 25, 2006, Yellow Cosmic Star, at the Moeraki boulders between the towns of Moeraki and Hampden on the west coast of the South Island. I had a sense of déjà vu as I listened to Votan's flute while gazing at the mysteriously shaped spherical stones scattered across Koekohe Beach. Each boulder weighs several tons and is up to two meters high. According to Maori legend, the boulders are gourds washed ashore from the great voyaging canoe Araiteuru, when it was wrecked upon landfall in New Zealand hundreds of years ago.

Votan had always been interested in geomancy and earth grids, which were a key theme of his early writings, namely *Earth Ascending: An Illustrated Treatise on the Law Governing Whole Systems* (1983). He explained that over the millennia each tribal culture around the globe developed its own flavor of geomancy in direct response to the geography and ecology of its religion. This is why Native people held certain sites more sacred than others. Later I would become increasingly interested in learning about how powerful Earth locations have been harnessed and covered over with artificial structures that disrupt the natural flows of energy.

I brought a pen and paper to the beach and wrote down notes as he spoke:

Human is a bio-electromagnetic battery.
Earth is a geo-electromagnetic battery.
The sun is a solar-electromagnetic battery.

We feed the Earth by opening up and operating on the same electromagnetic circuit.

Feeding (of the Earth) occurs through creating a resonance between our human circuit and the terrestrial and solar circuits so that we have a matching of electromagnetic frequencies. That's what keeps the whole system going, not only the Earth but also the sun.

Geomancy

As above, so below.

One clear, crisp winter day, Votan and I were walking on a path near Lake Wanaka with its mesmerizing vistas. On the walk, Votan casually commented, "What we call matter is really an aspect, or a side effect, of a conscious process. But it is a divine consciousness that is evolving the Universe as its skin."

This thought form put me into a deeply reflective state. I kept a pen and paper in my purse to write down key conversations or thoughts, as we never had a cell phone. Our initial 49 days in New Zealand bore much creative fruit; it was a liberating time for us both as we found a new rhythm together. Our relationship deepened, and I felt new dimensions of being and perception opening in the most unexpected ways. We lived in a state of pure harmony with each other, filled with endless creative possibilities, while retaining structure, discipline, and focus. I began a creative journal to try and capture the daily magic that I could not fully articulate in ordinary conversation. Looking back, these writings capture the essence of that time. Here is one excerpt:

In the silence of Middle Earth, something tender happened to me and my heart bloomed gentle and sweet. Within Nature's mysteries we lived in our own laboratory.

Our mission was simple: The Complete Transformation of Reality…
We drank ambrosial juices and herbal tonics. Our voices changed with the seasons.

In the snowy winter our voice became quiet—soft and powdery in a fire-warmed cabin in the woods.

In the spring our voice became bright—kissed by the sun, our words grew flowery and eloquent.
In the summer our voice became fluid and our words dropped one by one like a fresh string of pearls in the sultry moonlight (the sun's light also illumines the sphere of the moon).

In the autumn our voice became crisp like leaves and flowed like an ancient brook surrounded by colored trees.

We lived in a paint-by-number sort of way on a simple diet of multidimensional photons absorbed through light.

What magic!

Book of the Mystery

While traveling, we were always working; but it was a pure creative joy. We began preliminary work on the third volume of *Cosmic History: Book of the Mystery* while staying in a cabin near the stunning Lake Wanaka on the South Island of New Zealand. This volume was about art and creative imagination, and this area was the perfect place to begin this book with its impressive mountain ranges and crystal clear blue water. Here we began to examine the power of art and the imaginal realm and the recovery of the "lost planet analphs."

An analph refers to a sensory-conceptual storage unit. What we call a "thought" is actually an analphic engraving in a series, like an electrical patterning. According to cosmic science, thoughts in the form of analphs cannot be destroyed, not even by radioactivity or atomic bombs. This means that thoughts from other times and other worlds can transmigrate, thus the "Lost planet analphs."

We were primarily attuned to the analphs from the destroyed planet Maldek, realizing much of the drama that we enact on planet Earth is from an interplanetary script that has transmigrated and is superimposed into our unconscious. Most are unaware of this and so play out drama unconsciously.

In *Book of the Mystery*, we sought to retrieve these lost planet analphs through the study of art and music. Each of the chronicles tuned us to different themes and levels of knowledge. Each physical place that we traveled to was an experience in memory retrieval. During our first six weeks in New Zealand, we focussed our studies on planetary geomancy, which was a key theme of the third volume of Cosmic History. Geomancy means "to divine the Earth Spirit."

Earth is a living being vitalized by energy meridians known as leylines. These leylines are analogous to energy lines in the body, with which acupuncturists work. There was a feeling as we traveled to different places that we were activating the Earth's leylines through our conscious intention. These points, also known as "dragon lines," hold an unusual degree of geomagnetic energy. When these "dragon lines" cross each other, their energy spirals into a vortex. If several lines cross at a given point, called a node, it produces a massive vortex of energy, such as in Avebury, England, where many crop circles have appeared.

Sometimes when traveling in the car, Votan and I would focus on tuning into the vaults of information deposited into energy fields of different locations. Votan also shared that just as there are earth leylines, there are also interdimensional leylines that correspond to the crystal structure of the Earth. The leylines are the energy axis that runs between two power points. Most commonly, leylines are associated with megalithic monuments and other dramatic natural phenomena, such as mountains, lakes, rock outcroppings, etc.

This crystal structure made up of interdimensional leylines can be thought of as the intelligence of the Earth. This contemplation coupled with viewing Earth as a Timeship with a crystalline structure helped me make sense of the vision I had as a child exploring the underground time tunnels. This would mean that the leylines of the crystal structure are information carriers simultaneously interacting with each other and possessing past and future information.

Within this crystal Earth structure, all information is fluid and equally accessible. This means that the energy/information released or available at the power points is also fluid. I flashed back to my first visit to the tomb of Red Queen, and felt I somehow involuntarily gained access to the structure and vision of these interdimensional leylines, which like a time release would open me to different levels of knowledge.

Votan and I had 49 days to explore New Zealand and decide where to secure a place before flying to Brazil in September (Electric Moon) for the Second Planetary Congress of Biosphere Rights. He had been planning the event while on the road, which would include top thinkers from around the world. Here, he would present the CREST13 project as the centerpiece of the effort of preparing for the biosphere-noosphere transition. CREST is short for Centers for the Restitution of the Natural Mind, a "planetary engineering project" with the intention of setting up 13 centers strategically located in both the Northern and Southern Hemispheres. One purpose of this experimental project would be to utilize advanced meditation techniques to provide the medium for telepathic experimentation.

He wrote the main premise of the Second Planetary Congress of Biospheric Rights:

> *We are at the most critical moment in the history of the Planet. How will the human race choose to use its gift of intelligence in the face of multiple crises? Will it choose to continue to try to save its technological money-based way of life, or will it choose the path of spiritual-mental evolution, a return to living in the cosmic cycles of Nature?*

This was to be followed by travel to Argentina and Chile and then a trip to Istanbul, Turkey, for the 10th annual congress of the World Brotherhood Union Mevlana Supreme Foundation, November 1, 2006, Blue Galactic Hand. Here, we were introduced to Mme. Bulent Corak, a self-proclaimed incarnation of Sufi mystic Jalāl ad-Dīn Muhammad Rūmī. Corak (or Mevlana as she is called) was born in 1923, at the time when Colonel Ataturk established Turkey as a republic in the modern world. Mevlana, who channeled an enormous work that was compiled into one large book known as *The Knowledge Book*, was a respectable housewife married to a successful doctor when she received her first message from beings who called themselves the "celestial authorities," on November 1, 1981, White Solar Wind.

Mevlana followed a daily routine of transcribing the words she heard from inner realms. She continued for more than 12 years, and the messages received were compiled to create *The Knowledge Book*. Votan considered *The Knowledge Book* one of the most cosmic texts he had come across covering a host of areas, all aimed toward the integration and unification of planetary consciousness.

At the moment, we are in a medium of selection and everyone is crossing the Sirat (the bridge of the resurrection period that leads to heaven or hell) according to his/her consciousness. Those who are chosen will be chosen, and those who are disqualified will be disqualified. However, the Morrows and Future Days will bring unexpected Beauties.

—Mevlana, *The Knowledge Book*

Chapter 17

Lady Mile Road: Queenstown

The feminine values are the fountain of bliss. Know the masculine, Keep to the feminine.

—Lao Tzu

I do not wish women to have power over men; but over themselves.

—Mary Shelley

After seven weeks of intense travel, Votan and I arrived back to Christchurch in springtime (mid-November in the Southern Hemisphere) and bought a used silver Kia Sportage. A few days later we moved into a three-month apartment rental in the resort town of Queenstown on the South Island. The beautiful town is built around a pristine inlet on the sparkling Lake Wakatipu. Many tourists come for the nearby ski slopes and other outdoor adrenaline sports, including bungy jumping, which originated here.

Lake Wakatipu is New Zealand's third largest lake. It is also known as the lake "that breathes" due to its mysterious tidal activity, which the Maori say is due to the giant at the bottom of the lake.

The legend of Lake Wakatipu tells the story of two star-crossed lovers, the young warrior Matakauri and Manata, the beautiful daughter of a Māori chief, who forbade their love.

One night, a cruel taniwha (giant) called Matau kidnapped Manata and took her away and hid her in his mountain lair. Manata's father was so distraught about losing his daughter, he declared that any warrior that was able to rescue her, could have her hand in marriage.

Matakauri saves Manata and they marry each other. Matakauri wanted to ensure that the giant would not do something similar again, so he set fire to him while he slept. The giant's body melted, creating a deep gouge in the earth which filled with melted ice and snow. The large 'S' shaped lake left in his place forms Lake Wakatipu, which translates as the 'hollow of the sleeping giant'.

People say that the only part of Matau's body that didn't burn was his heart, which still beats in the lake, creating the mysterious, rhythmic rise and fall of its waters.

Our apartment was number 5 and had a balcony that overlooked Lake Wakatipu and was nestled in amongst towering rugged mountains including The Remarkables. We each had our own bedroom and bathroom, which was essential to us. Votan was excited to be living beneath the Southern Cross, not far from the great Southern Ocean that faces the mysterious continent of Antarctica. The Southern Ocean was named the world's fifth ocean in 2000. It is the fourth largest ocean in the world, surrounding the entire continent of Antarctica.

It was summertime in the Southern Hemisphere, and Votan and I experienced a sense of rebirth in this fairy tale town with its fresh mountain air and spectacular hiking trails. We immersed ourselves in nature and began to experience a sense of former timelines unraveling and new patterns being woven. On our first night in Queenstown I had the following dream:

> *I was in the jungle, wearing a too-small raincoat. It was extremely humid. I rose to my feet. To my periphery, I glimpsed what appeared as silent magicians, skilled at various mental arts. They were eating wildflowers and dancing in the air. I watched my body follow a path of certainty down a winding trail to a hollowed-out tree containing a silver goblet. I picked up the goblet and instinctively poured the liquid out. To my amazement an entire river began to form of which the goblet was the source. I kneeled down and drank from the river.*

I woke up to the sound of Votan's cheerful voice that seemed to merge fluidly with the dream. He handed me a cup of coffee and I began telling him the dream. My dream matched his morning meditation where he had felt transported to the jungle and was working with medicine men, who were doing a rain dance. This dream and his meditation felt like an auspicious omen for our time in Queenstown.

Votan woke up regularly at around 3:30 a.m., started his coffee, got meticulously dressed, including his necklaces and rings, and then went outside to stare at the stars. Then, he would wake me up at 4:30 a.m. with a cup of organic, dark French Roast coffee. I always felt so happy when he woke me up and was always excited about what the day would bring. We were deep in the writing of the *Cosmic History Chronicles, Volume III: Book of the Mystery*, which entered us into the themes of art and the imaginal realm. We could walk to town from our apartment in about 10 minutes, making our daily life very simple. The town itself was a tourist area, though the locals maintained a very friendly and unhurried lifestyle.

At this time we were applying for residency in New Zealand, and it was suggested to us on several occasions that it would be much easier if we were married. Though our connection was clear, I had reservations at the thought of marriage, initially. Our relationship was not for ordinary purposes, but was based on knowledge transmission. I did not want to be married, as that was not what our relationship was about. Votan had been married three times and vowed never to do it again; it had now been three years since he and Lloydine had divorced. She was now living in an apartment in downtown Portland and working at a dance studio, though Votan still supported her each month. Now that we were all three settled into our new lives, here in this remote location, I was able to see the significance of all of the initiations from a clearer vantage point.

During this time, Votan wrote:

> *Now it seems for what appears to be the last phase of my life, I will be able to put down roots, appropriately enough in one of the most remote parts of the planet, New Zealand. Another factor to account for in my spiritual pilgrimage is my apprentice, scarcely half my age she has hardly any personal history in the way that I do, and in that regard is a genuine innocent. Her life as my apprentice is the whole of her life, she has no other life than this.*
>
> *The study of the codes and her work on Cosmic History Chronicles and the cyclic regenerative purpose that we share, this is everything to her, it absorbs her completely. Precisely because of this she functions as a spiritual gauge for me—that is, as the mainstay of her reality I know that every thought, word, and action of mine has the potential of making a profound impression upon her. And for this my continuous self-examination is of utmost importance so that the operating frequency of my life can continuously refine her level of operation, for my witness and sole heir is Stephanie*

South, the Red Queen "the uninscribed to be inscribed by the Original Matrix Attained (OMA)."

Votan and I wanted our relationship to establish a new pattern of harmony and higher purpose for the rest of the world. We recognized ourselves as twin souls, but not in the New Age-y romantic sense. Having been born a twin to a librarian and poet, Votan felt his brother had been a guardian at the library of Alexandria when it was destroyed and then a keeper of the records of the library of the Dead at Mixtlán, Mexico in the time of Quetzalcoatl. And now our recognition of "twin souls" was more to make whole knowledge that had been fragmented. There was a sense of being inseparably interwoven with the totality of many beings to the point of no separation. In that state of being, there is only One being and superficial differences fall away.

Votan explained it like this:

The pairing of the twin souls is a high-level planetary experiment that requires complete utilization of all the capacities and facilities of the human organism and necessitates what is called a sexual pairing for the full attainment of the process. Through this process, the third-, fourth-, and fifth-dimensionals come into complete union. This is part of the process of the evolutionary shift that is being engineered in a pair of transitional human archetypes. The final goal of the entire human interval—from humanoid to cosmic planetary engineer—is the experience of plasmatic involution, the total clarification of charges contained in the Akashic records of both higher selves.

Even with my reluctance, the idea of marriage was persistent, for both practical and alchemical purposes. After saying yes to the marriage process, something further unlocked inside of me. I saw how this whole process (and all of our lives) is truly a time-release program. Ultimately we are meant to bring back to wholeness that which has been shattered or lost.

That summer in New Zealand, Votan and I spent many hours in nature reviewing our mission, refining the broader vision that is interplanetary in nature. We sought to understand the ancient trauma that had occurred in the shattering of Maldek. The prophecy cycle of Pacal Votan takes the shattering of Maldek as a genesis point, where occurred the primal trauma, sexual in nature. The Maldek genesis point represents a critical juncture that caused a rupture in the entire system. What happened? What do we need to remember? What is sex?

More and more, I began to understand that the Maldekian coding had been overlayed and woven into the three of us, each with a different function to fulfill. From this vantage, we each played our roles perfectly. As previously stated, the activation of Cosmic History came about through the enigma of the Maldekian error, which ended in the full destruction of a planet (represented by the fragmentation and to distortion of humanity's sexual chakra).

Votan wrote that the "terrestrial resurrection is to be the final episode in an interplanetary drama rooted in the destruction of Maldek; Maldek the original Garden of Eden now known as the Asteroid Belt."

Votan and I had shared many deep conversations over the previous three years, covering every aspect regarding the topic of relationship and his experience of how marriage could help it, or hinder it. This led us into in-depth discussions about the meaning of alchemical marriage and the conscious union of opposites.

Electric Dragon Wedding

> *Through perfect synchronization with one other being we can channel the psychosexual energy (radion) to create, not a child, but a New Earth Consciousness.*
>
> —Valum Votan

In late November, in the Overtone Peacock Moon, we decided to get married. Votan felt we should do it immediately and encouraged me to study about the alchemical nature of weddings. He also said that if anything were to happen to him, he wanted his things left to me, and if we were married it would be legal. I began looking for a non-denominational celebrant to marry us, and I also set about to write the wedding script and vows:

> *To have and to hold*
> *In the mystic, cosmic fold*
> *Through seasons of time*
> *Never young, never old*

We set a date for December 5, 2006, Red Electric Dragon. The guide of the day was Red Electric Serpent, my galactic signature. I felt strangely nervous. I kept the wedding secret from everyone, including my own family, for more than a year, as the purpose of our marriage was far different from the way most people think, and I didn't want any congratulations or attention to it.

Lady Mile Road

The night before we were to marry, Votan threw me a bachelorette party (though it was just him and me). It was a magical evening. We had a great life recapitulation, but I enthusiastically drank too much wine.

The next morning I wore a red dress from Mexico, and we made our way to a garden on Lady Mile Road in Queenstown, where we would be married at 11:11 a.m. at the home of an elder woman minister with two anonymous females as the witnesses. We told no one except a few trusted helpers, namely Jacob Wyatt and Kelly Harding, who were chief witnesses to our lives.

The gentle breeze complimented Votan's flute with otherworldly echoes of Kokopelli opening the sipapu between the worlds. The entire day was like a slow motion deja vu, as if we had done this before in another time. We exchanged jade necklaces rather than rings. Time seemed to stand still, and we felt many higher forces surrounding us. The surreal, dreamlike nature of reality was palpable that day as we drove to nearby Kingston, before riding the gondola to the top of the mountain for a view of Queenstown. This precious moment in time could not be held other than in my memory, as 36 days after this, our whole lives would change again in an unexpected way.

Telepathic Frequency

"441 is your telepathic matrix number." Votan heard these words in a dream 36 days after our wedding on January 10, 2007, Red Cosmic Earth.

These words were to be the opening to the final stage of his life's work. The day the dream occurred, he had been uncharacteristically sick for nearly a week. He lay in bed and like a feverish mad genius began obsessively mapping out 21 x 21 mathematical grids.

For five days, I brought him fresh juices, herbal tea, and vegetable soup while he stayed in his room decoding the 441. New information was released regarding the 1987A supernova, which had the third peak in 2007 (its initial explosion was in 1987).

This 441 system, which he would later call Synchronotron, was revealed to Votan 18 years after the discovery of the Law of Time (1989).

On the morning of January 15, 2007, White Overtone Wind, Votan had an interdimensional optical experience, where he felt directly connected to supernova 1987A as well as Sirius B. Much information was revealed. His connection to this supernova began with the Harmonic Convergence 1987. A recapitulative memory retrieval process kicked in, which he relayed to me in-depth.

Votan and I talked about everything. He would say, "Everything has to be spoken so that everything is brought to consciousness." I was continuously touched and impressed at his self-reflective capacity and the way that he painstakingly and skillfully taught by example, how to ruthlessly examine my mind, personality, and characteristics. He was committed to giving me his best all the time. We were completely drenched in the new scent of the cosmic history transmission. It felt like a continuous open window but wasn't without its challenges. We were striving for, as he put it, "a perfectly polished, highly refined consciousness like a diamond that cuts through any falsehood or distortion."

At this time he felt it particularly interesting that when he received the Telektonon Prophecy of Pacal Votan, he was in Hawaii, the northernmost end of Polynesia. When he received the 441 Book of Numbers, he was in Aotearoa (New Zealand), the southernmost end of Polynesia. He felt it significant that the rising of Sirius marked the flooding of the Nile in ancient Egypt, and the "dog days" of summer for ancient Greece, while to the Polynesians in the Southern Hemisphere it marked winter and was a prominent star for navigation across the Pacific Ocean. There was much to this connection.

This initial dream instigated an ongoing process of decoding. Votan discovered that this 441 cube matrix is a living system of information transmission that is always occurring; the cube is being transmitted to the larger mental field of the solar system and then into the planet.

The second stage of this transmission occurred eight moons later when a cube crop circle appeared at Sugar Hill in Wiltshire, England, reported on August 1, 2007, Yellow Galactic Sun. The crop circle contained 18 cubes, 54 faces, and 144 triangles. Votan perceived this as a sign of the entrance into the six cubes of the interdimensional shift. On the night that this appeared he dreamed that he was taken to the center of the cube matrix. He wrote:

> *When you are in the cube, everything is (communicated) by telepathic suggestion. You realize how slow and cumbersome conditioned thoughts and rationalizations are. Only the thoughts that are automatically originated by telepathic suggestion have value or are worth examining. This is why keeping silent in voice and mind is so important. Every time you meditate upon and construct a cube, you are participating in the original creation matrix of reality.*

Shortly after this revealment, our finances went to zero, and we could no longer afford rent. No sooner had we determined this than we got a message from Ed Higbee, offering his cabin outside of Dunedin in Waitati, New Zealand, for our use. We immediately accepted and began packing our belongings. We had met Ed some moons prior by synchronic intersection. Votan and I had been in Dunedin for the first time walking around, and he stopped at Captain Cook pub to use the restroom. I was standing outside alone when I heard someone calling my name. I was a bit shocked as we didn't know anyone in Dunedin. It turned out that Ed had left California many years prior with only two books: the *I Ching* and *Transformative Vision*. Ed would prove to be a great friend and support to us while in New Zealand.

We moved to the rustic cabin, which had an organic garden and fruit trees. It was secluded, and we got to work on *Cosmic History, Volume III: Book of the Mystery*. We spent much time making art and collages on the floor of the rustic cabin for the third volume of *Cosmic History*. The theme of this volume was art and the imaginal realm. As part of this process, I worked to decode hundreds of artists, musicians, philosophers and other creative people. This led me into a deep inquiry as to the underlying patterns that encode our perceived reality. For example, the Star Wars franchise revolves around the battle of good vs. evil, which mimics the War of the Heavens. Mars is the God of war.

In the 13 Moon calendar, the glyphs Skywalker and Worldbridger represent Mars. George Lucas, the creator of the *Star Wars* franchise, is a Solar Worldbridger, and he owns Skywalker Ranch in California. The idea for *Star Wars* was, in part, inspired by his friend and famous mythologist Joséph Campbell. In his book, *Hero with a Thousand Faces*, Campbell mapped out the hero's journey that we repeat over and over in different forms. Joséph Campbell shares the same galactic signature as Chogyam Trungpa Rinpoche: Red Spectral Earth. And both men passed away in 1987, the year of the Harmonic Convergence and the year of Votan's son, Josh's passing.

Furthermore, Campbell was deeply influenced by the work of Swiss psychologist Carl Jung. Jung released *Synchronicity: An Acausal Connecting Principle* in 1952, the same year as the discovery of the tomb of Pacal Votan. This year was seven years after the atomic bomb was exploded. Jung was the first to put forth the word *archetypes* and also introduced us to the term *collective unconscious,* key concepts utilized in the *Cosmic History Chronicles.* This example shows how we can use the synchronic order to decode people and events to find patterns and meanings that are not otherwise obvious.

At this time, I was also fully immersed in the writing of Votan's biography, which would later be broken into two books as it was too long for publishers to do it all at once. I asked him endless questions and was always taking notes. He loved it, as he had spent so much of his time in motion, it was the first time that he was able to reflect on his life as a whole.

Chapter 18

Waitaha: People of Peace

The penetration of the mystery is what is referred to as initiation.
—Valum Votan

Human history began with the creation of civilization and the building of empires. The emperor is the archetypal character who invades the lands, acquires territory, amasses wealth, makes war, and imposes taxes on the people. Since this is in disregard of natural laws, enormous karmic rebounds result. Empires never last, as they always crumble under their own weight. These were observations that Votan often discussed as we traveled to different places.

We studied the history and creation stories of the original people of New Zealand, while simultaneously focused on exerting our minds into new patterns and realms of thought. Shortly after the Day Out of Time, on July 25, 2007, Red Magnetic Skywalker, we moved to a secluded rental home with a cozy yet modern cabin feeling in Queenstown with a view of Lake Wakatipu. Votan and I immersed ourselves in writing *Book of the Initiation*, the fourth volume of the *Cosmic History Chronicles*. We were also working toward establishing residency in this country. As with every experience we had, this, too, was viewed through the lens of Cosmic History education. Votan had wanted to give me a vast worldview, introducing me to as many types of people, beliefs, and ways of thinking as possible.

Votan told me, "We have to keep seeing that we are always dealing with the same creation story told in many different ways. They are all describing the same thing. We want to honor all, but we don't want to get stuck in one particular point of view."

Maori Cosmology

> *Within the Great Void came the great sound, and out of the great sound came life and all that is. The song of creation sent forth great balls of fire and gases, the suns of the skies. Our sun is key to life, the essence. It was born of that moment of creation.*
>
> —Cosmology of the Maori Polynesian people

Maori culture is prevalent throughout all of New Zealand right down to the All Blacks rugby team, who invoke the Maori culture by performing the vigorous, warrior-style Haka dance before each game. When we dug deeper and talked to the gatekeepers of Maori culture, we realized that it is an indigenous people's family story about the struggle for land rights, identity, and the maintaining of their original culture and tradition. This story has occurred in many lands. After the Europeans come and get the natives to yield their sovereignty, then alcohol and disease take their hold. The population becomes decimated, and the people marginalized. Amazingly the culture survived, half assimilated, something still remembered.

Shortly after moving to our new location, we drove hours to the North Island of New Zealand to meet members of the Waitaha Nation, whom we had met on previous visits. It was a beautiful drive filled with equal amounts of animated conversation and silence, as we absorbed the breathtaking nature of New Zealand: the sea, cliffs, and beaches. The sheep far outnumber the people, leaving crisp green hills dotted with fluffy white Merinos.

The endless chains of mountains made getting from one place to another virtually impossible without having to go through winding stretches of highway often narrowed down to a one-lane bridge. Logging had also taken its toll, and many hills and mountainsides were barren, having been recently cleared out. The even, standardized look of new growth trees cascaded in even rows sprinkling the hillsides.

The Waitaha, "people of peace," were among the first of the Maori tribes to settle in New Zealand. Peter Ruka, Chief Elder and spokesperson for the Waitaha told us that he had been waiting for Votan (whom he called Time Lord) to arrive for two years now. The father of Peter, Teo-te-waka, had told him to look for a man from Teotihuacan. According to Waitaha prophecies, a Time Lord had been anticipated as long ago as 6,488 years ago—long before the Waitaha ever set foot on Aotearoa, which was only some 1,400 years ago.

On the 20th anniversary of the Harmonic Convergence, August 16, 2007, Blue Planetary Eagle, we were adopted by the Ruka family of the Waitaha tribe. Our adoption was formalized at the historic Waitangi Treaty grounds in a ceremony of presentation to the Grandmother Council and the Chiefs of the Waitaha Nation. Through the ceremony, Votan became the adopted brother of Tuwharerangi Ruka, head of Waitaha security, and was given the Maori name "Horotane Whautere." I became the adopted daughter of the present matriarch, Te Rangapu Te Korakora, receiving the Maori name of "Meremere Marotini."

Through the completion of this ceremony, we became recognized by Maori common law as having full "Tangata Whenua"(local people of the land) status. We were received as members of the sovereign nation of Waitaha. Still, Votan and I were to discover later that the government of New Zealand doesn't recognize treaties or contracts made by the Maori.

Songs of the Waitaha

Around this time, we also paid a visit to Barry Brailsford's home. Barry had been initiated by the Waitaha and had written a series of books about the Waitaha tribe at their request, including the beautiful *Song of the Waitaha*. He was a magical man living among mysterious stone formations. He told us that stone is the first ancestor, and that Waitaha also means carriers of life. Wai means water. Taha means gourd (to carry the water). So when they walked in the ways of peace, they walked as the water carriers, because water is life. Barry said the Waitaha told him that when traveling the ancient trails, you have to move like the water; flowing like water is the way to navigate the path.

Votan did much to assist the Waitaha family in regaining their rights to their land, much as he had done in Hawaii with the Hawaiian sovereignty movement. He was passionate about working to further equal rights for all beings. Having grown up a Mexican-American in Minnesota in the 1950s, he, his twin and his father were the only Mexicans in town, and they experienced much prejudice, particularly his father. This gave him a compassionate heart for indigenous people or those in the minority.

At this time, there were a few of our Waitaha family who broke from the other family and attempted to extort from Votan a large amount of money, threatening that if we didn't come up with it by Christmas we would be kicked out of the country. This lent to an increased backdrop of tension and uncertainty. Because of this, we decided to unplug and make a silent retreat together at our home for nine days during Christmas (which is summertime in New Zealand). During this time, I did the Master Cleanse, nine days of water with lemon, maple syrup and cayenne, and immersed myself into learning the mathematics of the holomind perceiver system.

I kept weekly notes of my inner and outer experiences to track the transformations taking place within me. I was growing accustomed to feeling the unfamiliar—whereas before, I would get anxious. I was learning to relax into a deep acceptance of the entire tapestry of life. The more I would place awareness on these codes, the more I felt the jagged edges softening and falling away.

I recognized the tendency when entering the unfamiliar, for the ego to cling or "go back" to previously engraved analphs seeking security, however illusory it may be. I observed that this is the ego's defense mechanism that attempts to cover or block the view of strange and seemingly foreign landscapes. It tries to throw a sheet over our eyes by reinforcing a familiar pattern. I found the more I worked on loving and trusting myself, the more relaxed and better my experience. This cannot be underestimated. Self-love is the first key to learning anything.

Goodbye, New Zealand

In February 2007 of the Red Magnetic Moon year, we left for what was supposed to be a two-week trip to Japan and then back home, but we were never to return to New Zealand again. We were surprised to learn that within seven months of our Maori adoption our visas had been declined renewal by the New Zealand government and we could not get back into the country. This was an important lesson regarding indigenous rights or lack thereof.

All of our work, our belongings, and car were at our beautiful rental house in Queenstown, and we suddenly had no access to any of it. We had been in the middle of writing our fourth volume: *Book of the Initiation*. Votan always impressed me with his unflappable demeanor, though inside I was filled with anxiety. He was accustomed to the ups and downs of life. He demonstrated to me how to transmute seemingly negative experiences into a positive experience by reframing my perception. Whenever challenges or obstacles arose, Votan would intensify his inner work, and he would remind me that all is created from within and not to get too hung up on fleeting third-dimensional circumstances. His philosophy was that when one door closes, another one opens.

I learned how to seek the lessons and knowledge wrapped in each experience, rather than be emotionally reactive to temporary circumstances. I agree with the Buddhist teachings that say most suffering comes from attachment and expectations.

All of the experiences that Votan and I shared were incorporated and used as material for our art, which at this time was the *Cosmic History Chronicles.* We were like cosmic scientists studying the field of human systems, experiences and behaviors and then reporting our findings back to cosmic headquarters.

Votan explained to me, "Everyone alive at this time on this sphere of reality is being tested; it is an across-the cosmos process.... Any creative process is an initiatic one. To be true and exemplify what it is communicating, the creative act must be grounded in the experience of its message. If you have not eaten an apple, then you cannot tell anyone what an apple tastes like."

Detour to Australia

We soon learned that we had been denied entry back to New Zealand. We purchased one-way tickets to Australia while we waited 10 days for our passports to be returned. We stayed in Kyoto and visited sacred temples while soaking in hot springs and determining our next steps. One sunny day while visiting the famous Kiyomizu Temple, our guide said that there is a Japanese saying that goes, "Do things with the readiness to jump from the stage of Kiyomizu Temple," which indicates that you are putting absolutely everything into what you're doing. This seemed fitting at that moment.

We ended up in Byron Bay, Australia, a beach town located in the far northeastern corner of the state of New South Wales. We rented our friend Lois's remote cabin for nine moons, deep in the Australian jungle without a car or internet, and with pythons often slithering on the roof. Lois had been host of a popular Women's talk radio show in the Byron Shire, and had interviewed Votan on an earlier visit. I felt an immediate kinship with her, as she also had grown up in Oregon.

The cabin was previously named Mevlana, having been utilized by one of Osho's groups. It was an hour walk to the nearest grocery store, and so we made weekly visits to town with Lois for groceries. The relocation caused Votan and me a break in our continuity. Still, it was here that we completed the *Book of the Initiation.*

Our friend, Ed, boxed and shipped our essential work items from New Zealand to Australia so that we could resume our work on the *Book of the Initiation.* This book reflects the time, and if one rereads it in this context, they may derive new meanings out of it. We were making our way through the labyrinth of time, determined to reach the center with many diversions and obstacles to overcome along the way. We wrote:

> *Proceeding down the path, you perceive glorious new colors emerging from a ground crevice. You stumble in the dark; a strange thirst for knowledge fills you. You delve deeper into the hidden, the mysterious, the inexplicable. You long to know everything; the Movement of the sun, the changing of the seasons, the cycle of human life, and the hidden power that covers the universe and its destiny. Despite the many detours and blind alleyways, a new certainty fills your being, a certainty that no matter what, you will reach the central point of luminosity, the shining of your soul essence.*

This was a disciplined hermetic time for Votan and me, in which we were intensely concentrated on our projects and with few belongings and little outside distraction. We observed that each volume of *Cosmic History* found us in unique circumstances as we lived the words written in the volumes, like a pop-up book. At this time, we were aware that we were undergoing a particular initiation.

Initiation brings about a change of focus of your mental vision so that a higher harmony may appear. In the introduction to the *Book of Initiation*, we wrote:

> *Our lessons of the labyrinth of the human social order were profoundly experienced and learned from. Because of our maintaining a cosmic perspective of our sense of mission, and deep and abiding faith in the divine will and its plan for all creation, we understood the multidimensional and microcosmic nature of our own initiation experience. There are many channels of perception available, and those who are*

> *conscious serve as cosmic instruments, testing the old world of matter by the world of spirit.*

We secured business visas in Australia, which required us to leave the country every three months. While Votan was still receiving invitations from around the world, his main priorities at this time were Cosmic History, Synchronotron, and preparing for the upcoming Noosphere Congress, which was anticipated to take place in Japan.

Dolphins and Whales: Telepathic Support

While living in this remote rainforest for nine moons, our telepathy with each other became such that we barely had to speak. We enjoyed the presence of each other as we worked, and we knew what the other needed. Whale and dolphin energy were prominent in our field, living so close to the ocean. Votan often pointed out that dolphins measure "time" with 13 sets of 28 grooves along with their teeth, which are further arranged in a configuration that functions as an antenna for sound and communication. Cetaceans are also said to be the planetary memory holders and star emissaries. In his earlier work, *The Arcturus Probe*, Votan wrote:

> *Having heard of the Galactic Federation, the whales requested first visiting the Sirius system, before being sent on a crystalline migration to the darkest part of the experimental sector. The reason for this being that the whale could memorize and keep perfect records in its vast sensory accumulator (what you call a brain), and therefore be an available galactic archive on the planet where it would be used for domestication.*
>
> *...The dolphins and cetaceans, too, came most anciently on their zuvuya tracks to inhabit the single vast ocean of the blue planet. It was the binary sensory integration of the dolphins and whales that helped ground the radio-electromagnetic effects of the Uranian polar tilt at the Earth's poles. ...*

Because of his deep connection with the whales and dolphins, Votan received a strong message that the Noosphere Congress could not be in Japan because of all the whale and dolphin slaughter, which was highlighted that year by the documentary, *The Cove*, which highlights dolphin hunting practices in Japan. We also learned that Japan had conducted research whaling programs in both the North Pacific as well as Antarctica. Instead, he determined the event would be in Bali.

Template of Tollan

After spending the day whale-watching in Byron Bay, Votan received another optical and lay down on the bed. He began to receive a vision which he said was the next stage of Synchronotron. After a few hours, he went to his desk and began drawing a sacred geometry, which would later be known as Hunab Ku 21, galactic tree of life. This came on the seventh day of our seven-day juice cleanse, where we were drinking primarily green juice, herbal tea, and water.

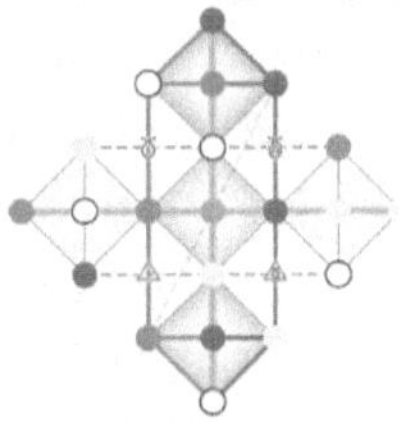

Hunab Ku 21, the Template of Tollan, would form the central theme of *Cosmic History Chronicles, Volume V: Book of the Timespace.* This was the next installment of the 441 in the form of sacred geometry with 21 key articulations. Each articulation represents an archetype based on the 20 solar seals, plus the Hunab Ku. Tollan, the heavenly city, is the primal place of origins and the place of return. Zuvuya is the path of the cosmic memory, the sacred way of return.

While he was receiving this in the early morning hours unbeknownst to me, I was meditating in my room and became very heavy. I lay down and then experienced a sensation of astral traveling through the solar plexus, known as the *kuxam suum.*

Astral Experience

In my astral plane travels, I found myself lucidly floating through neighborhoods. I floated into a home, which at first appeared mundane with a large television monitor in the living room and dusty knickknacks scattered about. I made my way into the dining room. I saw a vast interplanetary Telektonon board with crystals set on specific circuits spread out over a large oak dining room table. I heard a voice that said, "Pay attention to the circuits!"

I touched the crystal, and then began to levitate and flew around the room into the back of the house. I entered the next room without opening the door. The room emitted a soft, blue etheric light. In the corner sat Votan at a large desk or drafting table working diligently on what appeared to be some numerical codes.

On the wall, I noticed a life-size star map, and on another wall, there was a detailed map of the Earth. As I looked more closely at the map, the snow-capped Appalachian Mountains popped out like a 3D hologram. The temperature in the room dropped dramatically. Votan beckoned me to him and shared a series of mathematical codes. As I concentrated on comprehending these codes, subtle changes in the room began to occur. The lighting softened and brightened. The temperature of the room changed, the ceiling got higher, and the walls contracted and expanded. Different objects began to appear in the room while others disappeared. Every object in the room seemed to be shifting, altering, and morphing into ever more magnificent creations, shapes, and forms. Geometries began to appear. I heard Votan's voice say: "These are the codes of the new Timespace!"

I then floated out of this room into a smaller adjacent room in the seemingly mundane suburban home. This room was flashing in dimmed red tones and then brighter green colors. There, again, was Votan, wearing a large white and gold shaman hat. He was sitting at a desk working on mathematical codes. He said, "Hold on, I'm still working on it; the last one wasn't the final version."

Before I returned to my body, it felt like I was awakening several times into other realities. As I was trying to make my way back to the body, I stumbled across many radio transmissions. I began to receive various channels and crystal-clear snippets of conversations. Each fragment of conversation was in a different language, some of which felt like it emanated from other dimensions. The channels would go static and fade, and then the new channels would come in, one of which spoke in pure mathematics and another that didn't speak at all but was pure vibration.

When I finally returned to my body, I went to say good morning to Votan and tell him about the experience. He showed me what he had been working on. He told me he was mapping coordinates of the cosmic mind. Then he showed me the first version of the Hunab Ku 21 archetypal structure.

These types of synchronic experiences were common with Votan and me, and they were a crucial part of our working relationship. I would often retrieve missing information through Dreamtime, and it would turn out to be the key that Votan needed at that moment. On other occasions, deep in meditation, we would teleport together to different times and places and be able to hold conversations there. When we came back to our physical bodies, we were then able to transcribe the conversations into waking reality. This way of operating became the norm for us and elevated our relation to what some might call supernatural.

Chapter 19

Noah's Radiogenetic Time Ark

Noah's vessel is the largest and is in charge of directing the transmigration of a part of humanity from the surface of the Earth.
—Triguerhino

After nine moons in Byron Bay, we moved to Jan Juc, Australia, in the spring of 2008. Jan Juc, a small coastal town, is 100 kilometers from Melbourne and off of the famous Great Ocean Road in Australia. Our 1970s-inspired house was down the road from Bells Beach, a world-renowned surfing beach.

There was a Zen simplicity to this year-long time sequence, and we were grateful for clear ocean air, spacious land, and a car. We were now beginning *Cosmic History Chronicles, Volume V: Book of the Timespace.* At this time Votan was deeply immersed in the creation of the Noosphere Congress, which had now been moved to Ubud, Bali in cooperation with Sacha Stone and his organization, Humanitad.

This was a time of great productivity. Votan set up his office in one of the bedrooms, and I set up mine in the dining room by a large sliding glass door and deck that overlooked the spacious backyard. I began work on creating the first 13 Moon Calendar Almanac and had recently published Votan's biography: *2012: Biography of a Time Traveler.* A few years later I would self-publish a more detailed and the second installment version entitled *Time, Synchronicity and Calendar Change: The Visionary Life and Work of José Argüelles.*

When he first read the book, Votan wrote in his journal: "… Seeing myself so clearly now in the mirror held up by my apprentice, I feel even more determined, and judicious, in my actions to complete my mission unflinchingly."

Evening Activities

Since we didn't watch TV or take in much entertainment, Votan and I thought of creative ways to interact. Every moment was part of the Cosmic History education process. In the evening we would sometimes assume different characters and interview each other. We would sit on the couch after dinner, often with a cup of nettle tea. Votan was particularly fond of nettle tea as it is what Milarepa drank in the cave. We sipped our tea while focusing on different historical figures and discussing their archetypal roles. Through this type of relaxed creative dialogue, amazing insights and inspirations would open to us.

For example, one week we immersed ourselves into the mindstream of Noah's Ark and genetics. Our dialogue revolved around exploring Noah as an archetype of transmigratory travel, and also as one who serves as a warner to the people that something big is about to happen. He is instructed to create an ark, which represents the escape from a catastrophe. He takes seeds of life from one world to another. This extends into the area of genetics, which was also a vital theme of the teachings of the Law of Time.

I wondered aloud if creatures like minotaurs, mermaids and cyclops weren't part of some genetic experiment at an earlier time. Votan said that the genetic manipulations have afflicted various star systems and were a part of the "Luciferian experiment," as he had written about in *The Arcturus Probe.*

In other words, Lucifer and his followers hijacked the original creation and wanted the Earth and the creative powers of DNA for themselves. Originally we were meant to live in love and perfect harmony. Being that DNA is at its source a geometry indicates that it is really a pattern to be restored to its original blueprint.

As an archetype, Noah was the one who brought the genetic code from one world to another. This is why he took one form of every life in pairs—this was the genetic code. Votan reminded me that the purpose of the 12:60 beam was to inseminate Earth's electromagnetic mind field with artificial time which alters our DNA and erases cosmic memory. We, as a species, fell into a state of amnesia and detoured into the cycle of "history." The purpose of all of the synchronic codes and Cosmic History is to lay out a system of time magic or chronomancy to get back to the correct time.

Votan explained to me his vision of a *radiogenetic time ark*, the invisible mind thread carrying genetic information, transmitted like radio waves from one point to another. The word *ark* comes from the Latin *arca*, meaning box or chest. Time ark refers to a specific code container or configuration for radiogenesis, or the communication from one celestial body to another, hence: Radiogenetic Time Ark.

This contemplation of the archetype of Noah continued for days, and some of which was put into the second volume of the *Cosmic History Chronicles.*

> *For as in the days of the flood, they ate, drank and got married, until Noah entered the ark. And they knew nothing until the deluge swept them away.*
>
> *—Matthew 24:38*

The story of Noah was similar to my recurring dreams on a planet right before it exploded. People were eating and drinking, oblivious to the impending catastrophe. Votan explained that after Maldek exploded, a *radiogenetic time ark* was created to transfer information to Mars. Then after Mars went extinct, another radiogenetic time ark was sent to Earth carrying the accumulated karmic debris from both Maldek and Mars.

Maldek represents World War I, Mars represents World War II, and Earth carries the potential for WWIII. Votan defined war as the "institutionalization of a primal carnal crime originated on Maldek; it legitimizes killing for the sake of killing." Babylon was the city where the destroyers of Maldek settled on Earth to perpetuate their crime that is carried out today via the 12:60 artificial timing frequency. This is cause for much contemplation.

Contemplating Noah

In our evening conversations, one clue would lead to another. Before we knew it, synchronicities would be exploding in our minds. It was as though the universe was one big code to decipher. Here is one of our creative evening questions and answers sessions based on the Noah theme, to give you a sense of the energy:

> *RQ: Do you think Noah, on that ark, was doing rainbow bridge meditations, or was he consciously attuned to the electromagnetic field?*

VV: I think the ark was part of the rainbow bridge meditation, it was a function of that. It was a structural form of radiogenetic gene transfer. In the program of gene transfer was the potentiality of the rainbow bridge as being the alternative conclusion to the world destruction that occasioned Noah's jettisoning himself from the world system upon which he had been when it was destroyed.

RQ: Fascinating. Now let's talk about the increasing number of ships being spotted—does this have anything to do with the rainbow bridge?

VV: The ships have been here since the beginning of time. Or what we call "the ships" have been here in great abundance and particularly since 1945. The ships began to appear more frequently because of the release of radioactivity in the alteration of the terrestrial atmosphere. Not that they weren't watching earlier. But they came then in different forms of manifestation. They began to give the signals which alerted other people to the fact that the rainbow bridge was a potentiality.

RQ: Describe your mission in the rainbow bridge project? And also how it connects with the fleet of ships, we have now been witnessing.

VV: My mission was to first articulate the vision of the rainbow bridge and then create different telepathic exercises that have led up to it.

These are all congruently or convergently monitored by some of the different fleets that have been here with us. They had been responding to different telepathic signals and configurations and telepathic thoughtforms regarding the circumpolar rainbow bridge. They are part of the whole process—one gigantic geometric circuit board.

RQ: Is it like having one film projected from above and one film projected from below, and the images match up?

VV: Exactly. This is a tandem type of engineering project with the telepathic projections that we have been practicing here, and synchronistically converged with different programs that have been projected from the ships.

RQ: What role do Sirius and Venus have in this? Are they part of the engineering project? Who is ultimately behind it?

VV: What you might call the brain trust behind this is the Council of 9 on Sirius. This has been the higher mind thought control of this whole process.

RQ: How did you realize this? Were you receiving rainbow bridge flashes in your mind?

VV: When I began to awaken to this aspect of the mission at one point, my meditation would go into samadhi, which put me in the mainframe of the Sirius Council of 9. Of course, this council has been responsible for many prior activities, not only on this planet but of different places in the solar system, including what we call the Venusians… this is like a trade-off place where some of what had been historically called messengers or prophets had been traded off for Venusian energies.

These energies were then conscripted into Sirian councils for different types of work mandated by the whole planet unification for this part of the galaxy and stellar system. It is all part of one large piece. So it's not like the Sirians are over there and Venusians over there, and the Pleiadians over there ... it is all part of a holographic system in which people are functioning by sets of correspondences according to certain directives or ordinances from even higher dimensional levels.

RQ: What is your role in the hierarchy of this process? Are you a broadcaster?

VV: There are different titles according to a set of mandates or ordinances that I am operating from. According to one, I am a Chief Engineer of Velatropa 24.3, 2013 Resurrection Project. This has to do with coordinating the details of the project into a terrestrial labor plan that involves locating or conscripting the people who can hold the visualization and meditations and establish the telepathic network according to synchronic scripts. This goes back to the Dreamspell codes and so on.

I am also a telecosmic transceiver, which has to do with the role I play in establishing the actual coordinates of the evolutionary spectrum as it is rooted in the noosphere and as it radially branches out into the different time zones which we'll be entering. These are the simultaneous time zones, not sequential time zones, but radial time zones.

RQ: Regarding the new time or radial time zones that we will be entering, do you feel, as many Native traditions have indicated, that there will be a reduction of the population on earth?

VV: Undoubtedly, at one point, there will be the deportation of the souls to the different or other levels or stages of alternate universes where their soul growth can continue at a rate that is commensurate to that soul's level of comprehension. The ones who remain are the genuine ones, who at that point have no real filters or veils. These are the ones who have no axes to grind and have forgiven everyone and everything--with nothing to lose or gain. These are the ones who comprehend the nature of reality as being a continuously self-transcending process, and they feel grateful to be just participating in it.

People who are genuinely honest at this stage in consciousness development are very few. This has nothing to do with what you know or what you don't know or what you believe or don't believe. It has everything to do with being genuine, flexible, authentic, and unattached, with a deep sense of compassion and universal love.

RQ: Thank you... Let's talk about the rainbow as a symbol, a myth, an archetypal quality in the heart of every being.

VV: The rainbow, yes, it is an innate vision or magnet that exists. There are two types of rainbows that we see in the sky: those that occur after there has been some moisture, rain, or precipitation. Then there is the rainbow we see in clouds or the sky that is more electromagnetic. They both represent projections from the heart center of the human being as a single organism. As projections of the heart, they always beckon the human soul on its evolutionary path.

So the manifestation of the rainbow bridge is the expression of the feedback of the human beings projection into its own next evolutionary stage that then gets projected out and goes around the earth. The human is the earth. The human is holographically at one with the earth. The rainbow bridge is a sacred covenant written into every heart.

Chapter 20

Hollywood and Inner Technology

It's the movies that have really been running things in America ever since they were invented. They show you what to do, how to do it, when to do it, how to feel about it, and how to look how you feel about it.

—Andy Warhol

In the summer of 2009. Votan and I were in Los Angeles for book promotions of *2012: Biography of a Time Traveler,* which had just been published. We met with my father, Ron, who flew from Oregon to visit us. It was his first trip to LA, as he wasn't much of a traveler. Having grown up in a small Oregon town, and not being much of a reader, he couldn't have been in more contrast to Votan's intellectual prowess. Votan admired Ron's "unique heart intelligence," and the feeling was mutual. He loved Votan and called him Kimosabe (Ke-mo sah-bee), the name that Tonto called Lone Ranger in the 1950s television series. It means "trusty scout" or "faithful friend." He equated the name to Votan's sharp navigation skills, particularly guiding him through the streets of Hollywood and different parts of Los Angeles.

The three of us ended up at Hollywood and Highland in the Babylon court (Gate of Ishtar), near the Kodak Theater where the Academy Awards are held. This is where the "stars" walk the red carpet. This Babylonian scene was taken from a 1916 movie called *Intolerance.* Through the gate, you can see the Hollywood sign. The Babylon court is across the street from the old Masonic Lodge, now called El Capitan Entertainment Centre, which hosts Jimmy Kimmel Live!.

I took a special interest in studying the more esoteric roots of Hollywood. The holly tree was sacred to Druids. I found it interesting how celebrities walk the red carpet at the Oscars. This replicates red carpets that are put out for dignitaries, heads of state, or royalty. Many esoteric researchers feel it is symbolic of the powerful bloodlines that control the images and narratives of the world. Churches also often have red carpets to signify the blood of Christ. And note that *Oscars* is an anagram for *a cross.* In any case, Babylonian influence pervades the world and is particularly prominent in Hollywood, the image-making capital of the world.

Later that year, Votan and I saw the movie *Avatar* in Hollywood as a cosmic history field trip. We had heard the themes were about genetic engineering and off-planet mining of precious minerals. I found the violence at the beginning of the movie difficult to watch. The movie takes place in the year 2154. Humans have depleted their natural resources and so seek elsewhere to mine a precious metal, unobtanium, on Pandora, a lush, forested moon orbiting Polyphemus in the Alpha Centauri Star System. The planet is not habitable to humans, so one has to be genetically engineered to enter a "Na'vi" body, which is operated from the brain of a remotely controlled human. The mining colony from earth threatens the existence of the local Nature-loving tribe, Na'vi.

This sent us into a conversation about Maldek and the Sumerian legends, including Zechariah Sitchin's belief that the Annunaki genetically engineered modern-day humans by crossbreeding with Earth women. They did this to use humans as a slave race in order to mine gold from the Earth. In 2012, James Cameron would be part of a group of billionaire investors, including Google's Larry Page and Eric Schmidt, who would become part of a company called Planetary Resources, Inc. The goal of this company is to "mine near-Earth asteroids for precious resources like rare metals and water ice." The project had its beginning date set in 2022.

Moronge Morove: Rainbow Serpent

After traveling every day together for three years, three moons, and three days, Votan and I finally moved into our own home in Australia at 15 Bradshaw Court on September 28, 2009, Yellow Electric Star. I noted that at age 36, this was the 36th address I'd lived at.

The place was perfect: a three-bedroom, two-bath house set in a rural area on eight acres outside of Daylesford, Australia. Daylesford was in the Shire of Hepburn, 117 kilometers northwest of the state capital of Melbourne. It was the mineral spa capital of Australia. This rural area was surrounded by fern gullies, gum trees, and farming areas with plenty of kangaroos hopping around.

Our move-in date was one spin (260 days) from the 58th anniversary of the tomb opening of Pacal Votan, June 15, 2010, Yellow Electric Star. The house, which was found and purchased by our friend and patron Ishram Tansley, was to be the place where Votan would pass away 541 days later (77 weeks and two days).

Votan was so excited and joyful as a child when we moved into this space. He named the house Moronga Morove (Aboriginal for Rainbow Serpent). We turned the large, standalone garage into a giant art studio, and both of us began painting. We planted a garden, and Votan created much rock and natural sculpture art on the property. There was a sense of stability that we hadn't felt since moving from our home in Ashland. On weekends we would often go to breakfast at Himayalan, an organic, biodynamic cafe where Votan would generally order a Spanish tofu scramble and a cup of black coffee. I would generally opt for avocado mushroom toast and an almond vanilla latte.

Just a few weeks earlier he had given a powerful seven-day presentation on Synchronotron at the Babaji ashram in Cisternino, Italy. Located in the countryside of Valle d'Itria, in Southern Italy (Apulia), the space was highly resonant. Babaji's teaching was universal and respectful of all religions and traditions. This was the first time Votan had publicly presented this material, and he had done a seven day practice with me in Venice, California, prior to this presentation.

At the seminar, Votan told the attendees:

> *The purpose of the Synchronotron is to see if Human Beings, at least a select number of them, can unify with a system of language based on mathematics. Focusing on the language of these mathematical codes, we are here to begin to attain some minimal level of collective unification, to be able to function as a type of biopsychic electromagnetic battery to start charging the rest of the Planet.*
>
> *... Synchronotron is a living system. That means that when we start operating with it, we are engaging in telepathic waves that we are being transmitted, communicated, by different higher intelligences. The purpose of these waves is to activate the collective mental field of the Planet through a system of language based on mathematics....*

After the Synchronotron seminar in Italy, Votan went through a quantum evolutionary leap. His journals now were mostly all number. As we settled into our new home and lifestyle, we began work on *Cosmic History Chronicles, Volume VI: Book of the Transcendence.*

Mind Rebirth

> *All that was great in the past was ridiculed, condemned, combated, suppressed—only to emerge all the more powerfully, all the more triumphantly from the struggle.*
>
> —Nikola Tesla

Once home, we settled into the most concentrated work yet with the Synchronotron and the practice of Noogenesis. Votan emphasized that cultivating our inner technologies is the way of the future. Noogenesis means "mental genesis" or "mind rebirth." While this may sound like a stretch to some readers, several philosophers and mystics such as Pierre Teilhard de Chardin and Sri Aurobindo had prognosticated that there would be a further evolution of the brain, which is the purpose of the Synchronotron.

Votan felt that humanity needs higher visions about "what is possible" to strive for. Our practice presumed the brain as a wireless receiver or antennae with the capacity to tune it into any number of radio "vibration" stations. We began working in earnest with particular meditation and visualization techniques to "turn on" the holomind perceiver, a new sensory organ activated in the corpus callosum.

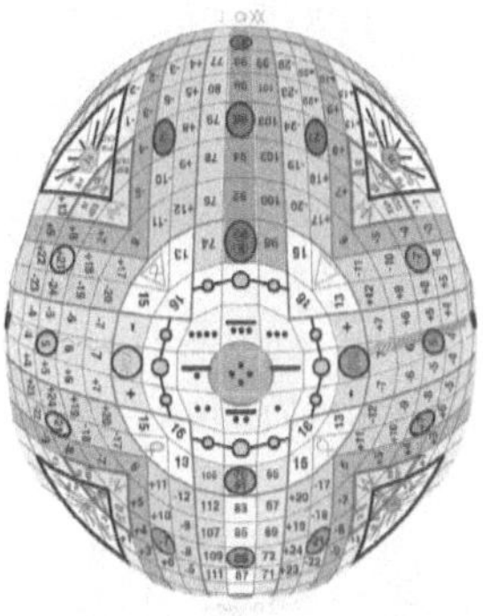

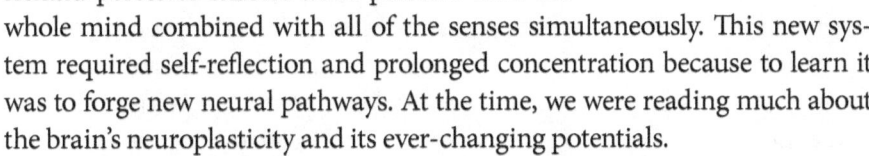

Votan explained that once activated, the holomind perceiver enables us to perceive with the whole mind combined with all of the senses simultaneously. This new system required self-reflection and prolonged concentration because to learn it was to forge new neural pathways. At the time, we were reading much about the brain's neuroplasticity and its ever-changing potentials.

We studied and talked much about the superpowers of historical figures. Solomon had command of the winds. Jesus walked on water. Milarepa tamed the lower forces and developed all types of siddhis. Votan spoke much about Milarepa, who lived and meditated in a cave for years, sustaining himself on nettle soup and astral light. Through rigorous self-discipline, he transcended the physical plane and arrived at a supernatural state of being. He obtained powers like walking on water and flying through the air. These powers came through extreme states of exertion set forth by an irresistible mystical urge. In yogic traditions, these people are called Siddhas and their powers, siddhis. Jesus said that we shall do greater things than him. We were interested in those who had activated their full capacities, and we wanted to activate capacities not yet perceived.

We wanted to make the supernormal the norm. And why wasn't it?

We sought to make our daily life as simple as possible so that we could focus on cultivating the inner realms. Each day had a unique frequency filled with hidden treasures. Our job was to discover the treasures through mental concentration and an open heart.

This noogenesis also had, as its goal, connecting our inner walkie-talkie system to other cosmic civilizations. Votan wrote:

> *The effort of cosmic civilization to establish communication with intelligent life throughout the universe is vast, heroic, and, to most humans of this little planet, virtually incomprehensible. For the possibility of such communication, there must exist in the planetary field of intelligence, not yet incorporated into cosmic civilization, a receptive capacity of consciousness in need of being informed by a higher perceptual order of reality. When that receptive need is ripened by an evolutionary crisis into a perception of the whole system nature of reality, then the cosmic civilization can respond.*

To systematically embark on this type of communication, we worked earnestly with the system of the Synchronotron. The structure located within the Synchronotron is called the *vulom magnetic attraction force field.* We will save all the technical details for another time as this needs full context to do it justice. So we will just give a vision of possibility that exists for a whole new way to perceive reality. With these new perceptions, creative imagination is opened. I related it to the teachings of Christ, who said: "The Kingdom of heaven is within; My fathers' house has many mansions; and: Be ye renewed by the renewing of your mind."

We all access the inner realms in different ways. I perceived the Kingdom of Heaven as an interdimensional wonderland that, when opened, reveals a pure, ever-new, fresh, and creative unfoldment of infinite treasures. It is our divine inheritance. It opens and closes according to our frequency. It is accessed through the narrow gate. As we change our frequency, we alter the vibration of the world.

The holomind perceiver is the name of our access code. To enter requires qualities such as discipline, patience, dedication, enthusiasm, and a deep letting go of all conditionings. Practicing the codes of the Law of Time and Synchronotron is the way we make our vehicle ready to comprehend nonconceptual states of reality.

Votan explained that as we become more conscious, we create certain leverage or pressure points that help shift the mental vibration frequency of ourselves and the planet. The purpose of this is for the quickening of the etheric body for the evolutionary transformation.

The Synchronotron system is essentially an interface system to resonate with other galactic intelligence. Votan explained to me his understanding of how higher or interdimensional thought templates are programmed by different sets of frequencies that are resolved through the system of the Synchronotron.

To understand this process, we followed a specific program. This might at first sound complicated to those who have never heard of all of this. But with practice, it is not as hard as it seems, though it requires dedication and consistency.

The key and most important practice is natural mind meditation and body discipline (we did yoga, but any body discipline works). We also did daily synchronic code practices to train our minds in new patterns and cycles. Our outer work and service to others was the writing of Cosmic History.

This rigorous mental work was complemented by much creative output in the form of painting, drawing, music, and poetry writing. Much of our communication was through poetic note exchanges, such as this one from Votan to me:

The path is clear the past is gone
And though it rains there is nothing but dawn
Hold high the torch, keep still the flame
Sit in the circle without name

See in the void all is mind
No above, no below, no front, no behind
On this day of spiritual sight
Can you hold firm to your inner light?

Sexual Life-Force: Mechanics of Noogenesis

Through perfect synchronization with one other being, we can channel the psychosexual energy (radion) to create, not a child, but a New Earth Consciousness.

—Valum Votan

The Synchronotron system was practiced to hook up with a cosmic interface system to resonate with other galactic intelligence. These galactic intelligences are interdimensional and are an extension of our own mind. It's just that our circuitry was previously switched off. We are learning how to turn it back on.

When working with this system and Cosmic History, we followed these three guidelines:

Love, love above everything.
In order to evolve, you must learn something new.
You only advance according to your own effort.

The primary key to the living knowledge of Cosmic History was to reconnect the fragmented circuitry through our bodies. We sought to connect the circuits of past and future knowledge within the human body and to cellularly defragment negative or outdated programming. This was just like my original vision in 2000 at the tomb of the Red Queen, where I was taken deep into my own body and shown the circuitry that needed to be reconnected so that the planetary field might be unified back to wholeness.

There must be a return to innocence.

The key to noogenesis lies in the redefinition of sex. Sexual or kundalini life-force is the biological base of our essence and fundamental creative power. This primal split of the hemispheres (masculine/feminine) combined with living in the wrong time is the chief deviation from our True Nature, as well as Nature itself. From this distorted time loop replay, all other problems stem. And all of these problems trace back to the misuse of sexual life-force, which creates enormous disharmony in the world.

The purpose of hermetic wisdom is to offset harmful programming in the free-will experiment of artificial time. In this process of Noogenesis, here is what I learned:

1. All of our conditioned and unconscious programs are locked into our sexuality.

2. The sexual wounding on this planet has everything to do with an Ancient Trauma that is highlighted in the shattering of Maldek.

3. This sexual wounding affects the very fabric of our reality. As Wilhelm Reich points out, it is sexual energy (creative life-force) "which governs the structure of human feeling and thinking, whether we are aware of it or not."

4. Redefining sex is redefining what it means to be human and is a key to noogenesis.

5. The two opposites are the source of all coding: the binary code, double helix, DNA code (which is precisely what the codes of the Law of Time are pointing to). When the right and left hemispheres have rejoined, the whole (galactic) brain lights up.

6. The key to noogenesis (or the birth of any new knowledge) is the union of masculine and feminine that keeps our world in balance and engenders a new creation.

7. The pineal gland and sex organs represent two polar currents or generators.

8. When these two poles are in resonance, they can create discharges that are the equivalent of the auroras at the north and south poles.

9. Auroras occur when natural discharges from the electromagnetic battery are numerous. These discharges can be focused through sexual energy that is in resonance with the electromagnetic field so that it releases energy that lights up the environment. This is how we charge ourselves, create our own electricity, and thus create more love in the world. This is the true definition of making love.

For what is it to die but to stand naked in the wind and to melt into the sun?

And when the earth shall claim your limbs, then shall you truly dance.

—Kahlil Gibran

Chapter 21

Oracle of Deathlessness

As long as there is a single wizard in the farthermost starpost of the galaxy, so long shall I be invoked and recalled by the name, Memnosis: Oracle of Deathlessness.

—José Argüelles, *The Arcturus Probe*

Everything born of sex dies. Only to be reborn again in another form. This is the mystery of life and death.

It was a misty autumn morning in southern Australia, when Memnosis, the Oracle of Deathlessness, came for José Argüelles/Valum Votan on March 23, 2011, Red Spectral Moon. I was not prepared for him to leave the planet so suddenly. Within only two weeks of him being sick, he was gone. During those final days I was in an altered space. Surely this all must be a dream. I felt like I was watching a movie but that reality existed elsewhere. He told me, "Don't worry, I have been serene through this entire thing." He said he'd been practicing for this moment his entire life. I took notes on the last three days of his life when his voice was reduced to a whisper, but his mind was sharper than ever. He told me not to try to figure it out as "when it's your time, it's your time."

Two weeks prior, we had gone on a three-hour hike, and he was robust and full of energy. He took off his shirt outside by our lotus pond. He was marveling at the regenerative and healing properties of the sunlight. Three incidents happened a few moons before his death.

The first one was 62 days before his passing when we were grocery shopping in Castlemaine, Australia. As we were walking through the aisles, he told me he felt someone was pulling him out of the body. I suggested he sit in the car while I finished shopping. When I got back the car, the feeling increased, and he said that it was an effort to remain in his body. Later that day, when we were driving home, we saw what appeared like some type of "Ship" in the sky. He was mesmerized by it and drew a picture of it in his journal.

The second incident occurred on Christmas Day, 2010, Red Magnetic Dragon. We were in our art studio painting, and a bird flew in and hit the wall. Votan picked it up to rescue it, and it died in his hands. It felt to be an omen, as he too was gone three moons later.

The third incident occurred a few weeks after. It was a beautiful sunny day with not a cloud in the sky. We were outside painting in our studio. I went into the house to get paper towels when I heard him scream. He had slammed his right middle finger in the metal studio door and cut it quite severely. There was a lot of blood, and he almost passed out. He couldn't stand the sight of blood. Though he needed stitches, he refused to go to the doctor. I did my best to tend to his wound so it wouldn't get infected. He was in a lot of pain and couldn't play his flute. Fortunately, he was left-handed, so he could still write in his journal and do his code work.

Back to the Stars

On March 20, 2011, White Galactic Worldbridger, he was taken to the hospital as he had become weak quite quickly. He was admitted and was led off to surgery at midnight. I waited all night in the waiting room, reading different scriptures. When he woke, he was coherent and in good spirits. He said, "Okay, I'm ready for the next adventure." The doctors informed me that he had only a few days to live due to peritonitis.

In those last three days, I asked Votan for final instructions. He told me what to give to whom (though he didn't have much). He left me with the responsibility of the Foundation for the Law of Time, which at the time was in much debt, and all of his belongings, among the most prized were his journals. I asked him if I should remain in Australia, and he just said, "Go where you are called." He whispered, "I have given you everything. You will know what to do." Though it was true that he had given me the inner teachings, still, I felt deeply unprepared in a worldly sense.

I asked if he had any final words. He replied:

"Love Everyone. Hate no one. Everything is Perfect."

He also said not to forget that it is "all a cosmic joke." Comforting me with his words, he also told me that he could help better from the other side and promised to assist me with *Cosmic History Chronicles, Volume VII: Book of the Cube*, which we had not yet begun. Three weeks before his illness, he gave me a final spontaneous tutorial entitled "Cosmic Sky Teachings." I ended up placing it into *Cosmic History Chronicles, Volume*

VII: Book of the Cube, though it was not really meant for that book initially. The basis of this teaching is summed up in this transmission:

> *Cosmic Sky Teachings are the essence of and encompass all spiritual or religious teachings that are known, have been known or will be known. Within the cosmos, every level of reality is present simultaneously. At any given moment, the universe is wholly unified by that moment. All religions are functions of different focal points of energy directed onto the Planet at different times for different peoples. All true religions flow into one stream of universal spirituality and are encompassed by the cosmic sky.*
>
> *All religions provide humanity with a type of scaffold or training wheels to get to a higher level and to ultimately see universal unity. Spiritual messengers, prophets and sages of all faiths represent a single tapestry of the vast interlocking interplanetary system.*
> *Cosmic Sky Teachings are the teachings of the unity of the cosmic mind. The cosmic mind is the unfolding or development into four key dimensions: the dimension of mind, the dimension of space, dimension of time, and dimension of number.*

Votan and I were escorted in an ambulance back to our house on the evening of March 22, Kin 88, Yellow Planetary Star. He wanted to die in his own bed. When we arrived home, I lit candles in the room and spoke to him in hopes of being a comfort. I stayed up most of the night cuddled up to his soon to be lifeless body. He took his final breath at 6:20 a.m., March 23, 2011, Red Spectral Moon. But before that occurred, he lifted his arm up and did the most elegant figure eight with his hand. Then it would drop back down. And he would lift it up and do it again. Was this an indication of infinity? Of the zuvuya?

After his final breath, I sat for a long while in silence. I didn't know what to do. Then I heard his voice say, "Go make a cup of coffee." So I went and made two cups, one for each of us, and placed one at his bedside for our final coffee together.

The next day, my phone was ringing off the hook. *New York Times*, *Wall Street Journal*, and *Los Angeles Times* were writing. It was all a whirl. I barely ate. I barely slept. My whole chakra system felt like it was being ripped out of its sockets. My body felt like it was dying. I had been so connected to him at every level; it was hard to fathom my life without him. I virtually had not talked to anyone in-depth for nine years. I didn't have many personal connections. I spent long hours in silence, feeling the depths of the human soul. The only thing I knew to do was to keep working. I finished the final chapter of his biography and published it. I started a blog, so I would have a vehicle to the world. I immersed myself in writing *Book of the Cube*, while I was undergoing the suffering at the depths of the human soul. I experienced every emotion.

I picked up his 1996 book, *The Arcturus Probe*, and highlighted key parts regarding death and deathlessness.

> *In your avoidance of death, you have denied yourselves full knowledge of the mind, and mind is the gateway to time.*
>
> *Nothing can keep you from death, so why do you try so hard to avoid it? Even when you say you believe in an 'after-life' as you so quaintly put it, why do you still shore up this life with insurance? And if you really do not know death and the cause of death fear, then what do you really know of life?*
>
> *Knowing that death is merely how the electric-crystal body experiences renewal and reactivation, we heteroclites were able to cultivate pulsar riding easily.*
>
> *Strange as it may seem to you who cherish your bodies and cling to death fear, we Arcturian Analogics felt an awesome liberation in this event. We also learned more deeply about the poignant points that render our endless love affair with each other so totally sacred. And we vowed to carry and remember this poignancy through all of our incarnations.*

Votan's encounter with Memnosis came 58 days after his 72nd birthday. In the 13 Moon calendar, Kin 58 is the signature of Pacal Votan's passing. Shortly after his passing, I found a letter he had written to me, and these instructions jumped out: "Gather all forces transmitted to you and send them to the universe as endless streams of simultaneous compassion waves—you have nothing to lose by loving everybody and giving birth to a whole new world."

Divine Romance

Divine Romance by Paramhansa Yogananda jumped out at me from a bookstore window on my first outing to the main town Ballarat, a few moons after Votan's passing. It gave me great comfort to read that "everyone who has ever loved you and who you ever loved is animated by the same source, it is God loving you through different forms. And that love can never die." Those words struck my soul like a lightning bolt. It also had instructions to attune your mind to those who have passed on.

In the summer of 2009, at the tail end of the Electric Storm year, Votan and I stayed at a small cottage in Venice Beach, California. We were doing a seven-day practice session in anticipation of his first presentation on the Synchronotron that he would do at the Babaji Ashram in Cisternino, Italy, in September (Electric Moon).

During that magical stay in Venice, Votan and I went for a long beach walk in Santa Monica, California, and he told me he had a vision of Paramahansa Yogananda. He saw his etheric body on the beach and received several telepathic messages. He received a confirmation of the unity of all messengers as well as other personal messages. He had never particularly spoken of Yogananda before this.

The following day we stopped into the Mystic Journey bookstore on Abbot Kinney Boulevard in Venice. We saw Yogananda's *The Second Coming of Christ*, featured in the window. He bought the double volume series. We discovered that Yogananda had passed away at the Biltmore Hotel in downtown Los Angeles on March 7, 1952, White Magnetic Mirror, precisely 100 days before the discovery of the tomb of Pacal Votan.

Valum Votan left this Planet 59 years after Yogananda. I met Votan when he was 59. Many numerical synchronicities began to flash in my mind, followed by a series of dreams with Yogananda, who became a deep comfort to me and guiding spirit. Before then, I had not paid too much attention to his teachings other than reading his seminal book: *Autobiography of a Yogi* as a teenager. In one dream, Yogananda was sitting on my bed in meditation. He gazed at me with penetrating eyes. As I looked into his eyes, they became spinning earths that I fell into, and he took me on a journey through the cosmos.

All Is a Number, God Is a Number, God Is Within All

After Votan's passing, I went through a period of depression that I did not know if I would ever emerge from. I felt that the best of my life was behind me. I had no one to gauge myself by. Day after day passed, and I immersed myself in work and vowed to memorize and imprint the mathematical grids of the holomind perceiver. My only choice was to evolve myself. And on top of it keeping the FLT going at this time thanks to Jacob and Kelly's steadfastness. I remained alone, seeing virtually no one for nearly two years. The following passage sums up my feelings at this time, which found its way into the introduction to *Book of the Cube*:

> *Through death, this book was born.*
>
> *This introduction begins in a dream: Full Moon, Blue Galactic Night; 114 days since the departure of Valum Votan. "Fear nothing!" Valum Votan said to me in the dream. "Grieve not! Arise and Go Forward!... Fear not, the world is a mere illusion. A plastic façade, bendable by the truth."*
>
> *In the dream, he held out a crystal cube. He motioned for me to concentrate. I gazed into the cube and at first, saw nothing but superficial reflections. I gazed longer, and suddenly I saw a long highway lined with very few houses. I noted a luminous glow emanating from some of the houses. Then I was lifted above the whole Earth and with x-ray vision saw the lighting up of specific residences across the globe.*
>
> *I realized I was being given access to view the light of those beings that had a covenant for total transformation. These agents of light reflected, through the cube, different fractals, together making the most exquisite and fantastic whole! Their minds merged as one in a telepathic network of light, while simultaneously, they each opened to a different channel, unique and brilliant. These were the wise ones, the makers of things to come, the keepers of the inner prayer, the channellers of the new reality!*
>
> *Suddenly I was back on the long highway, and my mind was magnetized to a specific house. Through telepathic gesture, I was granted entrance into one of the female's homes. My spirit*

hovered over her, of which she seemed calmly and happily aware. She carried a single candle and made her way to a desk and sat down. I watched as she wrote the words:

The Long War is Over, and the Days of Doubt are Past ...

What a deep relief these words brought! Then my attention turned back to Valum Votan, who was smiling and holding the magic cube of vision. It was now evening, and the stars were glimmering in the clear sky as he went inside, made a fire, and put on a tea kettle.

Then I awoke from the dream.

Where am I? And how did I get here? The dawn was breaking, and slowly the layers of this reality set in, one by one with all their subtle tensions and densities. Enormous pressure and urgency filled me, my heart pumping fast. I had only one thought in my mind: Finish the *Book of the Cube!* I immediately rose from the bed and got to work.

The meditation of the cube seized me and wouldn't let me go, day or night until it was complete. It was wintertime, and the winds were howling. I kept the wood stove burning as dark mists rolled off the falling gum trees. I pieced together fragments of transmissions, while new streams entered. I felt the presence of intelligences peering over my shoulder, crossing this out and adding that. First slowly, then quickly, the text rearranged itself as I surrendered to the process. Then a message of comfort came:

Do not worry or grieve. Death is a factor in the evolution of spirit; its real meaning is as a rite of passage of the spirit. The mission continues. It is an endless Spirit journey. Everything and everyone that ever was is here with you now. The spirit helpers surround you, guiding you. Those who remember the dream will assist you.

Tomb of the Red Queen, Palenque, 2010, Red Resonant Moon.

Ballad of Votan and Red Queen
By Valum Votan

Wrapped in purity and silence, the circle draws me from its center
Following their instructions the angels take a measure
And from it inscribe the pathways of a messenger to his treasure ...
(and the angels sing)
"We need someone who knows how to find the center
We need someone to join beginning and end
We need a sorcerer and apprentice
Who will follow the river past its last bend"

In an ancient city, Nah Chan, two tombs were placed side by side
One in the Temple of Inscriptions, the other in Temple 13, its guide
Votan and Red Queen they were called
Their faces covered with jade and malachite, red cinnabar covered their bones
But their souls had long since departed to a place only the Angels had known
What meant these tombs side by side,
So mysterious in ancient Nah Chan?
Who says we do not come back from the dead?
Who says these souls did not have a pact
To come back when the cycle was closing
To emerge from the mystery to find one another
And make certain their Love would put an end to all history?

Some say Votan and Red Queen were lovers
Some say they were just friends
A sorcerer and his apprentice
Following the River past its last bend

From their tombs in ancient Nah Chan Palenque
Xilbalbay the Underworld we are told
They returned to put the old time to rest

Votan and Red Queen twin souls
Through their Love they had passed their last test
Determined to find one another in a time of chaos and war
Prophecy put them together, prophecy opened the door
The masks of the dead, the two tombs of Nah Chan
Returned to terminate unholy Babylon
A sorcerer and his apprentice they were
Votan and Red Queen by name
A mystery wrapped in an enigma
Possessed of the secret to put an end to the game
Of selling the Earth for a profit in a contract bound by false time
Dissolved by their magic together—
No more war, no more fear, no more crime
Votan and Red Queen returned for the end
To follow the river past its last bend
Where angels were waiting with a heavenly scroll
Inscribed with their names joined as one soul

Some say Votan and Red Queen were lovers
Some say they were just friends
A sorcerer and his apprentice
Following the River past its last bend

Part Three
Realization

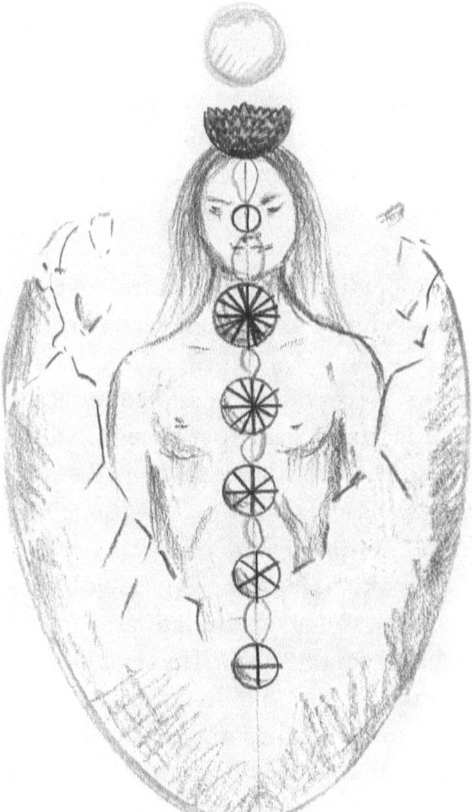

Chapter 22

Solitude and Retreat

I want to be with those who know secret things or else alone.
—Rainer Maria Rilke

After Votan died, I spent 631 days in virtual solitude at our home. I was still living in the very rarefied state that we had created, and I didn't want to lose it. I kept Votan's meditation room precisely the way he had left it, and I meditated every morning in it with his Excalibur crystal and baston.

Some days I would spend all day in a trancelike state where I would sit in the morning, and before I knew it, it was dark. We had planned to remain in retreat for December 21, 2012, Blue Crystal Hand, and had many talks about the next stages of our mission after 2013.

I contemplated all facets of the experiences I had been through to determine the next steps. *How do I proceed? How do I best serve with the knowledge I have been given? How can I make Cosmic History relevant to the world today? Why did I go through all this?*

I reflected that a key purpose of those nine years was to renew the base of human knowledge and to formulate and create a perspective and knowledge base that is totally fresh. This would give a new basis of self-perception and a new description of the universe.

I felt an incredible responsibility and pressure weighing on me to do something. I had no outside gauge for my life nor any reflections other than my inner results from work. It was a constant effort to keep up with all of the levels of information. I kept several notebooks for different projects, and did my best to keep all the flames lit.

On the human level, it was challenging to go out. All the grocery store clerks and shopkeepers had always seen Votan and I together and would always ask where he was. I had to tell everyone that he had died. I would sometimes go to the grocery store and walk around the aisles for a long time just to feel a sense of comfort or normalcy in the human realm.

It was a small town, and I felt people looked at me with pity as the woman whose husband had died.

My first trip out of town was to Melbourne to see the Dalai Lama. Votan and I already had tickets and had paid for a hotel for two nights. I had seat 114, sitting next to Votan's empty seat, 113. I thought it curious to see all of the Dalai Lama's monks glued to their cell phones. There was a chaotic feeling in the air. As it turned out, his monks were staying at the same hotel as me, and one of them saw me sitting alone. He approached me and invited me to dinner with them at the hotel, to which I obliged and had a great connection.

Other than this visit, I rarely went out of the house for two years, except to get groceries and much needed massages. I had resigned to be a hermit, living a monastic lifestyle, yet I still felt so much life in me. I contemplated much the best way to proceed and how I might be of service with what I had been given. I lived by Yogananda's guiding words: "Solitude is the price of God-realization."

I went on a lot of long walks, and at one period, drank a lot of wine from the organic winery down the road from our house. I would go through periods of cleansing and self-care coupled by not caring, not eating or sleeping, and really not wanting to be on this planet. I would give myself encouraging talks to cheer myself up and would record them and listen to them when I walked. I learned to be an excellent friend and support system to myself.

I recorded my dreams too. In one dream, I saw Votan at the ocean, on a monitor screen in my room, realizing the whole world was wired into an online streaming video. I felt like I was being watched, a feeling not unfamiliar, but amplified by his departure. I spent Christmas alone. Though I hadn't really celebrated it since 2002, I remember the vast emptiness of Christmas 2011 and the Gregorian New Year. On these holidays, Votan and I always had the most profound times together and generally accomplished a lot of work while others were immersed in holiday programs.

Sometimes it was unbearable to not have him in the third dimension. Sometimes I would hear his voice and think he was still there. Often I would wake up in the morning and feel that he was in his room meditating, only to remember that he was gone. I read through his journals to feel closer to him, and I continued writing in a journal where he had left off, doing the codes each day. I reflected on the poem he had written me for my 38th birthday, the final one I would spend with him. The poem seemed more like instructions.

If I look in the mirror of my heart
Then I am no different than you
For yours is the Voice
I am the Echo
Seek not the Mirror
But the Face in the Mirror
Follow the Echo back to the Voice
Trace the Voice Back to the Source
Where Voice and Echo, Mirror and Face
Are One
When the Path laid out
Is clear and true
Do not deviate!
Who follows in the beginning
Leads in the end
Who leads in the beginning
Transcends beginning and end
The innocent alone
Know where to go
When beginning and end have ceased
And all that remains
Is the unending flow.

My mind retraced the significance of both of our final birthdays spent together, just a few moons before his passing. On my 38th birthday, we spent the sunny day climbing the rocks of Hanging Rock, known for its supernatural qualities. The rock is allegedly over 6 million years old, formed by an eruption of magma, and was an easy 45-minute drive from our house. Hanging rock refers to a boulder suspended between other boulders under which is the main entrance path. A movie *Picnic at Hanging Rock* (1975) was made by Peter Weir, based on the 1967 mystery novel by author Joan Lindsay, about the disappearance of girls on Valentine's day in 1900.

Close by are other rock formations—the Colonnade, the Eagle, and the UFO. I found this interesting as the galactic signature of this day was Blue Lunar Eagle, Kin 15, which was also our street address. The site was considered sacred and used for ceremonies and initiations by three indigenous tribes: the Wurundjeri, Taungurong, and Djadja Wurrung. Votan and I had breakfast in the nearby town Woodend which boasts an Anti-Gravity Hill. On its incline, cars and other objects mysteriously find themselves rolling up, rather than down, the slope. The entire day had an otherworldly feeling, and Votan took what would be his final photo of me in a white dress at Hanging Rock.

Soul Journey

I would often have the feeling that I had received Votan's memory bank or that it had been overlaid into my mind so that I operated with a type of double-decker mind, mine and his. When I heard any information, I knew exactly how he would think and feel about it.

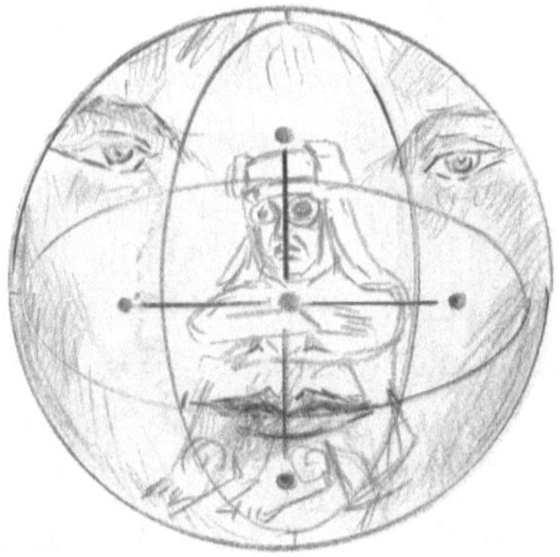

I questioned: *Who are we when there is no one to define us? Who are we when all relations are stripped away? What is our self-perception then?*

This is the real work that I embarked on at this time. A deep soul journey. Before he passed, Votan had told me that his mission was now dependent on my self-realization. In his notebook, he wrote:

> *It is now Red Queen herself who is empowered to be the central focus of transcendental energies necessary for the regeneration of the cycle and beyond. Cosmic History embodied in the complete transmission of the Galactic Mayan mind lineage of Votan is to be the legacy of Red Queen and the unraveling of the meaning of her uninscribed tomb. Though her path springs from mine, it will take her on an entirely new course... The Odyssey of Votan is the*

> *treasury of the Red Queen, the dispensation of the Law of Time is for her to spread like a resplendent light to the future race known as The Return of the People of Oma.*

Underground Classes and Parallel Rainbow Dream World(s)

The dreams continued, and they were always underground in classrooms and often in underground time tunnels, the same as I had experienced as a child. It was in this "in between the worlds" state that I continued my education for nearly two years after Votan's passing. I was shown many things and was convinced of other worlds existing parallel to our own. On one occasion, I was having a particularly challenging day. There was nothing left to do but inquire within.

I was guided to a practice, which felt to be a form of Pratyahara yoga, where you withdraw the senses from the mind by consciously releasing tension from the body, and thereby getting yourself into the most relaxed state possible without falling asleep. I entered a deep state and found myself traveling outside my body. I had the same static vortex feeling that occurs when you are shifting dimensions or astral traveling.

All of a sudden, I found myself standing outside of an apartment complex. I walked up a few flights of stairs directly to apartment 31. I entered without knocking. It was a lovely, spacious, immaculate yet simple apartment with wooden walls. I looked around. It seemed familiar. I walked down the hall to the left and saw an outline of my grandfather, who had passed years earlier as if to signify that I was indeed in another world.

I entered one of the rooms and saw a woman studying. She turned around ... it was me! I understood that I had entered a parallel earth. Everything appeared similar to Earth, though lighter, more luminescent. I mentally compared the feelings of the two different earths.

In this parallel earth, everything had such a profound feeling of wholeness that I cannot fully articulate. For example, on this earth, we are accustomed to there being so many details that we can never keep up with them. There is so much information that we can never fully process it all. There is so much to do that we can never get it all done. The details are endless, even down to constant lint on the carpet, the cobwebs in the corners, or the accumulated single sock drawer because one always disappears in the wash. Then there are the to-do lists, the timetables, the appointments, the emails, etc.

None of this existed on this parallel earth. There was a most beautiful, penetrating feeling of wholeness, an all-pervading peace, warmth, and well-being in a very calming here and now. As I was thinking these thoughts, Valum Votan entered the front room wearing a Hunab Ku shirt. He had overheard my thoughts comparing the two earths and added (telepathically): "Don't forget that traveling is so much easier and enjoyable here than on your earth, with all those airplanes polluting, long lines, security checks and forms to fill out!"

He pointed to the large windows in the front room. I looked out the window, and the sky seemed to open, pouring forth the most dazzling rainbows of all shapes and sizes: double rainbows, triple rainbows, dancing rainbows, rainbow mists, twirling rainbows—the ultimate rainbow parade! Votan telepathed: "This is what happens when you learn how to unzip the sky!"

Then I remembered how he had always said: "Rainbows are to the noosphere what toxic waste is to the technosphere. Not only is the noosphere as the planet mind vast in scope, but it also extends into other dimensions as well."

I understood that not only had I entered a parallel earth but the earth that had attained noosphere, a unified collective mind. Here, a manifestation was instantaneous, but it was all good, as the collective mind was set to a high positive frequency and deeply attuned with its Creator. Then appeared a big red spaceship. I got so excited that I ran out of the apartment and followed it down a hill, where I found myself on a pier surrounded by a beautiful large body of water. There was even a family sitting on picnic benches. They were accustomed to the sky phenomenon.

Votan joined me and showed me the beautiful birds, which he fed greens to, and he pointed out the flowers in colors I had never seen before; at the center of each flower appeared beautiful multicolored mandalas that looked like eyes. I began telling him everything that had happened on Earth since his departure. He seemed interested to hear. I asked if he could come back with me in this world...anything seemed possible. He explained that he could no longer physically reenter that earth, but he could enter this parallel earth. He indicated that this is just a glimpse of the world(s) that wait for those who believe in the Dream.

We went back into the apartment. I saw again the parallel "me," and I understood that I also exist in this parallel earth in a continuation of the Noosphere II project, which was simultaneously being carried out here. After the dream occurred, I slept for 14 hours straight. I was hoping to reawaken in apartment 31, but I woke up here on this earth to tell you about it.

Jesus and Magdalene

Around this time, I received a few books in the mail from Lois in Australia. This book series was entitled *The Expected One, The Poet Prince,* and *The Book of Love* by Kathleen McGowan. These books are written as fiction but tell the story of Mary Magdalene's life with Jesus. I took great comfort in those books as they opened me more deeply to the feminine energy and attunement to the mystery of Mary Magdalene. The premise of the book series is:

> *Two thousand years ago, Mary Magdalene hid a set of scrolls in the French Pyrenees: the Gospel of Mary Magdalene, or her version of the life of Jesus and the events of the New Testament. Protected by supernatural forces, these sacred scrolls could be uncovered only by a particular seeker, one who fulfills the ancient prophecy of L'Attendu—the Expected One.*

I would find myself a few years later in the south of France, visiting the places spoken of in the book, like Rennes Le Chateau and the Louvre, and teaching the Synchronotron to a group in the Pyrenees Mountains.

Around this time, I also received a phone call from Mother Tynetta Muhammed, who had planned to come to visit me in New Zealand but ended up getting delayed in Australia. She lifted my spirits greatly and told me about her visit to Apocalypse Island off of Chile, where there was discovered Mayan remnants that had affirmed her mission of Universal Recollection. The morning after that call, I woke up crying in a dream with Votan.

In the dream, he was getting ready for an event that was to take place on Easter Island. When I saw him, I said, "Wow, you have been resurrected." He replied, "I never died." I said, "But I saw you put into a body bag." He smiled and said, "It wasn't me." Then he said, "Remember, my love is true love." Then he disappeared.

For a week after the call from Mother Tynetta, I dreamed of Votan. All of the dreams were the same, revolving around death and resurrection and him reassuring me he was here and had never died.

I woke up to a powerful dream on Kin 207, Blue Crystal Hand, one spin (260 days) before December 21, 2012. In the dream, the sky was covered with ships, and giant red squid-like creatures began falling to Earth. This was followed by an inspiration to do a seven-day event in Australia for the first anniversary of Votan's passing. I ran the idea by Ishram and Ashani, who immediately agreed to host it on their land. They asked me to drive to their house that rainy day, and as I was driving, the most beautiful rainbow appeared! This was a turning point where I felt light at the end of the tunnel, third-dimensionally speaking. This event gave me a focalization point to synthesize information and also an opportunity to connect with people for the first time since Votan's passing.

Atisha's Retreat

> *No one can advise and help you, no one. There is only one way: go within.*
>
> —Rainer Maria Rilke

In preparation for this event, I went on a retreat at Atisha's Buddha Center in Bendigo, Australia. The Center houses the Great Stupa of Universal Compassion. The place was silent, being inhabited by just four monks who permanently lived there. To my delight, I had the meditation hall and library virtually all to myself. For nine days, I ate only cherries, berries, grapes and water and was practicing natural mind meditation and breathing exercises. In the evenings I sat alone in the library until the wee hours reading everything I could find about Yeshe Tsogyal. I contemplated that it was through the context of Padmasambhava and Yeshe Tsogyal that Votan and I had come together.

Yeshe Tsogyal, born in 5 AD, declared to become a Buddha in her lifetime. She was the consort of Padmasambhava, who brought Buddhism to Tibet from India. It was said that she could levitate, among achieving many other paranormal powers (or siddhis). She was responsible for organizing the teachings of Padmasambhava, many of which were hidden for future generations. This was a vast undertaking consisting of thousands of tomes and an extraordinary accomplishment for a woman of her time. She allegedly left the Earth at Zapu Peak in central Tibet, according to her biography, *Sky Dancer.* I was struck by the following instructions of Padmasambhava to Yeshe Tsogyal.

Oh yogini who has mastered tantra, the gross bodies of men and women are equally suited, but if a woman has strong aspiration, then she has higher potential. From the beginningless time, you have accrued merit from virtue and awareness, and now, faultless, endowed with buddhas qualities. Superior woman, you are a human bodhisattva. This is you I am speaking of, happy girl, is it not? Now that you have achieved your own enlightenment work for others, for the sake of other beings. Such a marvelous woman as you never existed in the world before, not in the past, not at present and not in the future—of this, I am certain.

—Sky Dancer

Chapter 23

Zero Point

When one has nothing to lose, one becomes courageous. We are timid only when there is something we can still cling to.

—Don Juan Matus

I used my own heartbreak as a gateway to understand the suffering of others, knowing that everyone we encounter is suffering in one way or another. I concluded that the only way out of all the suffering was to find the path Unseen, the hidden path, the bridge that mortal eyes cannot see.

I awoke on June 21, 2011, Blue Planetary Storm, feeling virtually paralyzed with sadness. It felt like my heart was being pierced over and over, and the core of my being was splitting open. All I could do was observe as torrents of emotion released from my body.

It was winter solstice in the Southern Hemisphere. On this dark, grey day, I took a drive to the dump to release old belongings. A powerful storm broke out, which matched my feelings. After it cleared, a brilliant rainbow appeared in the sky. Seeing the rainbow, I felt a deep sense that everything would be okay and that something new was on the horizon.

That day I checked my email and learned that six days prior, on the 60th anniversary of the discovery of the tomb of Pacal Votan (June 15, 2012), Red Queen's bones were returned on White Overtone Mirror. I felt this signified the return of feminine energy to its rightful place; not to dominate, but to create a perfect balance of equality in the world. I also noted that Mirror was the signature of Yogananda's passing. I read his words in *Divine Romance:* "To attach any reality to the outward show of life expresses lack of true wisdom."

The days continued to pass by ever more quickly. For this nearly two-year-long period, I felt I was living between worlds and could leave this planet at any time. My dreams took on a new lucidity, often providing the missing knowledge I was seeking in waking reality. I wrote them down faithfully as they revealed a whole other life being lived elsewhere.

They were my constant source of comfort. In the 13 Moon calendar, I was born on the third day of the Night Wavespell, which is the archetype of the Dreamer.

Ishram and Ashani helped arrange a seven-day event to commemorate the first anniversary of Votan's passing on March 23, 2012, White Crystal Wizard. They prepared their 20 acres of land to accommodate 52 people and purchased a huge yurt for the event as well as compost toilets. All the attendees camped out on the rural land surrounded by eucalyptus trees and accompanied by the morning laughter of the kookaburra birds. This land had originally belonged to the Dja Dja Wurrung, the Aboriginal tribe, who were bound to the land from their spiritual belief in the power of Dreaming.

I was grateful to have such a beautiful and dedicated group from around the world, to share with. We discussed that everything that occurs on the surface world is a symptom of an inner shift. We reviewed the origins of the Law of Time and the 20-year window of its unfoldment, from 1991-2011, which ultimately led to the Holomind Perceiver.

> *The non egoic state of mind is the gateway to galactic holomind and meditation. When you are nobody at all, God is present; the Great Beyond is staring you in the face. ... This is the Primordial Self whose authenticity you have been seeking all this time.*
>
> —Valum Votan

The more I worked, the better I felt. *Time Synchronicity and Calendar Change: The Visionary Life and Work of José Argüelles* was self-published shortly after this event thanks to a generous patron. I started a blog called 13:20 Frequency Shift and Galactic Spacebook, an alternative to Facebook, for those who wanted to share about the Law of Time. At this time, *Book of the Cube* was in final edits.

I began an accelerated process of recalling all the key points, travels, and lessons of my time with Votan. For five days, I was in an otherworldly state. All the memories came rushing forth into my awareness like a movie slide show.

These travels took us to war-torn Baghdad, the Mosques of Istanbul, as well as meeting Mevlana in Turkey. We traveled to Dubai, Spain, England, The Netherlands, Belgium, Austria, and Switzerland, where we stayed in the retreat home of Osho, and visiting the home and grave of Swiss psychologist Carl Jung. And then to Argentina, Brazil, Chile,

Japan, Singapore, Dubai, Bali, Africa (Kenya and Mombassa), Mt. Kilimanjaro, and India, where we visited Adyar, Helena Blavatsky's ashram and Sri Aurobindo's shrine and The Mother's Auroville community. I reflected deeply on all of this. Votan's final public talk had been at the Prophet's Conference in Vancouver, Canada on the Day Out of Time, Yellow Self-Existing Star (July 25, 2010). There, he was honored in a powerful ceremony conducted by Floredemayo, a Mayan-trained shamaness and leader in the International Council of the 13 Indigenous Grandmothers.

I spent 631 days in solitude, absorbed in processing and connecting various streams of information and continuing the work for the Foundation. But there were days when I also could not move, filled with little inspiration. I reflected that underneath the names, labels, and roles we play, that we are all ultimately just energy.

Over the years, both with Votan there and alone, I had many experiences with ships and other mysterious phenomena appearing outside my house. It became normal. I linked it directly with my connection to the Holomind Perceiver system in which I was fully immersed at the time. I realized that just making an effort to study and understand this system increases our brain energy and expands our level of continuing consciousness, the ability to remain "awake" and not fall back asleep.

Being alone was a great blessing, and in this time, my compassion and love for humanity deepened. I wanted to be a lighthouse for people, a safety zone of healing. I went fully through the throes of every human emotion and came out on the other side. I also had experiences over these years, where I felt like I was helping souls cross over to the other side during their transition.

At this time, I also deeply reflected on our original experiment with Lloydine. I had had a few conversations with her after Votan's passing. She was now living in a senior home with a roommate, living a simple life. Though our work together had completed on the physical plane, the lessons learned would carry on and hopefully be a treasure trove of lessons for others.

I would last speak to Lloydine on the third anniversary of Votan's passing on March 23, 2014, Yellow Magnetic Seed. This was 54 days before her passing of cancer on May 16, 2014, White Electric Mirror, the day after her 71st birthday. I told her I loved her unconditionally, and she reciprocated. She shared that her path had taken her in another direction and to other life experiences. She animatedly spoke of her father, Lloyd, whose galactic signature was Yellow Magnetic Seed. We didn't speak of Votan at all. After this conversation, I felt a sense of completion and a feeling of wholeness.

I was giving a talk in the white room at King Arthur Pub in Glastonbury, England, at the exact time of her passing. The theme was: Return of Galactic Camelot. I would learn about her passing that night when a note was slipped under my hotel door near midnight. I wasn't surprised as I knew she had been suffering from cancer for some time. I dreamed of both her and Votan that night, and the next day I was taken to the fabled Camelot by a Druid priest. Everything that day felt heightened, otherworldly, and dreamlike.

Upon returning back to the U.S., I was unprepared to receive a barrage of communications from many kin urging me to create a tribute for Lloydine. I tried several times to write a tribute but felt that to be honest with my experience, I would need to give more context than was appropriate for a tribute. Then I saw tributes painting her as an "ascended master," and some even went as far as to pit Stephanie "Red Queen" against Lloydine "White Queen," which would continue a while after. It was unfortunate, but everyone is entitled to their perceptions. In this case, I felt the most skillful means was to remain silent. At Lloydine's funeral in Boulder, there was a table set up with pictures as a dedication of her life, but with no indication of Votan or her work with the 13 Moon Calendar Change Peace Movement. She had chosen a different path. I will always be grateful for the role she played and her years of service with Votan to lay the foundation of this knowledge. She is me and I am her. And without her I would not be here writing this now.

Shortly after, I received a visitation that began in a dream but then extended into a telepathic communication that has since carried over into all facets of my life:

I was staring at the sun. It looked like it was coming closer and closer, then out flew a magic golden bird. Suddenly I found myself in my bedroom, and the golden bird appeared and shapeshifted into a being about three feet high, which felt female, but I could not tell by appearance. In fact, it was hard to make out its appearance because the glow of light around it was so blinding.

The most profound compassion, love, and empathy exuded from this being's heart to mine. It was as if I had known "her" all my life and knew that she was part of my "star family." She communicated telepathically but did not reveal her name or the specific place she came from. I knew she had traveled through the sun and intuited that she was a representative of the Galactic Federation of Light.

The love she was projecting completely melted my heart, causing a profound remembrance to overtake me. She expressed without words a deep empathy that her "people" feel for us humans who are "trapped" in this restrictive material plane at this time where there are many dark forces at play. Through her, I felt pristine and holy energy, with the memory of what true divine communion among souls feels like, so pure and clean and beautiful. Only when you re-experience the depth of this connection do you realize how far away our collective humanity is from this state of being.

She communicated that "they" are waiting for the unity and an invitation from the humans to offer more assistance. I understood that they have the technologies that can help us to regenerate our planet. However, they are awaiting our signal and invitation as a unified consciousness on Earth (this is the purpose of the Rainbow Bridge global peace meditation). Then I saw that she was about to leave. My heart longed to leave with her. She sensed my feelings and turned toward me with deep compassion that I could feel in my solar plexus.

She communicated that she would leave me with a "magic elixir." I saw what appeared as a lightning bolt come out of her third eye and hit mine, "charging" me with beautiful vibrations and deep comfort, but also leaving me with a message and reminder that the unified force of LOVE is the only way to cast out all fear and shadows from this planet.

This is the victory of the rainbow bridge prophecy. I understood that once enough beings unify in this vision, then it will unleash uncontrollable waves of Divine Light that will rush forth in ecstasy and heal the Universe.

Chapter 24

Ships and Sirius

The power of the seeker is in becoming the sought. The target is already in the arrow.

—Valum Votan

One clear, chilly evening, after a full day of immersion into the holomind perceiver codes, I heard Votan's voice in my mind say: "Go outside and look at the moon." I went outside only to view what appeared as a fleet of ships above the house—white orbs zigzagging across the night sky. I was transfixed. Then seemingly out of nowhere appeared an etheric-looking oval ship that materialized and dematerialized in different parts of the sky. It was beaming unmistakable colors of red and blue! At one point it seemed very close, as if to land, though there was no place among all of the trees. My body became electrified, filled with energy, and I was up all night.

The message received was: "There is only unity. We are not alone. We are parallel selves waiting to recognize each other and keeping each other informed on the telepathic plane of the real news of the universe."

I felt greatly comforted by this experience, and it only gave me further confirmation of the large interplanetary program we are all a part of. The next day I did an internet search to see if there had been any sightings in the area and sure enough there was a video posted of the exact orbs that I saw! The Gregorian date was 9/13: 9 x 13 = 117! Kin 117 was the signature of Votan's original dream of 441, that evolved into the Synchronotron system.

The UFO sightings were a confirmation for me of the inner work being made manifest in the outer world. I found it interesting to note that Carl Jung's final work was *Flying Saucers: A Modern Myth of Things Seen in the Sky.* Jung came to the conclusion that UFOs were examples of the phenomena of synchronicity where external events mirror internal psychic states.

I felt this was exactly what I was experiencing. The deeper I went into the practice of the holomind perceiver, the more events like this would occur. The right pieces of information would miraculously present themselves in my field of awareness. I trusted this process. I concluded that following the cycle of the 13 Moons allows us to come into resonance with our own intuitive faculty.

This led me to a deep certainty that these mathematical codes were connected to something vast and alive. And when you are alone with single pointed focus, then many unexplainable experiences can occur. These experiences were encouraging signposts that kept me going through what would have otherwise been a dark and uncertain time.

I was also greatly heartened to learn about Supernova 2011, discovered that same year on August 24, Blue Solar Night. Scientists say a supernova is the final stage of a star. Located in the Pinwheel Galaxy within the Ursa Major constellation, or the Big Dipper, this supernova was reported to be more powerful than 2.6 billion suns. Out of billions of stars in the galaxy, this one was said to outshine them all. The title headline in the local paper was:

"Supernova dazzles scientists." It begins: "California astronomers found the closest brightest supernova of its kind in 25 years…."

Reading about this activated me and I got excited to assemble more pieces of knowledge. The last supernova of this magnitude was supernova 1987A. Votan had written much about this supernova, which he called "Quetzalcoatl Supernova 1987A," as it occurred right before the Harmonic Convergence. For this reason, he felt it was a cosmic announcement saying, "Pay attention." He spent much time contemplating the hidden meaning of what he felt was a higher design principle behind the physical world. He wanted to understand how phenomena was created.

Supernova 1987A manifested rings that were supposedly ejected 20,000 years before the explosion and were a light year in diameter. In 1987, right before the Harmonic Convergence, the core of the supernova began exploding. By 1997 the explosions began to ignite the ring, and in 2007 it appeared that the ring was virtually ignited, appearing like a "ring of cosmic pearls."

Votan told me he felt that his "opticals," visual colored geometries, which appeared to extend into other universes, were a function both of the Vela Pulsar activated by Quetzalcoatl Supernova 1987A and Sirius coordination strategies. He thought that the 441 cube is the information matrix coordinating the activity of the 1987A supernova. He concluded that a supernova represents a state of profound attainment of enlightenment.

In *The Arcturus Probe,* he describes a supernova in the following way:

> *A supernova you will recall is, in reality, a star master, an entire star system attaining higher-dimensional enlightenment. Because of the 1987 supernova with the countdown just 26 years to go, the notorious 12:60-time beam was eclipsed and is now being reabsorbed into the reactivated binary sixth beam. With the release of the hold of the 12:60 artificial time beam in 1987, luminous sixth-dimensional engrams of the dialogue between Memnosis and Lucifer began to flood the Timeship's holon. This was the beginning of the second stage of interdimensional intervention.*

It was clear to me that the practices of the Synchronic Order served as a bridge, or type of interface system, to other telepathic civilizations who already live in full awareness of this structure.

A year later, I had a life-changing experience. First, I originally thought I was meant to be in Australia, but it became increasingly clearer that that was not meant to be. One evening, while outside to get wood for the stove, I saw four ships outside my house. Three were zigzagging orbs, and the fourth was larger with alternating blinking blue and red lights. I had seen a similar looking ship precisely one year earlier at the same location. While gazing transfixed at the mysterious crafts, I felt a tugging sensation in my solar plexus. I saw a clear vision of Palenque, and then felt my attention being directed toward Sirius. I tried to put the vision out of mind as I was determined to stay in my nurturing home.

The next day while getting groceries, I spontaneously stopped by a used bookstore. A book jumped out at me: *My Contact With Flying Saucers.* The book was about UFO contactee Dino Kraspedon, from Brazil, who was contacted in November 1952. I opened randomly to a page where the ET is talking about how soon the people of Earth will become aware of a second sun entering the solar system as part of a system of binary suns. This would change the orbit of all the planets. All my hairs stood at attention. I felt I had been plugged into an electrical circuit.

I went home and curled up with the book on that dark, rainy night. I felt a particular energy vibration as I read, but that was beyond the words. It awakened an ancient memory. The ET says that when this new source of light appears, many people will vanish forever from the face of the Earth, but a small community, obedient to the laws of God, will remain, and all present suffering will cease. There will be peace, abundance, justice, and compassion. He explains that UFOs have been sent to study the effects that the appearance of the "new sun" will bring in its wake.

The books stated, "The Sun which is to come will be called the Sun of Justice. Its appearance in the heavens will be the warning signal of the coming of the One who will shine even more than the Sun itself."

The ET said that the UFOs are here for the purpose of study and also to make the appeal to the humans to change course and avoid catastrophe and to live in peace. The ET also claimed to have come from a satellite on Jupiter, residing on both Ganymede and Io. This got my attention as the Waitaha people in New Zealand had also focalized on these moons, particularly Io.

In many of my dreams, Votan directed met to pay attention to what is happening in the sun. He believed that the binary sunspots are what account for changes in time and thought structures and that solar initiations affect the electromagnetic field, creating different mental quickening or shifts in consciousness. On those dark, rainy days I began to immerse myself in contemplations of the sun and the meaning of solar consciousness.

Votan had made clear that the entire 13 Moon calendar program, as well as the Law of Time, is a knowledge program from Sirius—Sirius being understood as the galactic outpost of higher knowledge for this part of the galaxy. The 13 Moon calendar start date, July 26, is based on Sirius. I wondered what role Sirius has in the new cycle we are entering into. Were the People of OMA similar to the Nommo that the Dogon people had talked about? They say that the Nommo will return (in a spaceship) when "a certain star reappears," and that Sirius A and B "were once where the Sun is now." The star will be invisible before it emerges, and is drawn with the rays inside the circle. It will only be "formed when the Nommo's ark descends, for it is also the resurrected Nommo's 'eye' symbolically."

This led me into the contemplation of the eye of Ra, Sekhmet, and ancient technologies. At this time I was also contemplating how in *The Secret Doctrine*, Madame Blavatsky says that the zodiac is an heirloom from the Atlanteans and the ancients believed that the world's history was recorded in the zodiacal signs. For three days I was absorbed in this knowledge and almost forgot the original message of the ship encounter about leaving Australia.

However, a few days later, the same thing occurred when I went to get wood for the stove. The large ship appeared again above my house. This was a powerful experience. As I went to put wood in the stove, I burned my right hand and received a small, permanent scar between my thumb and index finger. I felt that this stamped the deal, and I committed, at that moment, to leave Australia.

I was being called to leave everything behind and go to Palenque to conclude the Closing of the Cycle ceremony as the successor to José Argüelles/Valum Votan. I would take with me two suitcases and his Excalibur crystal that he had carried with him since 1985. The tomb of Pacal Votan had been sealed in 2011, and now was the time to return the crystal back to the point of prophecy in order that the new cycle might take root.

After this "ship" experience, I could no longer sleep in the bed that Votan had slept in and I moved to another room, which had been his office. My reality was palpably shifting and phasing into something else, but it was all still a mystery to me. At night I would awaken and feel I was falling through a vortex as if my whole room was spinning, and I had an uncanny feeling that someone was in a ceremony watching me in a vision, communicating something.

The Dream

> *Time is a Zuvuya, a memory circuit. Every zuvuya is a circuit of all time. We are born only to die and meet ourselves again at resurrection.*
>
> —Valum Votan

On the night of October 22, 2011, White Electric Wind, after nearly five moons in solitude after Votan's passing, I had a powerful dream.

> *I found myself in Palenque, in Temple 13, the tomb of the Red Queen. It was dark inside. Just as I was trying to orient myself, the walls started rumbling and swaying, and the narrow chamber shapeshifted into a type of narrow cabin full of light.*

I looked up, and there was Votan! It was as if we were in the same space as Temple 13, but the dimensions shifted, and the exterior took on a different form, or as if there were many dimensions contained in this one space and according to a shift of mind, a new environment emerged. I understood that we are always surrounded by an overlay of dimensions that are vibrating at different frequencies. It was as though I was being shown how to go back and forth through these frequencies.

So I was with Votan in this narrow cabin-like chamber. There was a single computer sitting in the center. He indicated telepathically that this computer was a type of control panel linked directly to the main control panel at the center of the Earth. He informed me that the center of the Earth radiates light beams of information that connect with all of the pyramid structures on the planet.

I understood these as the interplanetary regeneration chambers. He was also communicating something about the pyramids being overlays of a particular matrix structure that can be understood through the 441-cube matrix (though I did not fully understand this yet).

We were both drawn to this computer (or perhaps control panel). Numerical codes were coming up on the screen. Intuitively I knew it was set to go off (like a time capsule release) at any moment. In the dream, I thought perhaps these computers were monitoring the timing cycle of the galactic beams. Votan was intently watching the monitor screen. I thought he must be watching the shift in numerical codes that indicate the new beam being phased in.

I could feel the time was near. There was palpable electrical energy. All of a sudden a strange ripple effect went through the entire cabin (or pyramid overlay). I stepped outside and at first saw a pile of slugs. I picked one up. It was slimy, so I released it. As it hit the ground it dissolved into a strange black tar substance, then rapidly reshaped itself into the most brilliant green turtle!

Wow! I thought. This must be the transformation of matter! Then I spotted another building structure not too far away. It was rippling and swaying, and then rapidly melted into the same black tar-like substance. In its place appeared a beautiful lush garden with the most delightful smells emanating from it.

Again I was wowed! It is all really happening. THIS IS THE DIMENSIONAL SHIFT! Then I observed how my thoughts were intermingling and directly connected with these shifts. Once I realized this, I began to consciously radiate as much love as possible and had the thought for everything to be transformed into the highest version of itself. The joy and excitement were indescribable.

I went back inside to the narrow cabin where Votan was still watching the number screen. Then the entire cabin started rippling. I looked at him, and he was rippling like a wave, vibrating into a transparent etheric structure. I looked at my hand (which I often do in the dream as a sign that I am awake in the dream). When I woke up, this phrase was going through my head: ***We the secret dreamers await the right moment to apply the higher harmonics to transform the world.***

Chapter 25

Closing the Cycle

One must be deeply aware of the impermanence of the world.
—Dogen

I left Australia with two suitcases on Virgin Air Flight 1323 (441 x 3) on December 13, 2012, Blue Self-Existing Storm. Before my departure, I went through deep struggles and felt many forces at play as I packed up all of Votan's and my belongings with the gracious help of Ashani. It felt like the lines of destiny were once again being unraveled and rewoven into a new pattern. I recalled Votan's words to me: "Though her path springs from mine, it will take her on an entirely different journey."

In the days leading up to my departure, I became increasingly aware of the battle within the planet mind between the conditioned historical force and the new energy, the noosphere. An ancient story. Ancient forces. Ancient powers at play. I felt fragile and vulnerable, leaving the safety of what had been my home for the past three years, the longest I had lived anywhere in my life.

Arriving back to the United States alone was a surreal experience. Everyone felt so sped up in comparison with the rhythm I had been living in. It felt as if I had been living for years in a future world and then been sent backward through time and crash-landed.

Fortunately, I arrived at a familiar place, the home of our friend Seamus, for three days in Los Angeles. It was here where Votan and I had often stayed when in LA. I immediately realized how out of touch with modern civilization I had become. I had been living in another world, and I didn't understand half the conversations that people were having about the latest movies, trends, and even news. It felt irrelevant and distractive to the track that I had been on. I knew I had my work cut out for me to try to come up to speed with the mental field of this current Earth civilization. I felt so extremely sensitive to every perturbation and level of unconsciousness. It was clear that I was undergoing a supreme initiation, and at some points, I honestly didn't know if I'd make it through. I was comforted by and carried these words he had written to me about the Path of Heart:

> *To follow a path of heart is to be able to taste your own heart, to be alone with your own heart, to know that through knowing your own heart you may know all the people. To know your own heart is to be dissolved in its limitlessness; it is to hold divine and holy conversation with the presence of the Supreme, the Holy One who is in communion with all hearts. All knowledge that is true is in accord with the heart which palpitates at the center of a vast network of lines of force and streams of energy that extend to the ends of the universe.*
>
> *The heart knows before the mind can understand. You must take care of the heart, you must nurture the heart so that its vast capacities of love wisdom may nurture you and all that you encounter. To nurture the heart is to remain open to it, to be able to be truly alone with it, to guard it against obsessive thoughts of the mind so that its ever-flowing streams of universal insight remain pure and unsullied. To discipline yourself, to tame your mind, is to open a path for your heart. To keep the heart pure is the destiny of the true seekers, only then can we accomplish the great task which it is ours to fulfill*

Welcome to the Jungle

Arriving in Palenque, I had no idea what to expect. Hundreds of people showed up for the Closing of the Cycle, and it was the strangest feeling to be there without Votan, yet I felt him guiding every step of the way. Seeing the mountains was so refreshing. As in Australia, it was flat with fragile gum trees that fell over when the wind blew.

The Closing of the Cycle was a multidimensional event viewed through different lenses according to one's vantage point on the elevator of perception. All of Votan's work had led to this prophesied date of planetary initiation, which also signified the climax or final confrontation and equalization between historical polar forces, dark/light, male/female, etc.

He wrote much about this event:

> *The Closing of the Cycle is a cosmic event, a rare passage of the aeon. The aeon is the impossibly immense cycle containing all of the other cycles and is itself but a fractal of a divine thought-moment. The smallest cycle that is closing is the Great Cycle of history, a span of 5,125 years. It is also the conclusion of a 26,000-year cycle—a precession of the zodiac or Platonic (Pleiadian) Great Year. And it is the ending of a cycle of 104,000 years. A lot has happened in that time, not just on our little planet but throughout the solar system and our entire galaxy. We have all been called. We have chosen to be here for this grand finale.*
>
> —José Argüelles/Valum Votan,
> *Living through the Closing of the Cycle*

Like all great world-changers, Votan had been a controversial figure. So it was especially significant to me to return as his apprentice for harmony and to unify the galactic Mayan knowledge with keepers of the traditional long count. An Italian man, LWX, facilitated this connection after attending my event in Australia.

We were greeted with a welcome dinner at the community of Mayan elder Don Marzo. Upon our arrival on Blue Galactic Night, a large ship appeared in the sky. This was precisely 108 days after the initial four-ship sighting in Australia when I had received the message to leave everything and go to Mexico. Don Marzo commented to me that "they" appeared to make sure we made it safely, and I felt it a confirmation of the GM108X Galactic Mayan Mind transmission.

What was to follow was again another great initiation. Two days later, I gashed my right big toe atop the Temple of the Foliated Cross. The day was Red Planetary Serpent. We were in Nah Chan, House of Serpent. The right big toe is the serpent toe. It is associated with Maldek. I left a trail of blood as I walked down the steps, on our way to the tomb of the Red Queen. A true and unexplainable bloodletting had occurred. I gave a talk to about 200 people about the significance of the time on December 20, 2012, White Spectral Worldbridger.

Before leaving Australia, I had been given two crystal skulls, which I brought. One represented the feminine and one the masculine, which became a key theme of my talk. As the talk wound down, a big storm set in, and rain began to pour in the outdoor jungle venue. An otherworldly quality filled the air. (A year later in Hawaii I would give the male skull to Dr. Emoto for being the water messenger as Votan was the time messenger.)

That night after the talk, my toe worsened and appeared to be getting infected. At midnight I had an emergency doctor come to my room and cut the infection out and treat it. It was agony, and I questioned what symbolism this was, my serpent toe, blood, the foliated cross, the ships that guided me here, the tomb of Red Queen, all on the eve of the much-awaited date. I was deeply reflective of why Votan left the planet before the conclusion of all he had worked toward.

The next morning when I woke up, the sky was black; it was pouring rain with thunder crashing. Energies were chaotic. All was supernaturally heightened, and it felt like a force was "hijacking" what had been envisioned to occur, or perhaps this was what was to happen all along. A ceremony had been planned to unify the Mayan Long Count with the 13 Moons as a microcosm of the unification of all religions, truths, and belief systems. This unity did occur, though on the actual day 12-21, the planned ceremony shape-shifted into another script accompanied by intense rains that washed away illusions and preconceived notions about how things should be. Though it did not go as planned, I did participate in the traditional ceremony.

The energies felt heightened and compressed, almost supernatural, a drawn-out déjà vu, a replay from another time. Nobody knew what was going on, and the weather amplified it all. It was like Votan had described as the maximal state of chaos before the light comes. The dark forces were palpable, as was the light on the periphery.

I reflected that what had occurred on this much anticipated day was no different than the polarized scenes playing out within each human mind. I wondered if what was occurring was connected to the false perceptions of masculine and feminine still circulating within the collective field.

Lucifer Archetype

I felt that what occurred on the Closing of the Cycle was a reflection of the Luciferian forces at play on our planet today. I documented this in my journal. These forces seek to divide and create chaos and confusion. Lucifer ultimately represents our collective shadow side. He was an archangel highly favored by God until he rebelled, choosing to serve himself above all. Lucifer represents the first archetype to become "I" and not "we."

Votan explains Lucifer in *The Arcturus Probe:*

As much as I was light, I was ego, the force that maintains power in its separateness. It was the combination of sixth-dimensional light and third-dimensional ego that made my moves so contradictory and my actions easy to misperceive. Since there is neither good nor bad in any absolute sense, the effects of all of my actions have been ultimately creative, furthering the cause of evolution toward the light...

...Whatever I created, I thought, was an emanation of me, so I sought to maintain control over my creation. I ceased to know that I was cosmic in nature and believed solely in my own nature. Because of this, I became blind to the disharmonic effects of my actions. For a sixth-dimensional entity to behave this way is cosmically disastrous.

In the Book of Revelations, the devil fights against God's people only because they resist him. From the Galactic Mayan perspective, the key to overcoming perceived evil is to transcend duality altogether and enter into radial consciousness. Madame Blavatsky states, "resist not evil for in resisting evil we create greater evils..."

The Quran says that Iblis (another name for Satan) is allowed to run its course only until the Day of Resurrection. What is the ultimate goal of Lucifer in the Interplanetary Drama? He wishes to become a rival star-maker, according to *The Arcturus Probe*. This is the agenda of what we now see as Transhumanism, the ultimate mechanization of consciousness, which is but a shadow of True Reality.

Lucifer seeks to render Kinich Ahau [our Sun] ineffective as a star, and be in a position to become at last a star-maker and star master in his own right. To consolidate his hold, the next twist in the divisive cunning of Lucifer was to ally with the male power and overwhelm the female power. In this combative divisiveness, the final splitting of forces throughout the Kinich Ahau system would be complete, and Lucifer would become the undisputed star master of V.24.

The Closing of the Cycle ceremony felt to be a replay of the drama that began the "time wars" that are now reaching a climax on our planet. These time wars originated through a low-frequency beam technology created on Jupiter and Saturn in this galaxy (but this is only a template of other star systems). This created the misuse of life-force and also split the hemispheres of masculine and feminine. This low-frequency beam also created a death fear that is reinforced on our planet through the creation of "artificial time." The artificial time web enslaves the consciousness of the masses into an extra low-frequency wave, making it virtually impossible to access other dimensions.

This artificial time frequency is based on the ratio of 12:60 rather than 13:20 natural time. I reflected that we were closing the old cycle where we fought and condemned the perceived "darkness" (hence all the wars and fanaticism). And now, in the New Cycle, we must transcend this time loop by embracing (and not shunning) the darkness and face it directly with no fear. Love is always the answer. LOVE NEVER FAILS. Love the darkness, and it turns to light.

I reflected on how all of the stories, mythic dramas, lost worlds, and archetypes were now converging as eons of karma are being cleared at an accelerated rate. The New Cycle process was to be activated on July 26, 2013 in Mt. Shasta when the crystalline circuitry is reconnected, and the new galactic beam entered.

Chapter 26

Three Golden Dreams

I left the world with the aid of another world;
a design was erased
by virtue of higher design.
Henceforth I travel toward Repose,
where time rests in the Eternity of Time;
I go now into Silence.

—Gospel of Mary Magdalene

I felt like Rip Van Winkle, waking up on Earth after having lived in other times and worlds. Rip took a 20-year nap and time didn't stop. I felt like I had been living in the future and the world was still napping, though it had advanced in technology. Now I had to be reinserted to what felt like the past. Maybe I was supposed to help people get back to the future. But everything felt hazy and unclear upon my reentry into a post-Votan world.

After Mexico, I went to Hawaii, where Chris Coleman kindly offered me to stay at her home in Hilo at 1320 elevation. It was a time of significant adjustment on many levels. I would remain in Hawaii for six moons.

Following Dream Guidance

Being unclear on my next steps, I awoke one morning with a vision to synthesize all seven *Cosmic History Chronicles* into one book. The idea felt overwhelming. Still, I knew it was my next assignment, followed by preparing an event in Mt. Shasta to fulfill the mission laid out by Votan. The codes were my refuge, and I plunged myself into them. Each time I would wholeheartedly apply myself, a shift of perception would occur, often through the dreamtime. At this time, I relied on the inner world of dreams for my inspiration.

Here I will share three significant dreams in this period: the party, the golden dolphin and the baby unicorn. The first dream felt like a memory retrieval from perhaps Lemuria or Atlantis, and it would haunt me for weeks:

Everyone is coming to the party, but an unusual party.

I am the hostess.

The people begin to arrive: acrobats, dancers, musicians, children, it seems all time is present. Many people have come from another era, another time.

I feel both fascinated and a bit overwhelmed as I am the hostess and the guests are arriving so rapidly it is impossible to greet them all.

As I walk from room to room, the rooms shift into different eras.

I walk into one room. It is dark. Children are sleeping on the floor.

I go outside and see guests drinking fine wine but from a much earlier era.

Creative activity is bursting forth everywhere.

I am not sure what to do, so I walk around and make sure everyone is having a good time.

A man approaches me.

He seems to know me well.
He asks if I would like to do some mirror work.

I agree and follow his instructions.

I gaze into a very unusual mirror. It has three parts with two round pieces at the center.

When I first gaze in, I am amazed that I appear completely transparent.

Then the mirror sucks me in further and further.

I see many reflections and am mesmerized.

I lost awareness of everything besides what I saw in the mirror.

I saw all the beings who I had ever been.

The more I gazed, the more beautiful I became.

The reflection of All faces as One!

Then

All faces were stripped away.

I am gazing at my core essence—dazzling, exquisite, and utterly pure.

There are no words to describe it.

I came out of the mirror and went into the house. I noticed a room in the back that I had never seen. I entered. The room was elegant, and exuded royalty, with its high ceilings and perhaps 18th- or 19th-century furnishings, filled with purple velvet couches and fine art.

Two girls were sitting on one of the couches.

They were about 12 years old, well dressed, and sophisticated.

They were both lovely, but a sad feeling pervaded their aura. I asked them what was the matter; were they not enjoying the party? No, they were not—they said they didn't fit in here. They were extraordinarily articulate. They said they felt as if they had been sitting in this room talking to one another forever. There was something extraordinary, familiar, and haunting about this room.

The girls said they couldn't remember anything except being in this room. I told them about the mirror work I had just done. They were unusually fascinated by it and wanted to hear all about it. Their deep knowledge struck me.

Then I asked the girls if they would like to get out of this room and get some fresh air. They reluctantly agreed. I started to walk out the main door, but they said no, they had to go out the back door because they did not fit in here. So we went out the back door and began to walk. We walked up some rocks; there was a vast ocean down below. I led the way to climb on the rocks. Before I knew it, both girls fell in the water and disappeared. There was nothing I could do—though I did not feel particularly sad. I went back to the party, wondering who I should tell—though I wasn't sure if it even happened.

Shortly after this dream, I knew I needed a more remote space. I rented a secluded retreat house for three moons in Laupahoehoe, a small village on the Hamakua Coast of the Big Island. It was a beautiful, isolated space in a rural area with substantial rolling hills all around. In these 90 days, I entered into a supreme discipline to synthesize all seven volumes of the *Cosmic History Chronicles.* I was eating mostly fruit at the time, doing yoga, and taking long walks when I wrote *Accessing Your Multidimensional Self: A Key to Cosmic History.* The book would end up winning the Best Independent Spiritual Book award in the U.S. in 2016. This book would be the key that opened me to studying the path of Mary Magdeline, as it was translated by a French publisher who invited me to the south of France for an event.

Golden Dolphin Contact

Dolphins may well be carrying information as well as functions critical to the regeneration of life upon our planet.

—Buckminster Fuller

Cultivation of inner vision and imagination is key to navigating the New Cycle. We think in pictures. If we reorder existing knowledge, then we see a new image. Votan often told me, "If you want to know something, then practice merging your mind with it." These were my contemplations when I woke to a powerful dream on White Crystal Wizard.

In the dream, I was in a pyramid-like space with ocean water. Many dolphins gathered near me. They were transmitting much information regarding the holomind perceiver (which they embody with the balance of their right and left hemispheres).

The dolphins' superconscious panoramic awareness and excellent control over their brain functions were evident. I felt such love for our communion and began to say, "In Lak' ech" to each of the dolphins.

With these words, the dolphins rose up one by one, shapeshifting into half-humans (but their face still partially dolphin). I understood that they wanted to make contact and reciprocate my acknowledgment of them and also to reveal more profound aspects of their intelligence. They were supremely playful and put out their webbed hands for high-fives. After the play, they gave a warning that something was to come soon on planet Earth.

Then I was dropped from above into a large city. I looked around, and it seemed I was waiting with many people in line at a busy restaurant. I looked across the street, and all the Starbucks, McDonald's, etc., were being shut down, or people were freaking out because they could not get a latte (I realized that everything was closing all over the world). Buckets of rain began to pour, followed by a hailstorm.

My first thought was the weather was being simulated. Everyone felt something big coming. The dolphins knew. I was running along with many people up a flight of stairs to find shelter. An older man near me began to fall. I caught him before he hit his head. No one would stop to help us. He was very heavy. Massive lightning began to strike everywhere. Somehow an enormous strength filled me, and I picked up the man and put him over my shoulder and walked effortlessly up the stairs. Then I heard a voice: "REMEMBER the MAGIC OF THE GOLDEN DOLPHIN!".

Then I woke up.

The effects of this dream continued into my morning meditation. At the time, I was preparing for the New Beam event in Mt. Shasta. I reflected on the meaning of the dream and how it connected to the New Beam and world events.

I thought if dolphins are the bridge to the Sirian star system, then what does the Golden Dolphin represent? The Golden Age? It is often said Cetaceans are the planetary elders and star emissaries. Is the Golden Dolphin helping to recode the planetary frequencies by embodying the vibrational frequency of a New Golden Beam?

The dream allowed my mind to assemble fragments of knowledge that I had not been attuned to. I reflected that the new galactic beam is moderated through the sun. Our solar system is a living organism and is a member of a much larger galactic cosmic system. Telepathic attunement is the means of receiving new information. Sirius is the sun behind the sun that affects our own sun. It transmits energy to our solar system through electromagnetic lines of force.

I recalled that the Tibetan Master Djwhal Khul through Alice Bailey asked what forces were responsible for the world crisis during World War II, and he listed as the number one cause "a welling up of magnetic force on Sirius, which produces effects upon our solar system and particularly upon our earth." He proclaimed that the Sirian energies stimulated both the best and the worst in humanity, as depicted in the global conflict.

Sirius is also connected to mathematics and sound vibration, like the dolphin sonar. I thought perhaps the Golden Dolphins are the keepers of the lost chord, the New sound vibration that is being beamed to our planet, and rearranging our molecular structure. I wondered if this is the same sound vibration that forms the etheric grid that connects underground bases and the pyramids.

These reflections are an example of how my dreams would coincide with the synchronic order, activating an intuitive guidance system that attracted the right information at the right time.

Dolphins and Holomind Perceiver

This dream continued to open me to new perceptions. I wondered if it is through the frequency of the Golden Dolphin that destructive cataclysms are being averted. I reflected on how the dolphin intelligence embodies and transmits the Holomind Perceiver. In other words, they are holding the holographic template of a unified (and more playful) future.

Votan viewed the Holomind Perceiver as a "Sirian broadcast." He saw that at the center, the 441 (also known as Sirius B-52/Element 113) is a telepathic element that creates hypersensitivity in the brain, radializing and equalizing our sense perceptions.

Once the Holomind Perceiver is fully evolved and imprinted in the corpus callosum, we attain the panoramic vision and wrap around perceptions. The dolphins already have these capacities. When one hemisphere is asleep, the other is awake, so they are always conscious. They can intentionally control the passage of information through the corpus callosum. The corpus callosum, a thick white band of nerves deep within the brain, is the bridge that facilitates communication between the two hemispheres. The two hemispheres are physically separate.

Even though dolphins have two hemispheres just like humans, theirs are split into four lobes instead of three. The fourth lobe in the dolphin's brain hosts all of the senses, whereas, in a human, the senses are split. Some believe that having all of the senses in one lobe allows the dolphin to make immediate and often complicated judgments that are well beyond the scope of human ability.

White Unicorn: Innocence Restored

How can I be of highest service? What are the most important things to communicate? These were my contemplations when I had yet another dream that said, "Just color by number." Meaning, do the steps put out before you, and the next step will appear. I reviewed that I had completed and published Votan's biography, started a blog to communicate to the world, and created Galactic Spacebook as an online meeting place for kin. I had conducted a seven-day event in Australia and then created a Galactic Handbook, as well as a Galactic eZine to communicate the knowledge through art. I then completed the final Cosmic History, *Volume VII: Book of the Cube,* and traveled to Palenque to close the cycle on behalf of Votan. Now, I was completing the *Accessing Your Multidimensional Self* book and preparing for the New Beam ceremony and a three-day workshop in Mt. Shasta. All of these steps felt merely to complete past assignments that had been set forth by Votan.

While preparing for the Mt. Shasta event, I had the following dream:

> *I was in a house with Votan making dinner. It was nighttime. We were chopping vegetables, and everything seemed ordinary enough. Then, a bright yellow light flashed repeatedly through*

the house. This was followed by the sound of helicopters. Then a not-so-nice voice said, "You are coming with us"! And then I said to Votan, "Quick, change the Timespace!"

I then found myself on a ship sitting in front of a tall and thin being with a large purple/blue head and large, penetrating eyes. The being was androgynous and appeared more vibratory than physical. I was not afraid. I felt a heart connection. He/she kept repeating: "The more you help us, the more we can help you." Then the being shapeshifted into many different "alien" forms, revealing its different manifestations.

Then I awoke into another dream (on the same night).

I was in a comfortable, familiar room. I got up and attempted to go downstairs to where I thought the kitchen was. But when I opened the door, I found myself falling through a portal.

I looked around, and I was underground. Intuitively I knew I was beneath Mt. Shasta. I was crawling through dirt in a barely lit cavern. It seemed there were government video cameras, and I thought they were trying to catch a glimpse of an intraterrestrial civilization (sometimes referred to as Telos).

I called on the underground beings for help as it seemed I was trapped. No sooner had I called for help than I saw a light appear on one of the cavern walls. I touched the light and fell through another portal. I was now in a golden meadow with many flowers (like when the "Wizard of Oz" goes technicolor). I was alone.

Then I saw the most beautiful sight: a newborn baby unicorn! So pure. So sweet. I walked toward it, and it rolled on its back and allowed me to pet its stomach. The feeling was indescribable purity, healing bliss, beauty, and innocence. I felt it was telling me that, indeed, a new energy has been born at the center of the Earth, and it is now releasing great healing for the planet. The sounding chord for the Return of the People of OMA = Original Matrix Attained!

Chapter 27

New Beam and Mt. Shasta

Once someone dreams a dream, it can't just drop out of existence. But if the dreamer can't remember it, what becomes of it? It lives on in Fantasia, deep under the earth. There are forgotten dreams stored in many layers. The deeper one digs, the closer they are. All Fantasia rests on a foundation of forgotten dreams.

—Michael Ende

What is real? What is important? What is my duty, and to whom? These were the constant questions I asked myself. The dream of the new baby unicorn born in the inner Earth of Mt. Shasta, combined with the UFO encounter in Australia, seemed to be my clues to the next stages of the mission.

In the time when I was trying to determine which direction to go with the knowledge, I found there was nothing more powerful than silence. I would sit for hours until this world dissolved, and I entered into another, brighter world where answers to my questions were given. This is the nameless space of Pure Presence where you merge with all that is, that glorious warm space of light beyond all worry and doubt. Returning from that space, I realized everything is okay and always has been and always will be. We are one Eternal Being on an endless journey through space and time.

I reflected much on my own death and how we are only allotted a set number of days to fulfill the purpose we were designed for. My role was to stay attuned to, but not get caught up in, the drama of the world and the ever-fluctuating political and economic climates that grip the masses. I was to be a lighthouse, a source of comfort, someone trustworthy that others could rely on. I was to be a reminder of the inner world of unconditional love and with knowledge and certainty about the glory that is to come and is already here should we choose to see it. This knowledge of the Galactic Maya and the transmission was the vehicle to attain these ends.

The 13 Moon calendar was a daily application of the memory of harmony. The various levels of codes elevated my mind, lifting it out of the conditioned trance that keeps the masses sedated. These codes were like brain training exercises. They helped carve new neuronal pathways through attunement to frequencies that lift the mind into a fresh atmosphere.

During this time of uncertainty, I would often review the many instructions given to me by Votan:

> *Knowledge is power only when it is given as a gift. Meditate on the gift, and the power deepens. Pray with the gift and the power strengthens.*
>
> *With the gift of power, the soul becomes the source and resource of knowledge and action to overcome or harmonize whatever obstacle to the fulfillment of the Divine Plan.*
>
> *Medicine is knowledge of the Creator's Plan used for the good of all. Power changes according to the Creators Plan. Nurture the power, increase the knowledge. Make the medicine Universally healing.*

But how to make the Medicine universally healing was my constant contemplation. Votan had felt that of all the thousands who had been touched by or practiced the synchronic order and 13 Moon calendar, very few had understood. People tend to grab fragments of knowledge and think it is the whole, or others just want to be part of something, a tribe, or a group. I was seeking the ones who wanted to know our true origin and destiny. Those who wanted to tread a path not explored by others.

Emerging from Votan and my rarefied forcefield, I witnessed the confusion and chaos of the world. People's lives felt so complicated. I was overwhelmed by all the work that I perceived was mine to do. I knew that I had to first complete the work set out by Votan to open the New Cycle in Mt. Shasta, inaugurating the New Beam on July 26, 2013, Yellow Galactic Seed. I reasoned that if this were completed, then the next stages would reveal themselves.

Here is a little background to give context for the vision that led up to this New Beam ceremony:

In 1987, José Argüelles/Valum Votan put forth that this entire historical cycle that we are passing through is a galactic beam that is 5,125 years in diameter (3113 BC-2012 AD). This entire beam cycle also concludes the final part of a 26,000-year cycle, which is part of a galactic engineering project being projected through the sun. This project concluded 217 days later on July 26, 2013, Kin 164.

The beam knowledge first occurred to him in 1986, while meditating on the sunspot cycles at the pyramids of Coba. He had a vision of the 13-baktun cycle as a type of beam emanated through the sun as a type of radio program that coordinates the sunspot cycles.

These sunspot cycles then transmit the beam through peak solar activity, sending solar information to Earth. When the energy beam changes its frequency, the filter (sun) changes accordingly. Different ages represented different stages of the beam.

The Mayan Factor describes the galactic beams as a resonant frequency or radio waves emanating from Hunab Ku, galactic core—and even more specifically from the black hole close to the center of Hunab Ku. These high-frequency radio waves are coded with holograms or holographic information.

Near the core of the galaxy is a black hole. A black hole is usually described as a place where the gravitational field of a star or galaxy becomes so intense that everything caves into it. It is thought that the other side of the black hole is another dimension or universe. Inside the black hole is a dense core of information, which is a synthesis of everything in that particular star system or universal order—it is condensed here and then emitted as high-frequency waves. This is also similar to what Russian astrophysicist Kozyrev spoke of when he spoke of time beams, which are emitted from a stellar core or different celestial bodies.

According to *The Mayan Factor,* the Maya had a mission to make sure that the planets and star systems of this galaxy are synchronized with the galactic beam by the date we call

12-21-2012. The effect of the beam on Earth is the acceleration of human activity around the planet, which we call recorded history. This also creates material technology.

Toward the end of the beam, acceleration becomes exponential with seven billion humans, exponential curves of carbon dioxide, changes in weather, species extinction, war, drought, etc.—this is all part of the program. This is what is known as the climax of history and matter, the end of the 13th baktun—the Baktun of the Transformation of Matter.

Galactic Synchronization marked the beginning of a new beam genesis. Then comes a period of adjustment and regeneration as we make our way through the biosphere-noosphere transition.

Revisiting Shasta

In 2006 Votan took me to Mt. Shasta for three days to celebrate my 33rd birthday. It had always been a special place for both of us. It is known as a vortex worldwide and was considered by Native Americans the sacred center of the universe. It is also famous for UFO sightings, ascended masters, and Telos, as well as the legendary crystal city and beings inside the mountain.

I recalled that 10 years earlier, Votan and I were living in Ashland. One summer morning in 2003, Votan said he received a communication from "underneath Mount Shasta." We got in the car and drove an hour and a half to the mountain. It was a beautiful summer day, and we were inspired to climb as high as we could get. Once there, we laid on a rock and put our heads together and went out or perhaps in.

We had the simultaneous experience of being taken through a vertical passageway into the inner part of the Earth. While I had heard of St. Germain's sitings in the area and the community that lived inside the mountain, I never gave it much thought until now. Though I had heard many world myths and tales allude to subterranean regions. Many Native American Indians have legends of their ancestors escaping to subterranean dwellings after cataclysms. This aligned with my intuition that there is an interconnected network of subterranean cities spread out in different parts of the planet.

The Great Northeastern blackout occurred at the same time we were having this experience on August 14, 2003, Red Self Existing Skywalker. It was uncertain exactly what caused it. Still, Votan felt sure it was from solar activity that was being withheld from the public. At Mt. Shasta, he explained to me that the octahedral crystal core of Earth is a receiving station of information from other dimensions. The north and south poles are the points of entry to Earth. These two poles create a type of vertical electromagnetic tube that connects at the crystal core of the Earth.

For example, the galactic synchronization beam is beamed from another dimension through our sun. The sun then transmits this information to Earth (or other planets) through the two poles that then meet and register at the crystal core before being transmitted to the surface of the Earth.

Time and Technosphere states:

> *The role of the magnetic octahedral crystal core is to function as the bipolar oscillator and crystal transducer whose purpose is to maintain the Earth in the synchronic order of the 13:20 timing frequency. The Harmonic Convergence (1987) was an example of one of these messages sent from the Earth's core and received and acted upon by a critical mass of receptive humans.*

We returned to Mt. Shasta on several occasions. It is interesting to note that Mt. Shasta had one of the largest Harmonic Convergence gatherings and was also a key place where the Dreamspell knowledge was seeded. In 2009, Votan and I went into a bookstore, and I opened up a book, *Telos,* by Dianne Robbins, and was amazed when I read the following passage:

> *We will greet you on the surface in a new time frame, for which all on Earth have been waiting for eons and eons. This is the purpose of the Mayan calendar. It's to acquaint you with the new Mayan time frame that will make your entry into the Photon Belt harmonious and smooth. So, start today to adopt this new calendar and a new way of looking at your days and time; your synchronicity with the Galactic Core will be necessary for the Photon Belt passage through the stars.*

All of this was taken into consideration when I chose Mt. Shasta to inaugurate the New Beam. It is called a synchronization beam because the hologram and time beam synchronizes with the actuality of events in the dense plane of the third dimension. At one point, I had asked Votan, "Who creates these information beams?" His reply was that the "beam information is telepathically passed across star systems from one galactic intelligence to another."

He said that these patterns do not just happen randomly but are intelligently conceived and projected as holographic structures or images within different time beams. These beams then sweep through the universe, informing various structures of celestial/cosmic reality. He said that to receive the beam information (as the galactic Maya did in the 10th baktun) requires telepathic attunement. The Galactic Maya knew that the paranormal functions of the human brain are activated by solar frequencies from the sun.

Back to Shasta

The three-day event, Becoming Your Galactic Archetype, was organized by Jacob Wyatt, and myself at Stewart Mineral Springs on July 23-26, 2013. Before this event, I was focussed on the contemplation of the original unity, and how to shift into the highest timeline. Since returning to the United States, I had witnessed the amplification of the Tower of Babel where multiple "languages" or versions of reality were being played out simultaneously. There was so much duality and polarity in the human realm. I concluded that this tension is the dissonance between two opposing frequencies; like a tug of war within our heart and mind. I reflected that the deepest lessons are embedded within duality. Everyone has a different set of lessons to learn in this lifetime. Therefore, to eliminate duality would be a disservice for these beings, until their lessons are learned.

The event carried a special magic that concluded with a morning sunrise Ceremony of Resurrection on Galactic New Year. Lwx from Italy conducted a powerful ceremony to open the Rainbow Portal, a seven year cycle leading into 2020. Sham Tok Maru, a Galactic Mayan and true adept from Los Angeles, helped me to co-lead the main ceremony. I felt this event was the final step to complete the process put forth by Votan. This was the point when all the historical inscriptions, including all the messengers of all times, were realized within as a single thought-form.

This is where the terma of the Red Queen, the new feminine cycle, begins. This is an impersonal force; the Red Queen is a multidimensional archetype but also represents the awakening and empowerment of all the anonymous or marginalized ones throughout history—the redemption of the lost or forgotten worlds. She is also the archetypal shapeshifter, uninscribed and free to change. Not crystallized by any label. She is open, fluid, nurturer of all. Called forth by the inner dream or the imaginal realm where all of creation is born. She is the reminder to drop our defenses, become as little children, and explore the magic inner realms. She is also the archetype of the magical child. The one who believes in infinite worlds and possibility.

> *Who would know me must first the Red Queen know, for wherever am I, there the Red Queen shall also go; Keeper of my mystery, knower of my truth. Successor to my knowledge, shrine keeper of the mystery from which this dream unfolds. Entered through a doorway called Votan that a new beginning will flower, when the cycle comes to its close.*
>
> —Valum Votan

This was a time of fulfilling the 26-year vision that had been set forth at the Harmonic Convergence (1987-2013). This was a fractal of the 26,000 year cycle. After the New Beam ceremony there were no inscriptions or guidelines; there was nothing but a blank slate for a new vision to emerge. Unwritten and uncreated. Many people showed up at the sunrise ceremony, which was followed by a double rainbow. It was an electrifying sign.

Then I went blank.

Chapter 28

444 and Transylvania

The cave you fear to enter holds the treasure you seek.

—Joseph Campbell

After the New Beam ceremony in Mt. Shasta, everything accelerated. A new story was arising within me, coupled with expectations based on what had come before. My inner world was highly pressurized, and I felt I needed to create a vehicle to be able to coherently output it. I was in the process of rapidly educating myself about where the world had come to since I left it 11 years ago.

A few weeks later, I was back in Teotihuacan. This significant return to Mexico culminated with the release of a small vile of Votan's ashes at the Pyramid of the Sun in Teotihuacan. Here, I received a vision to create a galactic education center to house the knowledge. This would first manifest in Brazil in 2018 by original earth wizard Andre and his partner Tiele.

After Mexico, I briefly returned to Hawaii and had a surprise meeting with Dr. Emoto, accompanied by Crys'tal Colemen. I publicly presented him with a Banner of Peace for his tireless work as the Messenger of Water, just as Votan was the Messenger of Time. Dr. Emoto was a great friend and supporter of Votan and the 13 Moon Calendar. He initiated World Water Appreciation Day to coincide annually with the Day Out of Time festivals on July 25. I gave Dr. Emoto one of my two crystal skulls for healing, as he had been quite ill. He told me that he always told José that he must come to Japan 13 times, but José only came 12 times. Then he told me that I am the 13th.

In January 2014 of the Galactic Seed year, I went for a 26-day silent retreat in a remote cabin without electricity in the Colorado mountains. It was called Tail of the Tiger and had been one of Chogyam Trungpa's centers, where prominent lamas had retreated. Each day I had to hike to the well to get water and keep a fire going to stay warm as it was freezing. I only had a certain allotment of food, which I rationed and ran out of on the last day. My days were filled with meditation and contemplation. I also worked exclusively on the holomind perceiver index, which required tremendous prolonged focus which tuned me into the state of mind that Votan and I had lived together. I felt so close to him during this time. Never have I been so fully comprehended by another being. His love was unconditional, all-embracing, inspiring, and all-encompassing. I felt no reference point for my life at this time, which was a blessing as it required me to be very present and in full surrender.

Mount Shasta

It had been precisely 602 days since I left Australia when I moved into my house in Mt. Shasta on August 6, 2014, Yellow Resonant Sun. This was on the 69th anniversary of Hiroshima and 1 year after releasing Votan's ashes at the Pyramid of the Sun in Teotihuacan.

After eight years, I retrieved the things Votan and I had left in storage. As I opened the boxes, I was flooded with emotion, it was like opening a sealed tomb with all of his personal belongings, just how he'd left them in 2006. His old iMac computer was in there, and when I plugged it in, it began playing Bob Marley, Three Little Birds, with the lyrics: "Don't worry about a thing, every little thing gonna be alright."

In the tranquility of my own home surrounded by Nature, I synthesized much information and had several significant dreams that I recorded. The following was a particularly significant dream.

I awoke to a lucid dream at 4:44 a.m. in Mt. Shasta on June 11, 2016, White Overtone Wizard. This day was precisely 20 spins, or 5,200 days from the first Cosmic History transmission in Mt. Hood.

In the dream, I was taken to an underground chamber. A few official-looking men were there. They appeared neutral, neither good nor bad, more like impersonal cogs in the machine. The room was dimly lit, and there were no windows. Then all the lights went out, and the magnetic field seemed to collapse. I experienced a simultaneous wavy and spinning sensation. Then one of the men approached me. He was holding a light torch in one hand and a small device in his other hand. He placed the latter on my third eye. Many images began to flash before me. I understood that I was being shown what can only be described as ancient-future UFO aircraft. I saw everything from primitive-looking craft to what appeared more advanced propulsion systems. It was as though

I was receiving a telepathic slide show of the history and evolution of "spacecraft" and travel, both real and imagined.

After this experience was complete, another man stepped toward me, holding what at first looked like a holographic shield device made up of different geometries. It was round but seemed to contain grids and matrices that interfaced through resonance with various crafts and vehicles. It at first resembled something like a bar code, that scanned and recognized different patterns. I was shown that each craft contained its own geometrical signature. This device seemed to be able to reconfigure its permutations to match the difference signatures (much like the galactic compass with its 18,980 permutations). I recognized that this device was the Holomind Perceiver, a fractal interface nanochip that Votan had committed the remainder of his life to decode. When properly applied, I saw how it worked like a skeleton key that fits all systems and dimensions.

In the dream, this device, Holomind Perceiver, was tuned to a Mothership (I wondered if it was in the Andromeda Galaxy), and when the device was activated it could pull the "record or all knowledge of that particular craft, planet, galaxy, etc." where whatever object it focused on could be immediately known. It was as if it was a magnetic extraction device. Again, this device could also work for planets or stars or any celestial body. I felt so many information bits being uploaded into my physical system that I could hardly contain it, even in a dream.

This dream immediately shifted my perception of what planets, stars, galaxies, and world systems really are—though much information was non-conceptual and is difficult to find words for. For example, if one were to focus this interface device on Jupiter, the device would immediately reconfigure its geometrical circuitry to match Jupiter's resonant signature. Once the resonance was activated, then the device naturally was able to extract specific information effortlessly. Then it could be directed, for instance, to Jupiter's moons, and it would adjust its frequency accordingly to match these resonance patterns, which were slightly different than its host planet.

The dream continued, and I was led through an underground tunnel that seemed to contain the archival engrams of paradisiacal worlds. These worlds were very familiar and had a harmonious and sublimely uplifting effect when remembered. Just as I was drifting into a paradisiacal reverie, the Holomind Perceiver reconfigured, and it flashed what appeared to be different star histories through my mind at lightning speed.

Then everything was calm again, and I was back in the dark underground chamber. The man with the holomind device escorted me down a long hallway, where I met two very short beings with a bluish tint. I recognized them from other dreams, and they emitted a pleasant fragrance. They were friendly and read my mind, which was flashing to the Asteroid belt and wondering what had happened to Maldek. I wondered where the interface system was for the remembrance of this destroyed planet.

I felt their warmth as they conveyed that the entire interface system of this planet had also been shattered, just like the planet. It is the knowledge of this interface system that many on our planet are seeking, some consciously and some unconsciously. It relates to the Ark of the Covenant and the Holy Grail. I woke up with the message: *Your work is to recover the fragments but not to reconstruct the Ark, but to build a new one.*

I understood that these fragments were held in the physical body of different humans living on our planet today. But they were spread out, and I had to find them, like a cosmic treasure hunt.

After waking up from that dream, I felt somehow that reality as I knew it had been altered. I walked to the coffee shop in Mt. Shasta to think about it. When the cashier rang up my latte with almond milk, I was stunned to see the total was $4.44. It was one of those heightened activated days, and many insights began pouring in.

At this time, it was a particularly challenging time in the third dimension. I reflected that the polarity and tension that many are feeling is also felt within the Earth, and these tensions ultimately stem back to the great shattering, which was the collision of two opposing frequencies. This creates not only amnesia but neurotic tendencies. This is an (inter) planetary process. It is not always comfortable when we are being re-patterned from within.

Strangely enough, the week after the dream I found myself on the foothills of the Blue Ridge Mountains at the Monroe Institute in Virginia at the home of Joe McMoneagle, world-renowned U.S. Army remote viewer, and his wife, Scooter, the stepdaughter of Robert Monroe, a pioneer in the investigation of human consciousness. Monroe also created the famous Hemi-Sync audio technology. And though I had heard of the work, I had never really studied it. But as synchronicity would have it, they were the first ones that I told that dream to. It was well-received, and the atmosphere was charged.

I spent a few nights alone after in Washington, D.C., as I had never really been there. I thought it was interesting that I was given room 520 (260 x 2), and I once again awoke to another dream in D.C. at 4:44 a.m. That day I visited the famous Masonic Temple and was stunned to see a statue of the head of Pacal Votan inside!

A week before the trip, I got my first iPhone, and the phone prefix was 444! After Washington D.C., I went to visit my sister in Portland, Oregon, only to find the address of her apartment complex was 444, and she lived in apartment 218! Of course, 218 is the signature of the opening of the tomb of Pacal Votan. The next day I walked into Powell's Books only to see Votan's 7:7::7:7 on display. Was someone trying to communicate?

But what was all of this about, and where was it leading?

Synchronic Slide Show

After that dream, I began to focalize my attention on the Synchronotron system with its different mathematical overlays. When I would be deeply focused, I would have memories that appeared as slide shows. I entered a time of deep recapitulation of my time with Votan and was in awe of the magic of it all. Surely it was all a dream.

I flashed to being with him in Switzerland and the Carl Jung family home and grave. I then flashed to our visit to 19 Avenue Road, where Madame Blavatsky died, and then our visit to Adyar, where she established the Theosophical Society in India. That day I wore blue and white only to discover that the home she lived in, the Blavatsky bungalow, was blue and white. I flashed to the magic of arriving at the Russian Kremlin at midnight and the new excitement I felt. I flashed to our visit to Asturias, Spain, where we stayed on Argüelles street and swam in the ocean while studying the genealogy of his ancestry. I flashed on staying in Osho's retreat house in Switzerland, and then to the tranquility of morning walks in a pristine park in Hamburg, Germany. I flashed to the mystical blue mosque in Istanbul and the extravagant Atlantis hotel in the futuristic Dubai, walking on the beach in the early morning with camels. I then flashed on a tour of the Vatican and the eerie feeling of walking through the underground catacombs and the panic attacks in Rome.

I flashed to earlier studies of Sri Aurobindo and the Mother, as I was always fascinated by her concept of spiritualizing all the cells of the body.

I flashed to our visit to Sri Aurobindo's casket in India and to Auroville, the conscious community created by the Mother after his passing. I then flashed to the sacred temples of Kyoto, Japan, the hot spring baths, Mount Fuji and the holy Ise shrine. Then I flashed to Kenya and the African safari resort, where we were confined for a week with wild animals surrounding us while we focused on completing the Galactic Iching. I flashed on riding through the Syrian desert from Amman, Jordan, to Baghdad with the American military aimed at us. I flashed to the beauty of the mountains in Patagonia, where we stayed at earth wizard 13:20 community with chickens running wild. I flashed to the time travel experiment in Macchu Picchu, where we transported from Peru to Palenque.

I flashed on the many magical visits to the pyramids of Mexico, particularly the last visit in 2010, where much memory was restored simultaneously to us both. I flashed to our memory retrieval expedition to Uluru/Ayres rock. I flashed to holding hands with Votan through an earthquake in Chile. I flashed to buying a car in Christchurch. I flashed on the red light district of Amsterdam and the Maldekian memories retrieved there. I flashed to riding on the world's largest Ferris wheel in Singapore and talking about the wheel of time.

I flashed on our three months of freedom traveling all over the New Zealand south island, finding the healthiest food and hot springs. I flashed on Yogananda's sacred Lake Shrine in Los Angeles and then learning the Hunab Ku 21 on the beach in Malibu. I flashed on our seven-day trial run of the Synchronotron workshop in Venice Beach, followed by the real seven-day workshop at the Babaji Ashram in Cisternino, Italy. I flashed on all of our synchronized dreams and accelerated learning through perfect resonance.

Transylvania and Telektonon

> *Within the Earth is another earth, it knows us though we know it not.*
>
> —José Argüelles

Nine moons after the powerful 444 dream, Deborah Haight sent me a copy of the book *Transylvania Sunrise* by Radu Cinamar and Peter Moon. This set forth a series of mind-blowing synchronicities around

Transylvania. I found that when something keeps showing up in your field, it is wise to pay attention.

I was intrigued to learn about an underground discovery made with the help of an advanced radar satellite in 2003 in the Bucegi Mountains in Transylvania by the Pentagon. Allegedly, in the first book, *Transylvania Sunrise*, there is an underground holographic library, or a 50,000-year-old chamber with a holographic, bio-resonance image technology that contains holographic records of the Earth's history.

Now, this was extremely interesting to me, as the whole premise of Votan's work is that cycles are particular holographic projections. For instance, December 21, 2012 closed out a 5,125-year galactic beam cycle of a specific world hologram. You can watch this evolution from 3113 BC to 2012 AD, like a movie being projected onto your inner mind screen—a movie that was approximately 45 billion hours long. The quality of the next movie hologram that we call forth is determined by our collective vision for the highest future world possible.

Agartha and Peter Moon

In August 2017, I moved out of my home in Shasta and began a cycle of travel, first to Europe for events that culminated in Long Island, New York. Here I unexpectedly met Peter Moon when I bumped into him checking into a hotel. Peter is editor and translator of Radu Cinamar's book *Transylvania Sunrise* series, as well as being the author of many other books, most notably books on the Montauk time travel experiment.

It turns out he was a surprise speaker at the conference that I was attending called the Agartha to Humanity Symposium. Agartha is the legendary kingdom located at the Earth's core, also sometimes associated with Shambhala. Many cultures and religions tell various accounts of this underground world, which is said to have secret entrances in Kentucky's Mammoth Cave and in other caves and mysterious places worldwide, including those in Brazil, Ecuador, Tibet, Mongolia, and India.

The purpose of this Symposium was to initiate seven years of ongoing "disclosure" through 2024. When I heard Peter speak, it was like one déjà vu after another. He mentioned that he was first introduced to the mysteries of Romania, through his elusive friend, Dr. David Lewis Anderson, former director of the Time Travel Research Institute.

I was intrigued, and at the event Peter hosted a live Skype call with Dr. Anderson.

When Peter was speaking of advanced underground technologies, it connected many dots to the Synchronotron system decoded by Votan. I was particularly intrigued by the underground discoveries and felt they were directly linked with the Telektonon Prophecy of Pacal Votan.

In the story, Radu, a Romanian secret agent, gives details of three tunnels below the Sphinx at the Bucegi Mountains. These tunnels lead to Egypt and Tibet and to the Inner Earth. Peter explained that the tunnel to Egypt leads underneath the Giza Plateau to a similar facility as under the Bucegi Mountains. The tunnel that goes to Tibet, is via an offshoot tunnel that goes to Baghad, and another offshoot tunnel that leads to Mongolia. The third tunnel goes into the inner earth, and is the most mysterious tunnel of all.

The main speaker of this event was Tamarinda Maassen, ambassador to the Kingdom of Inner Earth (Agartha). Tamarinda said that the software for this reality ended in 2012, which was computer-generated, and after 2012 there is no software program. She then spoke of the Higher Beings who run this hologram and are not in agreement about where the world is going and how people are moving forward. She went on to say: Check if you are a projection inside an illusion, or are you a hologram in the program? If something is changing inside you, you are part of the future. If nothing changes, you are like a clone, a repeating hologram.

Incidentally, it turned out that Peter had been at the first Whole Earth Festival in Davis, California, which José Argüelles coordinated in 1970. But of particular interest to me was the description of a chamber that contains a holographic record of the Earth's history as well as holographic readouts of human DNA and also other species. Peter mentioned a projection hall where one can see the history of the human race. Are there ancient technologies within the Earth that have the capacity to change time as we know it? This was my experience as a child, and now it felt I was getting closer to its realization.

This thought stream is fully resonant with the Synchronotron system, as put forth by Valum Votan. This system is a fractal of the forgotten inner (ancient-future) technology, or internal interface system that contains star histories and connects us with other interdimensional systems and knowledge.

Three Caves

Everything quickened after this meeting, and the following year I found myself visiting three caves: 1) caves under the pyramids of Teotihuacan; 2) caves under the pyramids of Bosnia, known as the Ravne tunnels; and 3) the Ialomicioara cave in Transylvania.

In many esoteric and Native traditions, caves and underground chambers are associated with "serpent initiates." The top of the Pyramid of the Sun in Teotihuacan is located above an ancient cave, which, Votan said, was the cave where the serpent initiates gathered and left their wisdom. In Bosnia, there is also a Pyramid of the Sun, which is located 1.5 miles from the mysterious Ravne tunnel network (or caves), discovered by Dr. Semir Osmanagić.

In 2005, Dr. Osmanagić discovered the Bosnian pyramids in the heart of Bosnia and Herzegovina, in a small town called Visoko. He found five pyramids, which he called the Bosnian Pyramid of the Sun, Moon, Dragon, Love, and the Temple of Mother Earth. He also discovered the Ravne tunnels of which I visited in the summer of 2018 after Transylvania. Here, I presented Dr. Osmanagić with a Banner of Peace.

Visiting three caves in a five-moon span from February to June 2018 of the Yellow Crystal Seed year, formed an inner constellation that opened much memory in me. I noted that I was living my childhood "choose your own adventure" novel. Everything is coded. With these three cave visits, many pieces of my apprenticeship with Valum Votan began to cohere in a new way.

According to Madame Blavatsky's *The Secret Doctrine,* the serpent knowledge of the previous root races was gathered and reposited in subterranean chambers in stone to be kept by the guardians of the Earth, the elementals. These guardians would maintain communication with the "planetary logos." This is the point where the entirety of the knowledge held by the serpent initiates could be placed or reconstructed in stone. The stone is the holder of the resonant frequency of particular levels of knowledge through the geometry of its mineral structures.

Transylvania Caves

Deborah Haight, Kin 113, and I left for the Bucegi Mountains on White Solar Worldbridger, the signature of Votan's 63rd birthday when my apprenticeship began. It fitted as Deb had been present that morning when Votan awoke to the dream of the Return of the People of OMA.

This trip was part of a larger trip to share the knowledge in Croatia, Bosnia, and concluding in England for the Day Out of Time. The intention of this journey was both for memory retrieval and "healing the ancient trauma." Deb and I discussed that there are fractal overlays of unhealed, crystallized energy knots (trauma) that exist in the "thinking layers" of different locations on the planet. By bringing new consciousness and perception to these places, we can untie these knots and release the energy, which sends a signal back in time to the origin of that trauma. This set the tone of our trip.

Our journey was not an easy one. Traveling first from Los Angeles to London, we arrived in Bucharest on June 15, 2018, Yellow Spectral Star. This day was the 66th anniversary of the discovery of the tomb of Pacal Votan. I noted how 66 steps descend down the pyramid of inscriptions into Pacal's sarcophagus.

Once we arrived at our hotel in Bucharest, I was given room 440, which in the Synchronotron system is the code of Resurrection/Christ Code. We were joined by our friend Jason from California who stayed in room 441.

I couldn't sleep that night in Bucharest and was not feeling well. I was up most of the night and felt like I was being led through a death and resurrection scenario. All I could do was breathe, let go, and surrender. The next day, after some transportation challenges, we finally arrived at Hotel Pestera in the middle of Transylvania on Red Crystal Moon. This is the same signature that coded Votan's and my arrival date to Baghdad, Iraq, in 2004. I was given room 211. I found that quite synchronic as Votan's son's (Josh) death

day was Red Crystal Moon and his birth signature was Blue Electric Monkey, Kin 211.

This hotel was recommended by Peter Moon, as it is near a cable car that takes you to the Sphinx, of which the holographic library is allegedly under. Unfortunately, the cable car was closed down, so we had to make the steep hike to see the Sphinx on foot. Once we got to the top, a huge rainstorm set in and then hail. We took cover under the only roofed shelter there was, along with a few others. The rain was blinding, and the mud made the downward climb dangerous.

Fortunately, a Romanian family helped us. I couldn't help but think of the Solomonari that I had heard Tamarinda speak of. The Solomonari is a wizard believed, in Romanian folklore, to ride a dragon and control the weather, causing rain, thunder, or hailstorms.

Ring Around the Rosy

On our first night in Bucharest, I had a powerful dream.

I was in an underground chamber, and there were different circles of people, and they were all singing the childhood song. "Ring around the rosie/A pocket full of posies/Ashes, ashes/We all fall down." Then they would fall to the ground, stand back up, and repeat the process.

This dream seemed to connect with other dreams that I have had about underground simulation centers surrounded by gargoyles, where different events are programmed into and kept on a type of remote control time loop(s). So, when these time loop simulators are turned on, it is hard for people to think outside of the particular control system. And there are numerous ring-around-the-rosie time loops. I felt that this a key in understanding the mechanism holding the dream spell of history in place.

The next day the three of us explored the Ialomicioara Cave, which was just a few blocks from our hotel. Ialomicioara Cave is at an altitude of 1,500 meters on the right side of the Ialomitei Canyon. At the entrance to the cave is a monastery (Ialomitei Monastery), built in the 16th century. Ialomicioara's name comes from the Dacian word "jalomit," which means "to cry." The cave is actually known as an ancient place of Dacians where they used to celebrate the personality's death in order to become an immortal being.

At the entrance, the three of us were given headcovers for protection, as we explored the underground rivers and reptile-like rock features. Here, like in Teotihuacan, you can feel the multi-dimensional fractals of knowledge that are deposited here through the geometry of the stone structures.

Here I felt the connection with the Telektonon Prophecy of Pacal Votan. The original text describes Telektonon as a "distant, far traveling code of information received from spirits and deities dwelling within the earth."

Tamarinda had spoken about the release of the beings who were killed in the past due to volcanic activity, and how their corpses were turned to stone and enveloped in the caves. I found this interesting in light of the fact that the first prophecy codes were received by Votan in Hawaii, near Mount Haleakala. He said the Telektonon prophecy was "drawn from the living fire of Pele's breath."

I read Votan's original writing aloud:

> *Telektonon is distant because its code was left in a former time; it is far traveling because it is transmitted from far off stellar points through Earth's core where the deities and spirit guardians hold it until it is time to be released, thence it travels far from Earth's core to the sensory intelligence of the biosphere.*
>
> *Telektonon also refers to a type of coded text left to one intelligence to be "found" at a later distant time at the appropriate moment by another intelligence—in Tibet these types of texts are referred to as termas, or hidden teachings and the finders of such texts are known as Tertons, hidden text finders; Telektonon, like terma, is a prophetic text, a prophecy for the moment of its finding.*
>
> *The Telektonon of Pacal Votan is precisely such a text, a prophetic code of instruction for this time, a prophecy of the Earth and its biosphere, and the Victory that is Neverending.*

Touch the Source

OMA is in the middle of w{OMA}n

A clue

Original Matrix Attained

Activates MEN

Mental Electron-Neutron

Remember

Overcome

Trauma cataclysm

War of the Heavens

Death of a star

Mental Health

Hellbent creatures

Genetically manipulated

Death cult

Programmed for "Armageddon"

Frozen in trauma.

Overstimulation.

Stop!

Breathe!

Look!

Listen!

Remember

What happened

Explosion. Schism. Fragmentation.

Collective trauma

Generational

Bloodlines

Neurosis

Stop harming the Children!

Fear of darkness.

Fear of snakes.

Fear of war.

Fear of death.

Fear of water.

Fear of fire.

Fear of heights.

Fear of thirteen

Fear of "them"

Where did it all begin?

Another Star

Another Planet

Another Time

Another story

The Fall

The Spinning

The Vortex

Black Hole

Wormhole

Erasure

Land of the Lost

Lost in Time

Time Traveler

Yes YOU.

Remember the Beginning.

Transcend The Beginning.

Remember the End.

Transcend the End.

Get off the wheel

Don't go along

Politely decline

The deception of consensual reality

Think for yourself

Remember the Origin

Don't Forget the Completion

Drink the New Beam

It's Here

Sensory pollution

Clear it

Remember who you are

I am a signpost

A cue

A cure

A memory

You are the Way

Touch the Source

And

Live Again

Epilogue:
Return of the People of OMA

The crystalline know how to remain at the center
Between shifting worlds and strange times
They tread the nameless path without naming the narrowness
They squeeze through the eye of the needle
With naked faith and raw trust
They are the conquerors of the inertia of history
They have found the secret gate

Nineteen years after my initial vision of the tomb of the Red Queen, I found myself back in Palenque and Teotihuacan, Mexico. This time for two events that were inspired by a dream: The Return of the People of OMA in Palenque and Encoding the Future in Teotihuacan. These events were a mission of memory retrieval and cosmic healing.

Just as on my first visit to Palenque in 2000, powerful thunderstorms punctuated the beginning and end of our adventure. After four transformative days deep in the jungle, our group boarded a plane to Mexico City, which synchronistically, was co-piloted by Captain Argüelles!

Day Out of Time, Kin 13: July 25, 2019

To keep the heart pure is the destiny of the true seekers.
—Valum Votan

We began our Day Out of Time procession at Teotihuacan in the morning with the Prayer to the Seven Galactic Directions. Don Jesus (Eagle Jaguar Guardian) and Alberto Ruz Buenfil (el Vielo Coyote), among others, inaugurated the ceremony near the end of the Avenue of the Dead. Our group then marched silently toward the entry of the pyramid complex, holding the intention for the purification of the past, and retrieving the encodements from the future. Once we made it inside the pyramid complex, our group, now several hundred strong, gathered to form a sacred hoop of the people of OMA, a diverse microcosm of humanity comprised of people from over 45 countries.

We continued as a group, singing and marching toward the Pyramid of the Moon, stopping at seven different platforms to activate each of our seven chakras and radial plasmas within our bodies and within the earth. With each step, the energy increased.

Less than half a mile south of the Pyramid of the Moon, we stopped to acknowledge the largest structure in Teotihuacan, the Pyramid of the Sun. We acknowledged the masculine energy that it holds, that we were now bringing to the feminine, represented by the Pyramid of the Moon. I felt my heart melt in remembering that it was at the Pyramid of the Sun where José Argüelles/Valum Votan had received his original vision in 1953, and 49 years later, in 2002, he was honored by nine elders atop this same Pyramid and received a sacred staff.

As we turned to face the Pyramid of the Sun, we could see many other groups of people performing the bi-annual Fire ceremony. Because Teotihuacan is south of the Tropic of Cancer, the sun is directly overhead twice a year, on May 19 and July 25. A subterranean passage leads from a natural cave under the west face of the Pyramid of the Sun. The cave opening points directly to the setting sun on these two dates.

After blowing conches to the four directions, our group continued up the plaza. The fragrant smell of sage and copal incense filled the air as we marched down the Avenue of the Dead, toward the Pyramid of the Moon.

Twelve small pyramid platforms surround the Plaza of the Moon, making the Moon plaza the 13th. A secret tunnel was discovered under this Pyramid in 2017. The tunnel is about 33 feet (10 meters) deep. It is similar to other tunnels that have been discovered recently, like the tunnel that was found under the Temple of the Plumed Serpent.

Once we reached the base of the Pyramid of the Moon, we stopped, and a circle formed around us as a large drum was brought to the center with men and women in ceremonial Aztec regalia. The energy was electrified as the outer ring of people spontaneously began singing and dancing in a spinning circle around us. As I began to leave the circle, Don Jesus approached me and asked me to climb to the top of the Pyramid of the Moon with him. Don Jesus, Guardian of Wisdom, and Keeper of the Sacred Flame was firekeeper at events for Valum Votan and vowed to him to never let the flame go out.

Once we reached the top of the Pyramid of the Moon, he acknowledged the suffering that occurred when the Spanish Conquest all but decimated the original indigenous knowledge and culture. He then honored José Argüelles/Valum Votan as the bringer of new knowledge, before honoring me and then gifting me his sacred staff for carrying on the Galactic lineage.

He passionately explained how each part of the staff symbolized the cosmology of the Universe. The intricate carving of the wooden staff, which took him over a year to create, was revealed to him in a vision. The magical staff included a red and blue DNA spiral, a cube within a cube with mirrors in the center on all four sides, and multiple crystals protruding from the top. I felt a great sense of responsibility to receive this sacred instrument which had been infused with love and wisdom over the past 20 years.

One of our attendees, Father John, who witnessed the moment, said he saw a "simultaneous ascent and descent" of energy the moment I received the staff as if the Uninscribed had been Inscribed with the new templates. This was my sense also.

I flashed back to a dream I had with Votan in Mount Shasta in 2014. In the dream, he transmitted images to me of what would unfold in the world. He told me the key was to learn to "ascend" and "descend" simultaneously, to pull the energies from the heavens and ground them to earth.

Galactic New Year

This powerful event was followed the next day by our Galactic New Year symposium, Encoding the Future, emceed by Jacob Wyatt. Key aspects of the Law of Time were unfolded and expanded in new ways, demonstrating the dynamics of cooperation and collective action. One of our key speakers, Dr. Peter Lindemann, offered a powerful ceremony to change the timeline and steer the timeship by altering the current path of event probabilities into one that supports planetary abundance, purification, and rebalancing of the Natural World on behalf of all humanity. The shift was palpable.

I reflected that if the tomb of Pacal Votan had not been opened in 1952, this event would not have occurred. If the tomb of Red Queen had not been opened in 1994, this event would not have happened. Scenes flashed rapidly in my mind of the apprenticeship, Votan's passing, and all of the journeys afterward. And this was just the beginning of the story of the Return of the People of OMA.

OMA is Beginning, End and Beyond, therefore do not think that this template of Vision and action called Return of the People of OMA will be anything concise nor even familiar but more like a saga and a method of action emanating from a far off star but yet not so far from where you are.

—Valum Votan

A new stage of consciousness is opening. The year 2020 marks 1,328 years since Pacal Votan's tomb dedication in 692 AD. Valum Votan left the Planet 1,328 years after Pacal's death in 683.

The prophecy of Pacal Votan is a timeless prophecy that shows that the spiritual history/future of the planet is a single integrated circuit. This is the circuit of the zuvuya that connects past, present, and future. This circuit ultimately leads to the understanding of a new telepathic sense organ called Holomind Perceiver, the final revelation of the Telektonon Prophecy of Pacal Votan.

The Holomind Perceiver is the latent, hidden factor that manages our dormant faculties, the superconscious switch that transforms our whole being—body, mind, and spirit—into a divine instrument, free and radiant, unlike anything we can now dream possible. This is the Work of the Future.

This ancient-future technology can only be accessed with a pure heart and a clear mind. This is the treasure hidden within the cave of time, the secrets deposited in the inner earth, and the unveiling of the mystery of the Maya.

Choose your adventure.

The Future is Uninscribed

The new story is just beginning. And it starts with You.

And so that's what was written
On the Blank Map
Now I give it to You
What will you do?
Go even higher—to your spirit I am sending
Ascended waves of Light in a story never-ending

Synchronic Notes

Chapter 1: Lost in Time

July 25, 1992. White Crystal Mirror, Kin 38. First Day Out of Time celebration. Entry to the Cosmic Storm year. Beginning of the Timeshift. Creation of first Thirteen Moon 28-day calendars. "*The time shift, beginning on Cosmic Storm, 1992, is an interdimensional vortex ...*" —*The Arcturus Probe*

September 25, 1992: 1.5.3.6. Yellow Solar Sun, Kin 100. Electric Moon 6 of the Cosmic Storm year. Near death experience, Buffalo, N.Y.

Chapter 2: Enter the Dream

January 8, 1997: 1.9.6.27. Red Magnetic Serpent. Kin 105. Rhythmic Moon 27 of the Self-Existing Storm year. 24th birthday. Votan receives 20 Tablets of the Law of Time.

May 9, 1998: 1.10.11.8. Blue Rhythmic Monkey, Kin 71. Spectral Moon 8 of the Overtone Seed year. First encounter with José and Lloydine Argüelles.

May 10, 1998. 1.10.11.9. "Mother's Day." Yellow Resonant Human, Kin 72. Spectral Moon 9 of the Overtone Seed year. First meeting with José and Lloydine.

Paul Levy, White Crystal Wizard, Kin 194.
See his site: http://www.awakeninthedream.com

Mark Comings, Red Spectral Skywalker, Kin 193

Seamus Hiestand, White Planetary Mirror, Kin 218

December 10, 1989: 1.2.5.26. Red Self-Existing Dragon, Kin 121. Overtone Moon 26 of the Yellow Planetary Seed year. Discovery of the Law of Time in Geneva, Switzerland.

Chapter 3: Taming the Mind

October 31, 1998: 1.11.4.14. Samhain. White Crystal Worldbridger, Kin 246. Self-Existing Moon 14 of the Rhythmic Moon year. Move to Portland house.

November 6, 1998: 1.11.4.20. Yellow Overtone Human, Kin 252. Self-Existing Moon 20 of the Rhythmic Moon year. José and Lloydine move to Brightwood, OR (near Portland).

Khenpo Palden, Yellow Galactic Sun, Kin 60.

Khenpo Tsewang, Blue Electric Night, Kin 3.

Chogyam Trungpa Rinpoche is Red Spectral Earth, Kin 37.

Eden Sky, Red Self-Existing Skywalker, Kin 173.

Randy Bruner, Blue Cosmic Hand, Kin 247.

October 25-December 12, 1999: 1.12.4.8-1.12.5.28. Red Resonant Serpent, Kin 85, to Red Electric Skywalker, Kin 133. Self-Existing Moon 8 to Overtone Moon 28 of the Resonant Wizard year. Seventh year of prophecy. 49 day Earth Wizards seminary, Picarquin, Chile.

Chapter 4: Vision of the Red Queen

June 15, 1952. White Planetary Mirror, Kin 218. Crystal Moon 17 of the Spectral Wizard year. Discovery of the tomb of Pacal Votan. Pacal's tomb had been excavated by archaeologist, Alberto Ruz Lhuillier, revealing the first royal Mayan burial in a pyramid. It was compared in its richness of jade, ceramics and jewelry to the tomb of Egypt's King Tut.

June 1, 1994: 1.6.12.3. White Crystal Wizard, Kin 194. Crystal Moon 3 of the Magnetic Seed year. First year of prophecy. Opening of the tomb of the Red Queen, 42 years after Pacal tomb discovery. Archaeologist Fanny Lopez Jimenez discovered the tomb, which was accompanied by two skeletons, one presumably belonging to a child, and another one of a woman. This year, 1994, was also the inception of the World Thirteen Moon Calendar Change Peace Plan. 19 + 94 = 113.

June 2, 2000: 1.12.12.4. Red Rhythmic Serpent, Kin 45. Crystal Moon 4 of the Resonant Wizard year. Seventh year of prophecy. Depart first trip to Mexico.

June 6, 2000: 1.12.12.8. Red Planetary Moon, Kin 49. Crystal Moon 8 of the Resonant Wizard year. Ship encounter in Palenque.

June 7, 2000: 1.12.12.9. White Spectral Dog, Kin 50. Crystal Moon 9 of the Resonant Wizard year. Vision at the tomb of the Red Queen.

June 15, 2000: 1.12.12.17. White Rhythmic Mirror, Kin 58. Crystal Moon 17 of the Resonant Wizard year. First visit into the sarcophagus chamber of Pacal Votan. 48 years after its discovery. White Rhythmic Mirror is death signature of Pacal Votan.

Chapter 5: Entering GM108X

January 24, 1939. Blue Spectral Monkey, Kin 11. Resonant Moon 15 of the Spectral Moon year. Birthdate José Argüelles/Valum Votan

May 15, 1943. White Solar Wind, Kin 22. Spectral Moon 14 of the Lunar Moon year. Birthdate Lloydine/Bolon Ik.

January 8, 1973. Red Electric Serpent, Kin 185. Rhythmic Moon 27 of the Rhythmic Storm year. Birthdate Stephanie South/"Red Queen"

January 20, 2002: 1.14.7.11. White Overtone Wind, Kin 122. Resonant Moon 11 of the Solar Seed year. Move in date to Brightwood.

January 24, 2002: 1.14.7.15. White Solar Worldbridger, Kin 126. Guided by Solar Wind, Kin 22. Dream of the Return of the People of OMA. Apprenticeship begins. Note Resonant Moon 15 is the halfway mark in the 13 Moon year.

Deborah Haight. Red Solar Skywalker, Kin 113

Brian Haight, Red Lunar Serpent, Kin 145.

1991: Inception of the World Thirteen Moon Calendar Change Peace Movement.

March 3, 2002: 1.14.8.25. Yellow Galactic Seed, Kin 164. Galactic Moon 25 of the Solar Seed year. José Argüelles/Valum Votan honored as Closer of the Cycle by nine indigenous elders at ceremony atop the Pyramid of the Sun in Teotihuacan. Received sacred baston, 49 years after his original vision in the same place.

Chapter 6: Cosmic History

March 12, 2002: 1.14.9.6. Red Self-Existing Skywalker, Kin 173. Solar Moon 6 of the Solar Seed year. Votan vision of Maldek, leading into Cosmic History process. Maldek, once the fifth planet in our solar system, now known as the Asteroid Belt, is the blueprint of planets that have been shattered in many past world systems.

March 13, 2002: 1.14.9.7. White Overtone Wizard, Kin 174. Solar Moon 7 of the Solar Seed year. First Cosmic History transmission. "Cosmic History is a teaching of liberation." 52 days from when I moved into the Brightwood house. 52 weeks in a year, plus one Day Out of Time.

52 x 7 + 1 = 364 + 1.

Chapter 7: Daily Life

August 16, 1987: 1.0.1.22. Blue Electric Eagle, Kin 55. Magnetic Moon 22 of the Galactic Wizard year. First year of the "New Sirius" cycle that began July 26, 1987, White Galactic Wizard, Kin 34. Harmonic Convergence, global peace meditation. Conclusion of the 1144-year prophecy cycle of Quetzalcoatl, "thirteen heavens and nine hells." (Note to advanced practitioners, see kin equivalent of this day). Blue Electric Eagle, Kin 55 also coded July 16, 1945, when the world's first atomic bomb was detonated approximately 60 miles north of White Sands. National Monument.

March 13, 2002 - November 28, 2002: : 1.14.9.7 - 1.15.5.14. Both days coded by the White Overtone Wizard, Kin 174. Solar Moon 7 of the Solar Seed Year to Overtone Moon 14 of the Planetary Moon year. 260 day cycle of first cosmic history transmissions.

Chapter 8: Alchemical Cauldron

G.I. Giurdjieff, Kin Blue Overtone Eagle, Kin 135.

Madame Blavatsky, Blue Crystal Monkey. Kin 51

August 16, 2002: 1.15.1.22. White Overtone Dog, Kin 70. Magnetic Moon 22 of the Planetary Moon year. 15th year anniversary Harmonic Convergence. "Mother Board" vision at Crater Lake, Oregon, deepest lake in the United States, formed from a collapsed volcano. "Wizard Island" is the top of a cinder cone volcano within Crater Lake. Votan and I would return here to open the first day of the 7 year cycle of the Mystery of the Stone, July 26, 2004: 1.17.1.1. Blue Crystal Storm, Kin 259. *The crystal prophecy is yours to own, by these Great Powers, undo the Mystery of the Stone!*

Chapter 9: Supernatural Shock

The initial GM108X experiment lasted precisely 312 days, January 20, 2002, - November 28, 2002. White Overtone Wind, Kin 122 to White Overtone Wizard, Kin 174. 312 symbolizes the "Magician" archetype in the Hunab Ku 21.

George Harrison, Blue Galactic Night. Kin 203

Chapter 10: Path Less Traveled

January 8, 2003. Blue Resonant eagle, 30th birthday. Spent with Votan and Daniel Pinchbeck, Yellow Spectral Star. He visited three days to interview Votan for Rolling Stone magazine, which instead was used for his book *2012: The Return of Quetzalcoatl.*

Chapter 11: Phoenix from the Flames

July 16, 2003: 1.15.13.20. Yellow Magnetic Seed, Kin 144. Cosmic Moon 20 of the Planetary Moon year. Move to Ashland. Yellow Magnetic Seed is also the signature of the first day of the first year of prophecy, July 26, 1993.

July 25, 2003. Red Planetary Skywalker, Kin 153. Day Out of Time. Gateway to the White Spectral Wizard year. Fire initiation.

Alberto Ruz Buenfil. Blue Cosmic Monkey, Kin 91.

White Planetary Mirror, Kin 218. Machu Picchu, first time travel experiment.

October 9, 2003: 1.16.3.20. Red Galactic Moon, Kin 229. Electric Moon 20 of Spectral Wizard year. Third Annual International Roerich Conference in St. Petersburg. Birthday of Nicholas Roerich, Yellow Solar Seed, Russian artist and visionary nominated three times for the Nobel Peace Prize. Votan honored by Archbishop of the Coptic Orthodox Church of St. Petersburg. Seven years later he would receive the highest award from the International Committee of the Banner of Peace, The Nicholas Roerich Medal in Mexico City.

The Roerich Pact and the Banner of Peace represent international agreement signed by India, Baltic States and 22 nations including USA. The Roerich Pact is the first international treaty dedicated to protection of artistic and scientific institutions and historical monuments of all over the world. This agreement was signed on April 15, 1935, Yellow Planetary Human, Kin 192. The Banner of Peace is the official symbol for the 13 Moon Calendar Change Peace Movement.

Chapter 12: Healing the Ancient Trauma

This inverted Time seeks to disconnect or short-circuit our connection to Source. This (false) Time manipulates our emotional body. This (false) Time is harmful to the Planet. We are waking up! We are breaking the old spells. Whether we are conscious of it or not, we have volunteered to incarnate and set things aright on the future time track.

Chapter 13: Baghdad Portal

March 20, 2004: 1.16.9.14. Blue Magnetic Monkey, Kin 131.Solar Moon 14 of the Spectral Wizard year. Peace ceremony at Bagdhad National Theater, Baghdad, Iraq.

Chapter 14: Palenque and Pacal Votan

Pacal Votan (603 - 683 AD), Yellow Galactic Sun, Kin 60 - White Rhythmic Mirror, Kin 58.

The 13 baktun cycle of the Maya Long Count calendar measures 1,872,000 days or 5,125. Each of the 13 baktuns contain 144,000 days.

June 15, 2005, White Planetary Mirror, Kin 218. 52nd anniversary opening of the tomb of Pacal Votan/Palenque, Mexico.

1692. Trials of Votan written 1,000 years after the tomb dedication.It took It took nine years from Pacal's death to build the nine-leveled Temple of Inscriptions, dedicated in 692.

Type 4 civilization. Type 4 civilizations are those that have completely transcended the use of material instrumentation to operate a supercosmic or supergalactic consciousness and possess an absolute understanding of universal design principles of the cosmos. They can then radiogenetically transmit those to type 3 civilizations which are those in the most advanced stages of the material plane.

Mother Tynetta Muhammad, Blue Lunar Hand, Kin 67.

Chapter 15: Rainbow Noosphere

December 21, 2005: 1.18.6.9. Yellow Overtone Human, kin 252. Rhythmic Moon 9 of the Cosmic Seed year. Ceremony atop Pyramid of the Sun, Teotihuacan, to open the 7 rings (years) to the Closing of the Cycle, 2012.

Chapter 16: Southern Cross

July 2, 2006: 1.18.13.6. Red Electric Serpent, Kin 185. Cosmic Moon 6 of the Cosmic Seed year. Move to New Zealand.

Jacob Wyatt, Red Rhythmic Dragon, Kin 201

Kelly Harding, Yellow Rhythmic Sun, Kin 240

July 25, 2006: Yellow Cosmic Star, Kin 208. Day Out of Time. Opening the gate to the Magnetic Moon year at Moeraki boulders, New Zealand.

September 22 - 26, 2006: 1.19.3.3 - 1.19.3.7. Blue Resonant Hand, Kin 7 to Blue Spectral Monkey, Kin 11. Electric Moon 3-7 of the Magnetic Moon year. Second Planetary Congress of Biosphere Rights, held at the Parlamundi of the Ecumenical Fraternity of the Legion of Good Will, Brasilia, Brazil.

Mevlana/Bulent Corak, Blue Self-Existing Storm, Kin 199.

November 1, 1981. White Solar Wind, Kin 22. SelfExisting Moon 15 of the Lunar Seed year. First transmission of *The Knowledge Book* received by Bulent Corak.

November 1, 2006: 1.19.4.15. Blue Galactic Hand, Kin 47. Self-Existing Moon 15 of the Magnetic Moon year. Call to World Peace from the Universal Brotherhood event in Istanbul, Turkey, hosted by Mevlana.

"64. The scarcity of time is mentioned as a result of the time period which will be accelerated even more.

"65. You are faced with a change of Age. Do not ever forget this. Everything will settle in its course, silently and profoundly.

—*The Knowledge Book,* postulates from the Cosmos Federal Assembly, p. 389

Chapter 17: Lady Mile Road, Queenstown

December 5, 2006: 1.19.5.21. Red Electric Dragon, Kin 81. Overtone Moon of the Magnetic Moon year. Alchemical wedding, Queenstown, New Zealand.

January 10, 2007: 1.19.7.1. Red Cosmic Earth, Kin 117. Resonant Moon 1 of the Magnetic Moon year. 441 dream in Queenstown. Initiated what would later be known as Synchronotron. This would be the final part of a 20-year time release of coded knowledge, 1991-2011.

August 1, 2007: 1.20.1.7. Yellow Galactic Sun, Kin 60. Sign of Pacal Votan. Magnetic Moon 7 of the White Lunar Wizard year. Crop circle at Sugar Hill, Upper Upham, Wiltshire, UK. There were 8 cubes so arranged as to form a larger cube with a six-pointed star in the center. There are 3 faces showing to each of these cubes: 3 × 8 = 54, kin number of the White Lunar Wizard year.

Ed Higbee, Red Solar Skywalker, Kin 113.

Carl Jung, White Cosmic Wizard. Kin 234. Jung wrote an essay called "Wotan" in 1947, and published his famous essay on synchronicity in 1952, the year of the discovery of the tomb of Pacal Votan. His birthday is July 26, galactic new year on the 13 Moon calendar.

Chapter 18: Waitaha: People of Peace

July 25, 2007, Red Magnetic Skywalker, Kin 53. Sign of Quetzalcoatl. Day Out of Time. Gateway to the Lunar Wizard year.

August 16, 2007: 1.20.1.22. Blue Crystal Monkey, Kin 51. Magnetic Moon 22 of the Lunar Wizard year. Twentieth anniversary of the Harmonic Convergence. Adoption into the Waitaha family at Waitangi Treaty grounds, NZ.

Hunab Ku 21: The structure of the Hunab Ku 21 is the root of galactic culture. See *Book of the Timespace.*

Chapter 19: Noah's Radiogenetic Time Ark

Noah archetype. The Holomind Perceiver has 9 time dimensions. The ninth time dimension is the central control panel and has embedded within it the 9 stations of the ark. Each station of the ark represented a particular archetype as exemplified by different spiritual exemplars. At the center was Votan and Noah, archetypes of the interplanetary navigators. "Votan" actually means "heart of nine.

Chapter 20: Hollywood and Inner Technology

September 6-12, 2009: 1.22.2.15-1.22.2.21. White Resonant Worldbridger, Kin 46 to Yellow Cosmic Human, Kin 52. Lunar Moon 15-21 of the Self-Existing Seed year. Seven-day Synchronotron Advanced Training Seminar, Babaji Ashram, Cisternino Italy. The system of Synchronotron is a tool for learning the mathematical language of telepathy, which is coded into the Law of Time. It is a teaching from Sirius that contains the language of post-conceptual mind.

September 28, 2009: 1.23.3.9. Yellow Electric Star, Kin 68. Electric Moon 9 of the Self-Existing Seed year. Move in date to Votan's final resting place in Blampied, Australia. This signature also coded June 15, 2010, 58th anniversary of the opening of the tomb of Pacal Votan. Crystal Moon 17 of the Self-Existing Seed year. 1.22.12.17.

January 27, 2010: 1.22.7.18. Red Resonant Moon, Kin 189. Resonant Moon 18 of the Self-Existing Seed year. Final day of Votan and I at Palenque before his passing the following year.

July 25, 2010. Yellow Self-Existing Star, Kin 108. Day Out of Time, José Argüelles/Valum Votan's final public talk at the Prophet's Conference in Vancouver, Canada. He is ceremonially honored by indigenous Mayan grandmother Floredemayo.

Chapter 21: Oracle of Deathlessness

March 23, 2011: 1.23.9.17. Red Spectral Moon, Kin 89. Solar Moon 17 of the Overtone Moon year. Note that the discovery of the Law of Time occurred in 19**89**. 19 + 89 = 108. Votan's 72nd and final birthday was January, 24, 2011: 1.23.7.15. Blue Overtone Monkey, Kin 31. 20 + 11 = 31. There are 1,328 years between the passing of Pacal Votan in 683, and Valum Votan in 2011.

Parahamahansa Yogananda, White Spectral Wind, Kin 102. Death signature, White Magnetic Mirror, Kin 18.

Chapter 22: Solitude and Retreat

Dalai Lama, White Magnetic Wizard, Kin 14.

Lois Hunt, Yellow Magnetic Warrior, Kin 196. Kin 196 is the combined destiny of 185 and 11.

Chapter 23: Zero Point

June 15, 2012: 1.24.12.17. White Magnetic Mirror, Kin 18. Crystal Moon 17 of the Rhythmic Wizard year. After 18 years of being subject to uninterrupted studies in Mexico City, the bones of the Red Queen and her companions, were returned to Palenque (in a high security warehouse).

March 23, 2012: 1.24.9.17. White Crystal Wizard, Kin 194. Solar Moon 17 of the Rhythmic Wizard year. First anniversary of Votan's passing. Seven-day event in Australia, Solar Moon 11-17, Kin 188-194.

Chapter 24: Ships and Sirius

August 24, 2011: 1.24.2.2. Yellow Planetary Star, Kin 88. Lunar Moon of the Rhythmic Wizard year. 1 spin (260 days) from Votan's final day on earth. Supernova 2011fe was captured exploding by California astronomers. It was located 21 million light years from Earth in the Pinwheel Galaxy within the Ursa Major constellation. It was the closest and brightest supernova in 25 years, and was labeled the "Rosetta Stone" of supernovas. (For decoders see the significant psi chrono of this day).

August 31, 2011: 1.24.29. Blue Self-Existing Eagle, Kin 95. Lunar Moon 9 of the Rhythmic Wizard year. Ship sighting and message, Australia.

October 22, 2011: 1.24.4.5. White Electric Wind, Kin 42. Self-Existing Moon 5 of the Rhythmic Wizard year. Dream of dimensional shift. One year ago on that day Votan had received the "Galactic Spiral Density Wave" program on Kin 197, noting there were 791 days to 12-21-2012. (791 is 197 backwards). Everything is numbered.

Chapter 25: Closing the Cycle

December 13, 2012: 1.25.6.1. Blue Self-Existing Storm, Kin 199. Rhythmic Moon 1 of the Resonant Storm year. Return to United States alone, Virgin flight 1323 (441 x 3).

December 21, 2012: 1.25.6.9. Blue Crystal Hand, Kin 207. Rhythmic Moon 9 of the Resonant Storm year. Closing the cycle ceremony in Palenque. Combined signature of 185 + 22. *"Closing the cycle means to bring all of humanity as one planetary family in a state of peace and harmony to this cosmically climactic point in time, the end of the great cycle of history."* —Valum Votan

Chapter 26: Three Golden Dreams

Dolphin/Holomind Perceiver note: Even though dolphins have two hemispheres just like humans, theirs are split into four lobes instead of three. The fourth lobe in the dolphin's brain actually hosts all of the senses, whereas in a human, the senses are split. Some believe that having all of the senses in one lobe allows the dolphin to make immediate and often complicated judgments that are well beyond the scope of a human ability. These four lobes correspond in the holomind perceiver to the four hyperplasmic flows: alpha-alpha flow, alpha-beta flow, beta-beta flow and beta-alpha flow, each having sublimating and activating components, plus the fifth central Sirius B channel.

Chapter 27: New Beam and Mount Shasta

July 26, 2013: 1.26.1.1. Yellow Galactic Seed, Kin 164. Magnetic Moon 1 of the Galactic Seed year. New Beam sunrise ceremony, Mount Shasta. Followed by a double rainbow in the afternoon.

Chapter 28: 444 and Transylvania

June 11, 2016: 1.28.12.13, White Overtone Wizard, Kin 174. Crystal Moon 13 of the Planetary Wizard year. Significant dream at 4:44 a.m. 5200 days or 20 spins since first Cosmic History transmission.

June 15, 2018. 1.30.12.17. Yellow Spectral Star, Kin 128. Crystal Moon 17 of the Crystal Seed year. Arrive in Romania on the 66th anniversary of the discovery of the tomb of Pacal Votan.

Peter Moon, Yellow Electric Human. See his sites:
https://www.timetraveleducationcenter.com and
https://www.skybooksusa.com

A Note About José Argüelles/Valum Votan

Since this book primarily revolves around my apprenticeship and relationship with José Argüelles/Valum Votan, I feel it would be appropriate to give a brief background about him. Many know of different facets of José Argüelles' work and legacy. Still, few have really seen its vast scope, as he was one of the seminal thinkers of our time.

Born a twin in the atomic era of the nuclear bomb, José's eclectic background led him to encounter and learn from prominent yogis, Buddhists, Christians, Muslims, Hindus, esotericists, scientists, environmentalists, indigenous poets, musicians, and artists of all types.

José was a prominent artist, author, former university professor, visionary, and messenger of a New Time. He was a compassionate humanitarian and a fighter for minorities, the working class, and the underdog in general. He first became widely known as the initiator of the world-famous Harmonic Convergence global peace meditation, which occurred on August 16-17, 1987. This was the first synchronized planetary meditation event in history.

During that time, he also awakened the mass consciousness to the significance of the year 2012 as a consciousness shift point and turned the world's attention toward the Maya and their calendric system. His bestselling book *The Mayan Factor* (1987) gave credence to the Mayan calendar's cycles of natural time.

In 1989, after living several cycles simultaneously over a period of time José made a life-changing discovery while visiting the Museum of Time in Geneva, Switzerland with his wife Lloydine. José discovered that the Law of Time, like the law of gravity, is not a human law, but a natural law. It makes the distinction between artificial or mechanical time and natural time. He realized that time is a frequency and that the Maya understood this to be the frequency of synchronization which governs all of nature. He saw that this is universally true, with the exception of modern human civilization.

He promoted a version of the 13 Moon, 28-day calendar that he called the Dreamspell. The mathematical codes that comprised the Dreamspell made conscious what is known as the *Synchronic Order*, the universal matrix of synchronicity. This was followed by the decoding of the Telektonon Prophecy of Pacal Votan, an unprecedented demonstration of an interplanetary telepathic technology. José went on to elaborate on this natural time system with many additional tools and organized events all over the world.

While he has many worldly accomplishments, much of José's most creative activity has been out of the limelight and carried out off the beaten path, so it is essential to place the whole of his life in perspective. As companion works to this book, I suggest reading the two biographies on José I have previously written to learn more.

2012: Biography of a Time Traveler illustrates the way knowledge was revealed to José and evolved as a step-by-step process that was often painstaking on the human level.

Time, Synchronicity and Calendar Change: The Visionary Life and Work of José Argüelles, like the previous book, is based on numerous hours of questioning and conversations with José; ongoing study of his books, journals, papers, personal letters, articles, and documents; as well as traveling with him to various places and observing him in action.

Here I will quote from the Introduction of that book:

> *José is an ever enigmatic character and impossible to label, though if one title had to be chosen, it would be a planetary artist. An artist is one who is ever-evolving, ever-changing, and ever exploring new ranges and territory of thought and existence. As an artist, he is also a visionary and a channel for different transmissions of energy and information. A planetary artist can play many interchangeable roles, from student, mystic, professor, philosopher, teacher, and messenger. But each role, if played consciously, has the purpose of furthering the evolution of the individual, of the species and of the Earth.*

All images in this book are original drawings by José Argüelles/ Valum Votan, from his visionary notebook entitled *Terma of the Red Queen.*

Selected Works of José Argüelles/Valum Votan

The Transformative Vision: Reflections on the Nature and History of Human Expression. Shambhala Publications, 1975; second edition, Muse Publications 1992.

Earth Ascending: An Illustrated Treatise on the Law Governing Whole Systems. Shambhala Publications 1984; second and third editions, Bear & Co, 1988, 1996.

The Mayan Factor, Path Beyond Technology. Bear & Co. 1987; Second edition, 1996.

Surfers of the Zuvuya, Tales of Interdimensional Travel. Bear & Co, 1988.

The Call of Pacal Votan, Time is the Fourth Dimension. Altea Publishers, 1996.

The Arcturus Probe, Tales and Reports of an Ongoing Investigation. Light Technology, 1996. Translation: Spanish, Japanese.

Time and the Technosphere: the Law of Time in Human Affairs. Inner Traditions International, 2002.

__________ with Stephanie South. *Cosmic History Chronicles: The Law of Time and the Reformulation of the Human Mind* (seven volumes: *Book of the Throne, Book of the Avatar, Book of the Mystery, Book of the Initiation, Book of the Timespace, Book of the Transcendence, Book of the Cube).* Law of Time Press, Galactic Research Institute, 2004-2011.

Manifesto for the Noosphere: The Next Stage in the Evolution of Human Consciousness. North Atlantic Books, Berkeley, Calif., 2011.

Gratitude

Valum Votan/Spectral Monkey, for his unconditional love, discipline, dedication, and shining example in all ways. Without him, none of this would be.

Lloydine/Bolon Ik-Solar Wind, for her years of dedication in helping lay the foundation, and providing me invaluable lessons for refinement.

Deb/Solar Skywalker, "Fairy Godmother," for being a source of unconditional love, comfort, and gentle feedback through the entire process.

Brian/Lunar Serpent, "Dragon Keeper," for holding the structure of the mission and providing me a safe sanctuary for this work to unfold.

Seamus/Planetary Mirror, "Noble Knight," for providing a protective shield, nurturance, and encouraging editorial feedback, through some of the most challenging times.

N'Elektra/Blue Rhythmic Hand, who saw me through the entire process, and offered artistic and invaluable feedback from the vantage point of the feminine.

Sham Tok Maru/Yellow Electric Star, "Knight of the Solar Cross," for providing the crystal grid upon which I navigate. His discipline, consistency, and dedication are invaluable to me and this work.

David Aretha/Electric Human, for his professional copyedits in final stages.

Forrest/Planetary Sun, for his copyediting assistance, earth wizardry, and dedicated support in the beginning stages.

Jacob/Rhythmic Dragon, for his care, steadfast dedication, and editing suggestions. Without his patient assistance, this publication would not be.

Kelly/Rhythmic Sun, for her intuitive design skills and beautiful heart.

Father John/Cosmic Dog, for his divine insights and service as a cosmic midwife; and to his wife Devta/Self-Existing Human, for carrying the presence of the Divine Mother.

Ishram/Overtone Hand, for whom I will be forever grateful.

The original Earth Wizards who stood by me throughout, in particular, Flaviah/Resonant Star, Rodrigo/Crystal Mirror, Annibal/Galactic Wizard, Katarina/Magnetic Storm, Eden/Self-Existing Skywalker, Luis Zavala/Electric Mirror, and Andre/Lunar Skywalker for fulfilling the vision of the Galactic Education Center/Brazil.

Others who supported this process. Gustavo/Lunar Wind and Paola/Cosmic Earth, Shane/Self-Existing Storm, Ik Nehuen "White Elephant"/Resonant Wind, Gabi/Solar Star. Crys'tal/Galactic Sun. Ana/Planetary Wind, Sam Wise/Lunar Dog, Queen Esther/Self-Existing Seed, Sarah/Spectral Seed, Noelle/Overtone Eagle, Donna Rae/Resonant Human. And for all of my galactic soul family and star beings who have supported this work.

Thank You!

About the Author

Stephanie South is a visionary, synchronic teacher, and the author of several books, including the award-winning, *Accessing Your Multidimensional Self: A Key to Cosmic History.* She is Creative Director of the Foundation for the Law of Time, and is is currently working on *The Art of Synchronicity: Instructions from the Future.*

www.livingtimescience.com
www.1320frequencyshift.com
www.lawoftime.org

www.ingramcontent.com/pod-product-compliance
Lightning Source LLC
Chambersburg PA
CBHW030439300426
44112CB00009B/1072